Saklatvala
A Political Biography

Mike Squires

LAWRENCE & WISHART
LONDON

Lawrence & Wishart Limited
144a Old South Lambeth Road
London SW8 1XX

First published 1990

Photoset in North Wales by
Derek Doyle & Associates, Mold, Clwyd.
Printed and bound in Great Britain
at The Camelot Press, Trowbridge, Wiltshire.

Contents

Acknowledgements

Many people, organisations and institutions have helped me in the pursuit of my research. I would like to thank my mother and father for first stimulating my interest in Saklatvala, and Wally Barnes for his invaluable encouragement and support over many years.

The book has been aided greatly by the many people who have provided me with information both about Saklatvala and the Communist Party in the 1920s and 30s. My greatest debt is to Sehri Saklatvala and her brother, the late Beram Saklatvala, who generously gave their spare time to be interviewed at length about their father, and who allowed me to view and use what little was left of their father's memorabilia. In addition, I would like to thank Noreen Branson for guiding me towards little known resources, and the many Communist Party members who have shared their memories of the period with me.

I am also very grateful to Bradford College which gave me a term's secondment in order to begin my research, and to the Greater London Council (Ethnic Minorities Unit) for a grant which enabled me to complete it.

My thanks are also due to a number of people whose contributions are less easy to define: Phil Read, Robin Reeves, Dave Gadian, Ian Buckley and Jane Thurlow. A special mention must be made of Bernadette Loderick for her consistent encouragement over a long period.

In conclusion I should like to thank my sister Pat Squires, and Robin Solomon, for their devotion, tolerance and proof-reading capabilities. Without their help, this work would not have been possible.

Foreword
Keith Vaz

It is impossible not to feel a bond of friendship with Shapurji Saklatvala, even though he was born over a century and a quarter ago. Indeed, in Saklatava's maiden speech to the Commons on 23 November 1922, he raised issues which are fascinatingly relevant today, concerning Ireland, South Africa, Russia, and unemployment. I chose to quote from the glorious final line of his maiden speech in mine, his exhortation to his contemporaries to 'burst out of these time-worn prejudices and boldly take a new place'.

Certainly, though his parliamentary career was brief, Saklatvala's political influence was very far-reaching, and his own hallmark was, unmistakably, boldness. He had unflinching commitment to the socialist struggle to relieve the abuses endured by the working masses in Britain, and throughout the world, and a passionate concern for the right to national independence of the Indian people; these mark him out from his contemporaries as a personality of outstanding principle and idealism. Born into a wealthy parsee family, he was driven, not by material necessity, but by simple conviction, to take his place in the front line of the popular movement against the injustices of class inequality.

The path he chose was personally costly, for the stand he took both inside and outside parliament attracted almost universal political disapproval, resulting in isolation within the Commons and, elsewhere, in frequent threats against his physical safety. His refusal to bend to unscrupulous pressure from all sides, and his readiness to go to prison and to submit to a permanent restriction on his entry to India rather than compromise his position, are vivid testimony to an exceptional courage and strength of purpose.

In the end, the reader may well feel that Mike Squire's penetrating commentary is more significant for the light it sheds on the history of the Communist Party, and the birth pangs of the labour movement, than as an account of how Saklatvala emerged as the third person of Asian origin to sit in the House of Commons. There can be no doubt that the man himself would not have wanted it otherwise.

Chapter One

Early Life

Shapurji Saklatvala was born in Bombay on 28 March 1874. His father was Dorabji Saklatvala, a Bombay merchant. His mother's brother was J N Tata, the owner of India's largest commercial empire. The Saklatvala children were raised alongside those of the Tatas, and they shared the same household.

Jamsetji Tata's wealth was phenomenal. Three years after his death, it was estimated that the trading firm he had established in 1868, with a capital of 21,000 rupees, was worth 15 million rupees. His commercial interests were wide-ranging, including cotton mills, coal mines, steel factories and, in his later life, hydro-electric power. The Tata company built the Taj Mahal hotel, the most luxurious hotel in Asia, at the cost of a quarter of a million pounds. Some of his wealth was used for philanthropic work; for example he granted the government, in 1898, a property valued at £200,000, to found a post-graduate institute for scientific research. All these were considerable sums of money at the time. It was a very wealthy family for a future revolutionary to be born into.

Both families were Parsee, and for many generations had been adherents of the Zorastrian religion. Saklata-vala's devotion to this ancient Persian faith was a recurring theme throughout his life, and in his speeches he often referred to the spiritual side of humanity. He was for many years an active member of the Parsee community in Britain, and despite his lifelong commitment to socialism he never relinquished his religious beliefs. Like many Parsee boys he was sent to a vernacular school where

1

Gujerati was the medium of instruction.

At the age of sixteen he went to St Xaviers School, an exclusive private school run by Jesuit priests. Here boys were prepared for the equally exclusive St Xaviers College, which Saklatvala entered three years later. The college was a university for the sons of the Indian upper class and Saklatvala was entered to take a Batchelor of Arts degree. It was at St Xaviers that Saklatvala learnt the art of public speaking. He was one of the instigators of the 'Gwalia Circle', a debating club with a mainly literary theme.

His sporting ability, and more particularly his health, at this time, was the subject of some dispute. His brother maintained that he seldom took part in any games and did not enjoy the company of rowdy boys, and that though in fairly good health he was physically never very strong.[1] This observation was disputed by one of Saklatvala's friends and contemporaries at St Xaviers, who remembered meeting almost every day at Markers ground in Bombay to play cricket or football, or some other sport.[2] Apart from these disputed sporting activities, Saklatvala's interests at college included mathematics, English literature, religion and philosophy. Mr Spittam Cama, a colleague at St Xaviers, described him as a brilliant student, yet he failed to obtain his degree, even after a number of unsuccessful resits, leaving St Xaviers without a qualification.

At this stage of Saklatvala's life there is much speculation as to whether or not he became a catholic. He was certainly influenced by the Jesuit priests who taught him, and there is some evidence that at about the age of 25 he underwent conversion. A friend claims that when he visited Saklatvala in 1900, there was a figure of the Virgin Mary above his bed. Apparently this so incensed J N Tata that he threw it out of the window. Another of Saklatvala's old school friends maintains that he was baptised at the Meadow Street Convent in Bombay. This claim was refuted by Saklatvala some years later, when he insisted that he participated in the baptism merely out of curiosity.[3] Despite Saklatvala's denial of his early flirtation with Christianity, he did have two of his children educated at catholic schools, although he stipulated that they were to receive no religious instruction. When he was married, on the eve of his 'conversion' to socialism when the vicar complained that he could not marry a heathen, Saklatvala assured him that he was a Christian. Whether or not Saklatvala embraced Christianity is not known, but his questioning of the family religion led to a number of quarrels. The outcome was that Saklatvala moved out of the Tata residence at Espalade House in Bombay some time in 1902, and moved in with his mother and sister at nearby Hornby Road.

Saklatvala's dabbling in an alternative religion seemed to have little lasting effect on his relationship with J N Tata. The family godfather had an affection for his nephew, akin to the feelings that he felt for his own two sons. He had two boys, Dorabji and Rattan, and the three were all brought up together; there developed an animosity between Saklatvala and the eldest son Dorabji however. Their disagreements, which in their childhood were personal, became political as the boys grew older, and were to have a far reaching effect on Saklatvala's life. J N Tata was a liberal nationalist. He was a member of the Indian National Congress from the time of its formation in 1885, and was an active member of its Bombay branch. He favoured the development of industry and commerce by Indian nationals, using Indian finance. This approach was supported by his nephew, but his views were not shared by Dorabji, who was something of an anglophile.

At J N Tata's instigation, Saklatvala joined the family firm in 1901. A year later he was selected by his uncle to lead a prospecting expedition for iron ore and coal deposits, in the Chandra district of Central India. When this proved unsuccessful, the prospectors moved on to the Dondi-Lohara region of Northern India. Here their efforts were much more fruitful, and the expedition, nearly three years in duration in all, led to the creation of Tata's iron and steel empire. For part of the time in his travels Saklatvala was accompanied by Dorabji, and also by an American engineer, an employee of the company called Weld. As well as difficult living conditions the prospectors faced competition from a rival English company who were

also investigating the area for mineral deposits. Frank
Harris, in his biography of Jamsetji Tata, gives an account
of the hardships experienced by the group:

> In April, 1903, Mr Weld and Mr Dorabji Tata joined Mr
> Saklatvala and entered upon a period of adventurous
> wanderings which was often marked by much privation.
> The heat in the Central Provinces in April, May and June is
> intense. The prospectors were generally moving far from
> the railway line, and sometimes had difficulty in obtaining
> food. Water was frequently scarce and bad, and they were
> often compelled to make their tea with the soda water they
> carried on their carts. There were times when they could
> not make any progress at all. The district includes large
> forest areas, which are the joy of the hunters because tigers
> are numerous; but prospectors for iron and coal regard a
> multiplicity of tigers with more apprehension than delight.
> Roads were few and indifferent. Sometimes, the party
> found shelter in a village house, but there were nights
> when they had to sleep in their carts. At first they lived very
> roughly indeed.[4]

During his extensive travels, Saklatvala had a number of
brushes with the British authorities. On one occasion he
locked up a number of the native police, after they had
tried to extort money from labourers in his employ. He
also incurred protests, particularly from British officers,
because he paid his employees more than was usual and let
them rest during the afternoon. A rest period was
customary for the British in India, but not for their Indian
servants.

During this period, although by no means an active
nationalist, Saklatvala was sceptical of British rule, and by
1902 there is evidence that his views were beginning to
turn in a reformist direction. At this time there was an
outbreak of plague, and Saklatvala, who was enjoying a
rest from prospecting at the time offered his assistance in
the relief work taking place in Bombay. It shows that he
was already sufficiently concerned about the poor to give
up a much needed holiday in order to help the plague
victims. It was in doing this work that he had a bitter
first-hand experience of the attitudes of the British
authorities. It is worth relating this experience in full,

because it gives a graphic account of race relations in British India at the turn of the century. It further shows the influences that were at work on the young Saklatvala, influences that were still plainly visible twenty-five years later. Addressing the House of Commons in 1923, he referred to this part of his early life:

> If I may be permitted just to give something from my memory of a personal character in this matter. In 1902 a plague was having devastating effects all over India. It was to be taken in hand not merely as a grave problem, but as something to save human lives. There was a Professor Haffkin in those days who was the first man who with some measure of success gave out an anti-plague serum for innoculation. His experiments were being conducted on a large scale. I was then associated as secretary with an important committee of welfare work. The Governor of Bombay, who was then himself staying out of Bombay, immediately sent a telegram to Professor Haffkin to go to him with certain facts and figures because the matter was becoming of vital importance. Professor Haffkin asked me to go and assist him. I gave up my work in the office and I went to the place where he was staying, and that was his European club. People talk about untouchability! Although I had facts and figures at my disposal, I was actually prevented from entering the white man's club. Ultimately, when it could not be helped, the messenger of the club, after telephoning to various government officials, took me to the back yard of the club, led me through the kitchen, and an underground passage to a basement room, where the professor was asked to see me because I was not a white man. That happened twenty-five years ago.[5]

After the plague subsided, Saklatvala returned to prospecting, which was his major concern, until J N Tata's death. The head of the company died in May 1904, and after his death there was no longer a restraining influence on the growing antagonism between Saklatvala and Dorabji. Dorabji's power increased and the arguments between the two also grew. Saklatvala's greatest worry seemed to have been the relative importance of mining within the company which he regarded as very important. Some time after his arrival in England, he was to express his concern in a letter to a friend, and also the idea that he might be able to direct mining operations from England:

> I'm afraid the Tata office might give up mining enterprises in my absence, especially if Mr Padshah retires from it. I shall always urge my best to keep up the mining department and develop it gradually from here.[6]

The differences between Saklatvala and Dorabji came to a climax in 1905. Their views clashed over the direction that the company should take, and as a temporary solution it was decided that Saklatvala should go to England. He was perfectly happy with the idea, and was to take over the running of the company's Manchester office. There was also other reasons for Saklatvala's departure. He was becoming too critical of the British authorities and might prove an embarrassment to a growing concern like Tatas. In addition, the exploration work, which had been extremely arduous, had taken its toll on his health and he suffered from recurring illness, particularly malaria. The stay in Britain, it was hoped, would help his recovery.

The move to England

It was clear that Saklatvala did not consider that England would be his permanent home. Writing to a friend in 1906, after he had been there for almost a year, he said, 'While I am here I am preparing myself as a barrister, ultimately I mean to return to the Tata office and attend to mining more than to law, but who knows how the future turns.'[7] These were certainly prophetic words – romance was to intervene and alter his proposed course of action.

Saklatvala's political development during these first few years in England is significant. It is difficult to assess how radical he was when he left India. There is no evidence of any association with nationalist groups, and there were no socialist organisations of any size in existence to which he might have belonged. His views had not progressed beyond the mildly reformist stage. He had been in opposition to the British authorities, and had developed a social awareness, as evidenced by his work for the plague victims, but beyond that the rest is speculation. There are no private papers left and very few letters relating to this early period.

One indication of his early political ideas was that on his arrival in England, after a short stay in Manchester, he moved to London and took up temporary residence in the National Liberal Club. It would not have been unnatural for Saklatvala to have had Liberal sympathies; the Indian National Congress relied on Liberal support and the Liberal government of 1906-1914 had instituted a number of reforms that were welcomed by the nationalist movement. The most significant of these were the Morley-Minto Reforms. Lord Morley, a Liberal Lord and Secretary of State for India, was introduced to Saklatvala soon after his arrival from India – this gives some indication of Saklatvala's status. According to Reg Bishop, Saklatvala's secretary while he was an MP, the meeting was not a happy one and led to Saklatvala's rejection of Liberalism.

> His family made him a life member of the National Liberal Club. Here, so the idea went, Sak would meet all the really respectable friends of Indian freedom. He did, and having met them he didn't think much of them. Among those he met was Lord Morley. The outcome of a furious argument with 'Honest Jack', as Morley liked to be known, was Sak's resignation from the Liberal mausoleum and his entry into working class politics via the Independent Labour Party.[8]

In order to assist in the recovery of his health, Saklatvala stayed for some time, during 1906, in the spa town of Matlock in Derbyshire. There it was hoped he would be able to rest and recuperate and the medicinal waters would do him some good. It was here that he was to meet his future wife. Working in the town at the same time was a Miss Sarah Marsh of Tansley, a village a few miles from Matlock. Saklatvala, on first meeting her, was immediately impressed, and what followed was a quite romantic courtship. In a letter to her son, written some time after his father's death, she described what happened.

> He first saw me on his birthday, March 28th 1906. He asked Maria Marsh who I was. She said her cousin, so he asked her to call me to him, which she did. With his beard I took him to be an old man. He gave me flowers almost every day, and asked me to go for walks. I was too frightened to do so but kept saying I would just to satisfy

him for the time being. One day I got a note from a shoe
shop, would I go in to try on some shoes. There was a note
inside a special pair of shoes which I was to try on from him
saying that he hoped to be able to buy all my shoes from
now on. I happened to say I would like a cycle so he bought
one and pretended to give away raffle tickets to several
people and I was given the winning ticket. The day he left
the Hydro he asked me to see him off on the 2.19. I said
yes but had no intention of going, my friend and I went out
in the afternoon. When we returned we got a phone
message from Daddy to say he was on Matlock Bath Station
and he intended to remain there however long it was until
I went to see him. I went at 9 o'clock at night and said
goodbye to him. He wrote twice a day after he went away.[9]

Over the next few months her attitude obviously changed
and they were engaged in November of that year, and
were married at Oldham in August 1907. The marriage
was successful, the couple were devoted to each other, and
they had five children.

Saklatvala's political ideas at this stage were still in a state
of flux, he was undoubtedly moving towards socialism, as a
few surviving letters from friends indicate. During his stay
in Matlock he befriended a Mrs S Richards, and she
testifies, in a letter to Beram Saklatvala, to his interest in
socialist ideas.

About November or December 1905, your father came on
a visit to Smedley Hydro, Matlock, in which town I was
managing a glass and china business. He came in one day
to make a small purchase. During his conversation then,
and on subsequent occasions, I soon discovered that he was
very interested in politics, at that time 'socialistic'. Your
father found out I was interested and he would quite often
come into the shop (which was opposite the Hydro) and
talk long and earnestly of the injustice meted out to the
working class.[10]

That his conversion to socialism took place at around this
time is affirmed by no less a person than J R Clynes.
Clynes, who was an activist in the General and Municipal
Workers Union, attended a number of meetings in
Matlock in 1907. Here he came into contact with the
young Indian. According to Clynes, Saklatvala attended
these meetings, and what he heard there was influential in
recruiting him to the socialist cause:

I attended a number of meetings under the auspices of the above union [General and Municipal Workers] held in Matlock and one or two adjacent places during 1907. We of course spoke not only on trade union and industrial matters, but dealt with the political questions from the socialist standpoint. Your father attended these meetings and in due course he asked me to arrange a talk with him. We had very pleasant conversations, and as I learned later he gave me some credit for turning his views in the socialist direction.[11]

After Saklatvala's marriage in August, 1907, the couple moved to London and took up residence in a bed-sitting-room in Holloway Road. It was from these fairly modest surroundings that Saklatvala's organisational commitment to socialism began. Towards the end of 1907 he joined the Social Democratic Federation, a small marxist group formed in 1884, led by H M Hyndman. The nearest branch was in East Finchley, and it was here that Saklatvala heard Bernard Shaw speak for the first time. Here too he renewed his love of debating, first practised at St Xavier's, by regularly attending a mock parliament at Finchley. His links with the area were broken when his mother died in America, in November 1907. Her ashes were buried at Brookwood in Surrey, and the couple moved to the area to be close to the grave. Because of the move Saklatvala was no longer involved in an active S D F branch, but this did not prevent him from pursuing other progressive causes. At this time he was a keen supporter of the women's suffrage movement, and over this issue he took part in his first public protest. This was a votes for women demonstration, which marched to Hyde Park in the summer of 1908.

Saklatvala remained a member of the Social Democratic Federation (later renamed the British Socialist Party), until that organisation, along with several others, became the Communist Party of Great Britain in 1920. However, it was not the main vehicle for his socialist activity. At that time it was quite common to be a member of move than one socialist organisation, and Saklatvala concentrated most of his efforts on working in the Independent Labour Party. The ILP was the largest of the socialist groups. It

was affiliated to the Labour Party and it was through the
ILP that Saklatvala became a Labour Party member when
he joined in 1909. Although there were differences
between the two parties, membership was open to all, and
there were no bans. It is significant, given his future political development, that Saklatvala chose to be active in the
ILP, and not the avowedly marxist BSP.

After their stay in Surrey, the Saklatvalas moved back to
London. Temporarily Saklatvala stopped working for
Tatas, and made a half-hearted attempt to become a barrister. He joined the bar at Lincoln's Inn and took the first of
the exams, but then decided against a career in the law. It is
a matter of some speculation whether this was because his
socialist ideas were unpopular amongst the predominantly
conservative trainee lawyers, or because by this stage he had
developed political ambitions. From Lincoln's Inn he went
to the firm of British Westinghouse where he stayed until
the spring of 1909. His next career move was to a firm of
consulting engineers in Manchester. It was from this Lancashire city that Saklatvala made his first modest impact on
the labour movement nationally.

In Manchester, as well as joining the Independent
Labour Party, he also became a member of the Manchester
Clarion Club. And, his delight in debating was given a
further opportunity to develop at the local discussion
group, the County Forum, where he regularly attended the
weekly debates.

But it was not directly in the arena of socialist politics that
Saklatvala made his first attempt to influence national
events. His first intervention was on behalf of the workers
of India. Although this attempt was unsuccessful, the unity
of British and Indian workers was to be a recurring theme
throughout his life. He was the instigator of a move to
interest the British trade unions in the formation of a
General Workers Union in India. Early in 1911, he was a
member of a committee, which included J R Clynes, which
petitioned a number of trade union leaders with the aim of
giving 'an opportunity for the expression of national concern for our fell (*sic*) workers in India'.[12] The attempt came
to nothing, and even those within the labour movement
who were interested in colonialism knew nothing about it.

This endeavour apart, Saklatvala's new found convictions seemed to have lain dormant until the outbreak of the first world war. He was a member of two socialist organisations, but there is no evidence that he was an active member of either body. His political inactivity during this period can be attributed to two reasons. First, as a married man with several young children there was little time available; second, and most important, he was planning to return to India, and if possible to settle there permanently. There were certain dangers attached to this course of action, which reinforces the view that when he first came to England it was partly because he was in serious conflict with the authorities. His father wrote to him warning that he might be arrested if he set foot on Indian soil; however Saklatvala disregarded his advice, and with his wife and family set sail for Bombay in May 1912.

The attempted resettlement did not last the year. Even though he took no active part in politics, and there were no reports of any conflicts with the British authorities, by 1913 he was back in Britain. The reasons for this sudden return are unclear, but once again the animosity between Saklatvala and Dorabji Tata may have been decisive rather than any political cause. Despite this conflict, Saklatvala's prestige with the company remained high, and on his return he was again employed by Tatas as a departmental manager, first in the Manchester office and then in London. There was no attempt by Dorabji, at this time, to force Saklatvala out of the company's employ; he seems to have been content with simply ensuring that he was out of India. This attempt at a permanent return to the subcontinent was not repeated; from then onwards Saklatvala looked upon England as his home.

On his return to England, after a brief stay in Manchester, the family took up residence at 51 Lebanon Park, Twickenham, which was not far from the home of J N Tata's other son, Sir Rattan Tata, who had recently acquired York House in Twickenham. Unlike Dorabji, Sir Rattan took little interest in the company and lived the life of a leisured aristocrat. He was affectionately described by a younger relative, who said of him that 'work was not his line, he was the artistic dilettante, chestnut headed, frock coated, picture collecting, armour loving member of the family'.[13] Saklatvala got on well with Sir Rattan, and the reason he moved to Twickenham was to look after his eccentric relative.

A year after Saklatvala's return from India, the first world war broke out. The attendant horrors, and the political and social repercussions of the conflict, had a lasting effect on the development of his socialist ideas. The war itself, and its almost inevitable product, the Russian revolution, galvanised Saklatvala into activity. This clash between the major colonial powers pushed Saklatvala, as it did so many others, in a leftward direction. It was during the war period that his nascent socialist views took shape and developed, and by 1919 he had become something of a national figure in the ILP. He had also embraced the revolutionary brand of socialism and was a committed supporter of the Russian experiment. In the space of four years, he had changed from being a card-carrying, though inactive socialist, with no worked-out perspective, into a virtually full-time agitator whose main ambition was to overthrow capitalism.

Notes

[1] Letter from Sorab Saklatvala to Beram Saklatvala, dated 12 April 1937.
[2] Material supplied by Mr Spittam Cama, a friend of Saklatvala's, from their days at St Xaviers.
[3] *Ibid*.
[4] Frank Harris, *Jamsetji Nusserwanji Tata*, Blackie & Son (India) Ltd. Second Edition, 1958, p169.
[5] *Hansard*, Vol 213, 2274, 25 November 1927.
[6] Letter written by Shapurji Saklatvala, 29 June 1906.
[7] *Ibid*.
[8] *Daily Worker*, 20 January 1936.
[9] Letter from Mrs Saklatvala to Beram Saklatvala, undated.
[10] Letter from S Richards to Beram Saklatvala, 15 March 1937.
[11] Letter from J R Clynes to Beram Saklatvala, 2 March 1937.
[12] Circular dated 7 February 1911, entitled 'General Workers Union in India'.
[13] Interview with Beram Saklatvala on 18 August 1976.

Chapter Two

ILP Days

The Independent Labour Party was Saklatvala's political home for twelve years and for five of these years he was an active and prominent figure within the party. Although his activity started slowly, once it gathered momentum he became totally absorbed in ILP politics. From 1916 onwards he was a fervent campaigner and propagandist for ILP policy, addressing numerous meetings throughout the latter half of the war, particularly on the subject of imperialism. He also raised this issue at ILP national conferences. This was a forerunner of what he was to try to do some years later as an MP – to raise matters at national level while at the same time mobilising support amongst the rank and file. It was during his period in the ILP that Saklatvala developed his passionate and absolute commitment to socialism, an obsession that was to remain with him for the rest of his life. It was also through his activity in the ILP, locally and nationally, that he gained notoriety in the labour movement: his adoption by the Battersea Labour Party and Trades Council as their parliamentary candidate in 1921 was in part due to the number of contacts that Saklatvala had made in the borough through his involvement in the ILP. It was through the ILP too that Saklatvala's ideas about socialism and colonialism developed and matured.

During the war the ILP's membership tripled, reaching over sixteen thousand by 1918. Despite the restriction placed on the party by the war situation there was a good deal of activity. Many ILPers were opposed to the war, and after the introduction of conscription there was an escalation of activity which resulted in an influx of new recruits. Prominent ILP leaders such as Ramsay Mac-Donald and Clifford Allen were opposed to the war, and the party was seen by many as the party of peace. However, while some members, whether for pacifist or socialist reasons, were in opposition to the conflict, many others supported the war and enlisted in the services. It was from among the anti-war elements that support for the Russian revolution and the Communist International found a ready following after 1919. Saklatvala was a part of this trend and he played an important role in trying to win the ILP for affiliation to the Communist International. When this was rejected, Saklatvala, reluctantly, left the ILP, and joined the newly formed Communist Party.

Saklatvala's initial reaction to the outbreak of the war was not that of a revolutionary socialist. Many in the ILP, and on the marxist left, saw the war as an opportunity for perpetuating civil war. Their declared aim was to use the conflict in order to overthrow their own ruling class. Saklatvala's first response was that the conflict should be utilised for practising individual acts of terrorism, and that the object of these attacks should be the British troops in India. He openly consorted with other Indian residents here with the aim of converting them to this point of view. His public expressions of hostility to the rule of the Raj made even some of his friends nervous.

> As soon as the war began a small group met in a restaurant on the corner of Dean Street and Oxford Street to discuss India's attitude in the affair. Bhownagree, Parikh, Delgado, Shapurji and myself used to meet there regularly. But his attitude, which, to put, it bluntly in his own words, was, 'to kill as many Englishmen as possible', soon frightened off Bhownagree, who left us. He used to discuss such schemes as poisoning the British troops in India by infecting the Bombay water supplies with cholera. All this in a public restaurant in time of war, when the waiter might have been a detective.[1]

This early reaction soon changed and by 1917 Saklatvala was in opposition to the war and in sympathy with the conscientious objectors. This transformation was brought about by two influences. First was the terrible carnage wrought by the war, and its subsequent effect on public opinion. Although a majority initially supported the war effort there was a significant minority who increasingly questioned the government's actions; many found their patriotic fervour dampened as the numbers of war dead began to grow. Saklatvala was affected by these national stirring, and as a socialist already, it was not difficult for him to accept the arguments of the revolutionaries in the ILP, that the underlying reasons for the war were economic. He increasingly came across this view the more he became active in the party. Thus the second factor to influence Saklatvala's change of heart about the war was his greater involvement in the ILP.

He joined the City of London branch of the party in 1916, and the discussions that took place there contributed enormously to Saklatvala's political development. It was a large branch, covering the West End and the City, and parts of North London. The branch had a number of left wing activists within its ranks. One of the members was J T Walton Newbold who was the first elected Communist MP in 1922. He served alongside Saklatvala who was elected as a Labour MP at the same time. C H Norman was also a member of the branch, and a prominent supporter of the Communist International. He and Saklatvala were later to become close political allies. When the ILP decided against affliation to the Communist International, C H Norman resigned from the branch, but, unlike Saklatvala, he did not join the Communist Party. Another member of the branch was Clifford Allen, one of the leaders of the ILP, who lived in Battersea and was tried before a military tribunal in the borough for his refusal of military service. The historian, Raymond Postgate, was another branch member who also, for a short period after its formation, became a member of the Communist Party of Great Britain. Arthur Field, who also lived in Battersea, and was a close friend of Saklatvala, and a co-founder in 1917 of the Workers' Welfare League of India, claimed the credit for his recruitment to the branch:

I was invited to lecture to the City of London ILP on

'Constantinople and the War' early in 1915 and there asked to rejoin my old love, which I had helped to create, the ILP. I did. From one of my meetings at Prince Henry's Rooms, Fleet Street, I carried Saklatvala off to the City of London ILP, and he joined.[2]

The importance of the City branch in Saklatvala's development as a revolutionary cannot be overestimated. He made an important contribution to the branch, particularly in developing its international links. The City branch, due to Saklatvala's influence, became a bastion of anti-imperialist solidarity. It was also during his time in the branch that Saklatvala began to make a national impact on the ILP. On two occasions he was elected as a delegate to the ILP national conference. The conferences gave him an opportunity to address a wider audience, and added to his already growing stature within the party.

The first record of any public activity by Saklatvala on behalf of the ILP was not until April 1917, when he addressed a meeting of the branch on the subject of 'Socialism and Racialism'. The meeting was reported in *Labour Leader*, the ILPs weekly paper, and Saklatvala's address received glowing praise. This initial meeting provides an insight into two aspects of his thinking at this time. One was to be a permanent feature, the other was merely a passing phase. The first was Saklatvala's insistence on the ethical appeal of socialism; the second was the notion that socialism must be international in order to be successful:

> On Friday last Mr Shapurje [*sic*] Saklatvala delivered a very interesting lecture on 'Socialism and Racialism'. He pointed out the utter inconsistency between aggressive nationality and socialism. He thought that socialism rested on an ethical principle – it was a desire for the benefit of all and unless it was worldwide at the same time, it would be unsuccessful. His address was well worth hearing.[3]

This emphasis on the morality of socialism was to be a recurring theme, and was a reflection of Saklatvala's Parsee beliefs. The idea that socialism must be global was widely held by socialists at the time. It was generally agreed by marxists that socialist revolutions would occur in a number of countries at the same time. Europe, and Western Europe in particular, was considered to be the most likely setting for such an uprising, because it was industrially developed and the working class was large and fairly well organised. It was thought that socialism could only be successful if it took place on a worldwide basis, since it could not survive in a democratic form surrounded by hostile capitalism. However, after the Russian revolution, the Bolsheviks, faced with the failure of revolutionary movements in the West, developed the idea of the possibility of building socialism in one country.

Saklatvala shared this early belief in the necessity for socialism to be universal, and told the readers of *Labour Leader*:

> Socialism must realise that within the inseperable economic unit of an empire, internationalism is not a secondary and remote stage of evolutionary development, but it is a primary and unneglectable factor of achieving the first stage of success.[4]

Indeed, this approach to internationalism, with a clear commitment to colonial freedom, was later to be one of the main attractions of the communist movement for Saklatvala.

Saklatvala joined the City branch of the ILP in the year that compulsory military service was introduced. Conscription posed a serious problem for the ILP since many people in the party were pacifists, and refused to enlist in the armed forces. They were hauled before military tribunals, where in most cases their objections were over-ruled, and were then sent to centres of forced labour for the duration of the war. For the City branch, and others like it, with a high proportion of the active membership in opposition to the conflict, the problems of maintaining a continuing organisational structure were great. Because of this, a certain amount of reshuffling of personnel took place, and Saklatvala was given a post of responsibility in the branch. But despite the loss of a number of of active members through internment, the City branch was in a buoyant state. It had over three hundred members and a bank balance of thirteen pounds. This reflected the growth of the ILP nationally, from 5,534 in 1916 to 16,631 by 1918.

By the time of the ILP's Annual Conference in 1918, Saklatvala was sufficiently established in the Branch to be elected as a delegate, along with A L Bacharach, B M Landen-Davies and Harold Wratten. It was his first national conference and he used the opportunity to raise the issue of India's independence. He was sceptical about the approach to international affairs of his colleagues in the ILP. He told the delegates that they should be 'more definite in their talk of internationalism'.[5] He successfully moved a resolution on India urging the ILP to take a more active interest in the work of the Indian National Congress. As was consistent with the view expressed in the circular of 1911 referred to earlier, this resolution demanded that the national movement in India should adopt specific measures that would alleviate the lot of India's workers. Saklatvala argued that there should be closer co-operation between the growing Indian labour movement and the Congress. The resolution called for immediate legislation to improve the hours, wages and general conditions of the workers, and supported the long term aim of nationalisation of the land, railways, mines and other important industries. The issues raised by Saklatvala at this conference were to be consistently put forward throughout his political life. Although his attitude towards the Indian National Congress varied, his commitment to promoting the cause of colonial liberation within the British labour movement never altered.

Saklatvala exerted considerable influence in the City branch and this was most marked when it came to issues of international solidarity. Although the branch had a reputation for taking up these questions, Saklatvala's recruitment gave them an added impetus. He was helped in his endeavours by a number of other committed internationalists who were also branch members. The City branch actively encouraged solidarity with national liberation movements, which at the time of the first world war were in their infancy. This kind of activity, which was common in the 1930s, through the work of the League

Against Imperialism, was unusual at this time; the City branch were pioneers of such work. Saklatvala was a fervent advocate of this approach, and he spoke at a number of meetings with representatives of the emerging freedom movements within the British Empire. In 1919, the City Branch organised two meetings in solidarity with national liberation movements. The first was about labour conditions in India, and was attended by delegates from the Indian National Congress. The second was a public conference addressed by members of the South African Native National Congress, and was quite an ambitious venture. India had an established independence organisation, which had support in Britain, and India's independence was a political issue, however remote its attainment might seem. South Africa, on the other hand, had no developed liberation organisation, and there was little support from outside for the African colonies to be freed. It was a noble venture from the branch, showing that while others in the labour movement may have made a distinction between African and Indian freedom, no such dilemma faced the City Branch activists.

Saklatvala began to extend his speaking engagements beyond his local branch, and from 1917 onwards he travelled extensively on behalf of the ILP, addressing meetings in all parts of the country. By 1918 he was totally immersed in and committed to the ILP. He told the delegates at the 1918 conference that he was there as a 'socialist, a sincere, earnest wholehearted believer and supporter of the policy of the Independent Labour Party'.[6] In the same speech he gave an insight into what was to be his life's obsession:

> those of his comrades who had known him since he joined the party in 1909 would know that he only wanted to do one thing, and that was to spread socialism from one end of the world to the other.[7]

Saklatvala's intense level of activity brought him into contact with a large number of people involved in the labour movement. These contacts, which included a number of leading figures in the ILP as well as members of the rank and file, were to prove useful when he later

secured the parliamentary nomination of the Battersea
Labour Party and Trades Council. At this stage Saklatvala
had tremendous respect for the ILP's leader, Ramsay
MacDonald. It was not until some years later, after
Saklatvala had been elected to parliament, that antagonism developed between the two men. MacDonald's
support for India's freedom had made a deep impression
on Saklatvala, and at the 1919 annual ILP conference, he
lauded MacDonalds with great praise. He told the
delegates that MacDonald, and others like him, perso-
nified all that was best in Britain, and claimed that Indians
only submitted to British rule because of their faith in
people like MacDonald; it was not because they had any
confidence in the British ruling class:

> They might wonder that from time to time people in India
> had aquiesced to their presence in the country. The true
> reason was not because they were enamoured with Lord
> Curzon or Lord Harding, but now and again they had seen
> on the horizon an Englishman of the type of Keir Hardie.
> When they had seen a Ramsay MacDonald and had pinned
> their faith in Philip Snowden, they had been living in hopes
> that England was full of Englishmen like these, and it was
> for this reason alone that India had acquiesced to the
> presence of the British.[8]

Saklatvala's admiration for MacDonald was not just
expressed verbally; during the Kharki Election of 1918 he
gave unstinting support to his leader. MacDonald was the
Labour candidate for Leicester, and although Saklatvala
lived in Twickenham in Middlesex, it did not prevent him
from actively participating in MacDonald's campaign. One
of his contemporaries commented that it was this kind of
total involvement that contributed towards Saklatvala's
poor health:

> The most striking instance I can remember at the moment
> of the way in which he used up his physical strength for
> propaganda purposes was during the General Election of
> 1918. For some time during the election Sak travelled from
> London to Leicester evening after evening to speak for Mr
> Ramsay MacDonald and travelled back to London again
> the same night.[9]

Saklatvala's reverence for MacDonald was not unusual. Because of his opposition to the war MacDonald was supported by many of the ILP left, and although Saklatvala, as yet, belonged to no organised left pressure group within the party, he shared the view of other left-wingers that MacDonald was the best leader available.

Saklatvala's activities within the ILP were at every level. Apart from the numerous branch meetings which brought him into contact with the rank and file, by 1919 he had attended two annual conferences. He had made important contributions at both, and was beginning to emerge as a national ILP figure. In the same year *Labour Leader* published two major articles by Saklatvala on India. These articles, which were later reproduced as a pamphlet, established Saklatvala as the ILP's expert on India and India's economic development. At the middle level of the ILP too Saklatvala was starting to make an impact. The ILP was organised in divisions, and each division had representatives on the National Administrative Council. In 1919 and 1920 he unsuccessfully sought to win a seat on the Divisional Council. He also offered himself as a speaker and was on the ILP's annual speaker's list.

On numerous occasions tributes were paid to his oratorical skills in the reports of his meetings that appeared in *Labour Leader*. Throughout 1919 the paper was littered with examples of his obvious ability to recruit to the party. One report claimed that twenty new members were gained through 'our comrade's magnificent address'.[10] Cardiff ILP claimed he was 'India's finest orator'.[11] Other Branch reports verify his popularity as a speaker ... 'each address was an educational treat in itself. Our grateful thanks go out to our comrade and we earnestly appeal to members everywhere when they have the opportunity to hear him to seize it'.[12] His endurance was also remarkable. On a speaking tour of Cleveland, he addressed the Cleveland Federation of the ILP during the day, and then spoke at a public meeting in Middlesborough in the evening. The next day he was in Stockton, speaking at a meeting there. This was just one of the many examples of his absolute dedication to the party.

The effect of 1917

The effect of the Russian Revolution on the European labour movement was profound. Although at first information was difficult to obtain, because of the war and the internal military situation, it did not take long before its importance became apparent. Snippets of news began to filter through, and the achievements of the Bolsheviks were applauded by the more militant sections of the labour movement. Saklatvala, like thousands of other socialists, was transformed by the events in Russia. For him the revolution had a dual significance. Not only was it the first successful attempt by socialists to achieve state power; it was also the first time that a major country had broken free of colonialism. The parallels between India and Russia, for Saklatvala, were striking. For the rest of his political life he made constant comparisons between the two countries. He argued that the advances made in Russia could equally well be achieved in a free, and socialist, India.

Soon after news of the revolution had reached Britain an organisation in support of the Bolsheviks was established, called the People's Russian Information Bureau. The group was short-lived, and there is little surviving material on its origins or work, but according to two contemporary reports Saklatvala was one of its founders. The *Daily Herald* claimed that he took a leading part in its establishment and this assertion was supported by S V Bracher in, *The Herald Book of Labour Members*.[13] The City branch affiliated to the Bureau Conference in October 1918 and was represented at a Bureau Conference the following year, and these actions were probably partly due to Saklatvala's influence. Apart from his activities in the Bureau, he spoke at a number of ILP meetings in support of the revolution. At Swadlincote branch of the ILP in December 1919, he addressed three meetings on, 'What has happened in Russia' and 'What has happened in India'. These meetings, and the attempt to link events in Russia and India, typified his post-1917 view of the world.

In the wake of the Russian revolution the Communist International was founded in March 1919. Its role was to be to establish and organise the work of Communist

Parties throughout the world, and to assist in the spread of revolutionary politics. After the collapse of the Second International at the outbreak of the war, it was inevitable that an international realignment of socialist forces would occur. The Second International, which had previously been the international centre for socialist parties, was discredited in the eyes of many socialists because of its failure to oppose the war. Even before the Communist International was established Saklatvala argued for a new international body. He told an ILP meeting in South East London in October 1918 that the workers needed to organise across national boundaries in order to defend themselves against capitalism:

> In a powerful speech he demonstrated the futility of pursuing political forms which are mere shams and emphasised the need for a world-wide organisation of the workers in the face of the ramifications of industrial and commercial capitalism.[14]

For the next two years the ILP was embroiled in an argument over the merits and demerits of affiliation to the Communist International. During this period Saklatvala emerged as one of the leading spokesperson's of CI supporters within the ILP. The new International laid down twenty-one conditions for affiliation to which any organisation wishing to join would have to adhere. These conditions included the acceptance of the Soviet system of government, the necessity for armed struggle in order to overthrow capitalism, and the dictatorship of the proletariat. Ultimately, agreement to these terms proved impossible for a party like the ILP. This meant that despite some initial success by communist supporters within its ranks, it remained outside.

The emergence of an organised group within the ILP with the express aim of agitating for affiliation to the Communist International took place on the eve of the 1920 annual conference. The Left Wing Group, as they became known, were confident that they could be successful. Before the conference took place a number of important ILP divisions had already voted in favour of affiliation to the Third International. These included Scotland, by 150 votes to 28, and Wales, by 91 votes to 61. Saklatvala was associated with the group from the very beginning. At the London and Southern Counties divisional conference in February 1920, he spoke in favour of a City branch motion which called for the ILP to affiliate to the CI. He opposed a suggestion that the National Administrative Council should first draw up a memorandum on the CI. He claimed that 'to ask the NAC to draw up an impartial report upon the Third International is like asking Sir William Carson to draw up an impartial report on the Sinn Fein Movement and the demand for an Irish Republic'.[15] He was unsuccessful and the motion from the City branch was lost.

The 1920 annual conference marked the high point of communist advance within the ILP. The delegates voted to withdraw from the Second International and to continue negotiations with the Third; but they stopped short of calling for immediate affiliation to the CI. A resolution along these lines was defeated by 472 votes to 206. After the conference, Third International supporters within the ILP began the publication of a journal, *The International*. The aim of the paper was to win support for the Communist International before the crucial conference of the following year. During that year the ILP would continue to negotiate with both the Communist International and a number of other non-committed socialist parties who were outside both Internationals. The aim was to create a new all-embracing world wide organisaton. The ILP sent Clifford Allen and its chairman, R C Wallhead, to Moscow for discussion with the Executive Committee of the Communist International. There were serious disagreements between the two organisations, particularly over the dictatorship of the proletariat, and the establishment and function of Soviets. They could also find no compromise over the Third International's commitment to revolution, and the ILP's equally strong affinity for pacifism. Wallhead and Allen returned from Moscow with no agreement, and immediately the ILP began negotiations to establish a new Socialist International.

This objective was ridiculed by the communist section of

the party, who pointed out that it had first been mooted by the French and German socialists, who had since rescinded their decision and had decided on affiliation to the Communist International. The ILP Left Wing Group issued an appeal to ILP members entitled 'The ILP and the Third International' in January 1921. The appeal, which was signed by Saklatvala and a number of other prominent Left Wing Group members, argued strongly for CI affiliation.

> The French Socialists and German Independents, whose move for a 'reconstructed' International influenced the ILP's attitude last Easter, have now realised that a 'reconstructed' International means the Second International all over again, with all that the Second International implies. They have accordingly, by decisive majorities, rallied to the Third International, and we ask all members of the ILP to consider the facts given in this statement, to realise that the issue lies between the Second and the Third International, and to vote for the affiliation of the ILP to the Third, on which alone a vital and truly international organisation can be built.[16]

Saklatvala played an active part in both *The International*, and in the move for Communist International affiliation. *The International* was published fortnightly in Glasgow and first appeared 19 June 1920. Issue Number One contained an article by Saklatvala on 'Freedom and the International'. He wrote again for the journal in September, this time with a contribution on, 'Ireland and the ILP'. This was the last edition of the paper, which was rather surprising given the imminence of the 1921 conference. Those who supported the journal included a number of important ILP figures. Many of these, like Saklatvala, were later to become prominent in the Communist Party. J T Walton Newbold was a member of the group. So too were Helen Crawford, Emile Burns and J R Wilson, who were all at one time members of the Executive Committee of the CPGB. Rajani Palme Dutt, one of the party's leading theoreticians for over half a century, was associated with the Group.

Within the City branch the influence of Communist

International supporters was strong. In August 1919
Saklatvala was nominated by the branch for the position of
ILP representative on the Executive of the London
Labour Party.[17] The same meeting elected him as a
delegate to the London Labour Party Annual Conference.
C H Norman, another leading activist in the Left Wing
Group, was, during 1920, the acting chairman of the
branch. The City branch was consistent in its support of
the Third International. In September 1919 the branch
passed a resolution supporting the action of the Swiss
Socialist Party in withdrawing from the Second and
joining the Third, Moscow International, and hoping that
the British section would not be long in following their
example.[18] This decision was reaffirmed at a special
meeting held in January 1920.

At the same time as the struggle over the Internationals
was taking place in the ILP, moves were afoot outside the
party to establish a new revolutionary organisation.
Negotiations towards this end had been taking place for
some time and had started even before the founding of
the new International. The ILP had been involved from
the beginning in discussion taking place to unite several
left parties to form a new revolutionary organisation. The
other main participants were the British Socialist Party
(the renamed SDF) and the Socialist Labour Party, which
had split from the SDF in 1900. The BSP was affiliated to
the Labour Party and had a membership of 6000. The SLP
was mainly based in Scotland and its membership was only
around one thousand. After the Russian revolution and
the formation of the Third International, the majority of
the participants in the discussion agreed that the new
party should be based on adherence to the principles of
the Communist International and support for the Soviet
system. These terms proved unacceptable to the ILP and
the party withdrew from the discussions.

The Communist Party of Great Britain was formed at a
Unity Conference held in July/August 1920. The 160
delegates came mainly from the British Socialist Party and
the Socialist Labour Party. The ILP Left Wing Group sent
greetings to the Conference. Saklatvala was one of the
four signatories to this message and this gives a further

indication of his importance within the group. The group's strategy, which was fully supported by Saklatvala, was to welcome the formation of the Communist Party, but to stay outside its ranks in the hope of winning the ILP for Communist International affiliation. In their message to the conference the four spokesperson's for the group made their position clear.

> Our main objective is to adhere to our organisation, which logically in our opinion can have no other course open to it but to act with other internationalist comrades along the lines of the Third International and to which end we are now unceasingly devoted.
>
> You will readily understand therefore the necessity of our absence from your convention, though the rapid establishment of a strong Communist Party in Great Britain is as dear to us as to you.[19]

The group's policy towards the newly formed Communist Party was contradictory. While welcoming the formation of the new party, they also called for a strengthening of the ILP left wing. It deplored the fact that a number of ILP left-wingers had left to join the new party thereby reinforcing the hand of the anti-communist section within the ILP:

> We are holding a position of great strategic advantage, at the present time against odds. If we give way or we are scattered the loss will not be ours individually, but the movement generally, just as much as the gain would be a successful issue of our perseverance. We want our ranks to stand firm as well as solid, we can ill afford to give away our fighters. We even need reinforcements. We therefore trust you will take no action which might scatter or thin our ranks, and we even hope that you will do everything in your power to reinforce us with every fraternal assistance, so that we may ultimately hold the ILP citadel in the service of communism here and on the continent.[20]

The first indication of how the 1921 annual conference would vote over this issue came with the Scottish Conference of the ILP in January 1921. At the previous conference, Scotland, an important and usually militant

division, had voted overwhelmingly in favour of Communist International affiliation. This decision was now
overturned, and by almost two to one the Scottish
delegates voted against joining with Moscow. Soon
afterwards the Welsh division too revised its earlier
decision, and by February 1921 a number of important
ILP divisions had voted against CI affiliation.

The all important 29th annual conference of the ILP
was held at Southport on 27-29 March 1921. Surprisingly,
and for no apparent reason, Saklatvala, although still a
member of the City branch, was one of the two delegates
to conference from the Clapham branch.[21] Early on in the
proceedings he made his presence felt by speaking in the
debate on the Report of the National Administrative
Council. He used the occasion to try to win support for the
Russian government and the Communist International.

> How could they ask Lloyd George to enter into closer
> political and trading relations with the Russian govern-
> ment when they said that for socialist purposes their own
> representatives must not sit round a table with the Soviet
> representatives or enter an International with them.[22]

Saklatvala further argued that over a number of important
national and international questions the ILP had not
remained true to its socialist principles. It was this view
that the ILP had renounced its socialist heritage, rather
than the ILPs rejection of CI affiliation, that ultimately led
to his resignation from the party. Even before the debate
on affiliation took place the ILP left received a rebuff. The
chairman reported that a letter had been sent to the
conference informing the delegates that Arthur Mac-
Manus, the Chairman of the Communist Party, would
attend the conference as the representative of the CPGB
and the CI. Rather presumptuously the letter stated that
the intention of the MacManus visit was 'for the purpose
of addressing the delegates on behalf of the Communist
International ... we are sure that your NAC will give
Comrade MacManus every facility for this purpose'.[23] The
ILP's secretary had declined the offer, an action that was
endorsed by the conference delegates.

In the crucial debate concerning affiliation, Saklatvala

was one of the principal participants. In a rather rambling speech he again accused the ILP of not being militant enough in its socialist endeavours:

> British Imperialism, with its great idealist opponent the ILP, had today managed to get a million more square miles. British militarism today had reached the highest point of brutal bestiality and had gone beyond all bounds of honour. If that was the potency of the ILP idealism, why were they offended when others came and said, 'keep your idealism, but make it more potent'.[24]

He recognised that one of the major obstacles to winning the debate was the Third International's own terms for admission, and urged the delegates, rather like a doctor, 'to go to Moscow, accept the Twenty One Points and those who felt the points were too bitter, swallow them'.[24]

On this occasion Saklatvala's eloquence was not enough. In reply, MacDonald, at his rhetorical best, accused Saklatvala, and Communist International supporters, of disruption:

> They were all grateful to Saklatvala for his very noble sentiments about brotherhood, but he had the greatest difficulty in banishing from his mind the activities of the Party with which Saklatvala was associated. He had informed them he did not want disruption, but his Party had been officially instructed from Moscow to remain inside the ILP to disrupt it.[25]

These accusations of disruption must have been particularly hurtful in view of Saklatvala's long record of work in the ILP. Furthermore, Saklatvala may have been 'associated' with the Communist Party, but he certainly did not join that organisation until some time later. Even then it was only after much soul searching, and after he had suffered a number of defeats at local level in a last rearguard attempt to undo the work of the conference.

When the motion for affiliation to the Communist International was finally put it was defeated overwhelmingly by 521 votes to 97. This heavy defeat for the left was not helped by the absence from the conference of Clifford Allen. Allen had negotiated in Moscow on behalf of the

ILP and was known to be much more sympathetic to
affiliation than his co-negotiator, R C Wallhead. But it is
doubtful if even his presence could have swayed the
delegates, in the face of such determined opposition to the
conditions for affiliation.

Not only were the left defeated over this issue, but their
candidates were trounced in the elections to the National
Administrative Council. Only Helen Crawfurd obtained
enough votes to go forward to the second round, and then
she came bottom of the poll. All the other members of the
Left Wing Group were defeated on the first ballot.

The high hopes of the previous year had not come to
fruition, and after the conference the members of the Left
Wing Group were undecided as to what to do next. Should
they stay on in the ILP and work for its transformation
along communist lines, or should they leave and join the
Communist Party? The group had never had a clear
strategy in the event of its defeat and as a consequence the
membership went in both directions. Estimates vary, but
anywhere between five hundred and one thousand joined
the Communist Party.[26]

There were some moves at local level to set up entirely
new socialist organisations, but without much success. This
was the case in Saklatvala's branch. Soon after the
conference, at the annual general meeting in April, he
moved a resolution that the branch be dissolved and
reformed as the City of London Socialist Society:

> In view of the now declared opposition of the ILP to the
> Third International and its adhesion to the Vienna Union
> of Socialist Parties and in view of the general conduct of
> the business of the Party by the NAC, the members of this
> branch are of the opinion that no advantage can be gained
> by continuing the City of London Branch of the ILP, but
> hereby form themselves into the City of London Socialist
> Society for the advocacy of the principles of Socialism and
> the policy represented by the Third International.[27]

This resolution was defeated by 22 votes to 16. An
amendment, which favoured an en bloc secession to the
Communist Party was defeated by 11 votes to 8. There
were 45 members present at the meeting.[28]

A month after his first attempt, Saklatvala tried again to get the branch to sever its links with the ILP. This time he moved a resolution that payment of affiliation fees to Divisional and National funds be suspended.

> In view of the unconstitutional action of the Southport Conference in deciding in favour of affiliation to the Vienna Union when the delegates had no instructions whatever from the branches, and when the branches were not given an opportunity of seeing the Report before it was accepted. In view of the ill-advised step of the Conference being induced to withdraw the new Policy and Programme clauses which were practically accepted by all the Divisional Conferences, and in view of the attitude of the ILP delegates towards the Vienna Conference of anticipating a direct opposition to the Third International, when they were on a supposed mission to approach it through indirect channels, this branch of the City of London decides to hold in suspense all affiliation fees to the Divisional and National Funds for at least six months, or till such time as the ILP movement adopts a proper Socialist and anti-capitalist Policy and Programme, severs its imposed connection with the Vienna Union, and starts on a fresh and sincere effort to seek fraternity and ultimate affiliation with the Third International.[29]

The resolution was not seconded, whereupon Saklatvala tendered his resignation from the ILP, which was accepted with regret. At the same meeting nine other resignations were received by letter, including that of C H Norman.

In his attempts to get the City branch to break with the ILP Saklatvala made clear that it was not just over the affiliation issue that he was at variance with his own party. His exasperation at the direction in which the ILP was travelling was much in evidence in his own letter of resignation. The letter made no mention of him joining any other party and he was at pains to explain that his resignation was not brought about by a single issue. Such was Saklatvala's standing in the movement that *Labour Leader* decided to publish this letter in full:

> On the failure of my resolution tonight to hold in suspense the affiliation of this branch with the ILP. I have resolved to tender you my resignation as a member of the branch,

thereby severing my connection with the Independent
Labour Party of Great Britain.

I need hardly say that it gives me considerable pain to cut
myself off from the association of the comrades of this
branch, but perforce that is left to me as the only mode of
retiring from the ILP. I do not think it at all necessary to
elaborate upon the reason for my doing so, but I may say
that it is not merely upon the issue of my comrades not
finding themselves as ready to join the Third International
as hastily as I have been. Looking back at the entire
proceedings of the Southport Conference, I fail to see any
resolution carried there as a measure of socialism, and
even in several of them I painfully discover a spirit not at
all creditable to socialism or communism.

It also appears to me that this was not a chance voting at
a single conference, but it is the new life on which the ILP
members are launching out, namely of seeking municipal
and parliamentary advantages at the sacrifice of the spirit
of the true socialism. Holding such a view, rightly or
wrongly, I find myself unable to continue my membership
in the movement. I can scarcely let this opportunity go by
without expressing my thanks and gratitude to the
numerous comrades in the movement whose hospitality,
good fellowship and pleasant friendship I have enjoyed. I
still hope that even in the newly acquired temperament of
the ILP the spirit of persecution will not form part, and we
who hold different views and opinions will continue to
have the privilege of occasionally expressing and discuss-
ing our views.

The ILP comrades know very well how Labour Party
and Trade Union organisations though differing in views
from them, have extended to ILP members unstinted
invitations for addressing meetings or for social amenities,
and I have little doubt that ILP members will show to their
potential adversaries the same spirit of fairness.[30]

Saklatvala's fond farewell to his old party was marked by a
high degree of comradeship and tolerance. There was
little animosity, and he was not slow to commend the many
pleasures that party membership had brought him.
Although he made no mention of joining the Communist
Party, within a few months that was where he had made
his political home. This was not inevitable. Such was his
love of the ILP that it was conceivable that he could have

stayed on to carry on the political fight. This course of action was taken by a number of ILP left-wingers. But Saklatvala, like many of the activists in the Left Wing Group, opted for immediate membership of the new party. Given his commitment to the Russian revolution and the Communist International there seemed little other choice. The decisive rejection of CI affiliation, by such a large majority, held out little hope of winning the ILP for communism. Once the choice was made, Saklatvala put at the Communist Party's disposal all his considerable talents and energy. The party gained a first class propagandist, with the added benefit that within a few weeks of his joining he had been adopted as the Labour parliamentary candidate for Battersea North. It was the securing of this nomination that was to help make Saklatvala one of the best known communists in Britain during the 1920s and early 1930s. But had it not been for the large number of people he had met through his activity in the ILP, and the oratorical skills he had learnt in that organisation, it is doubtful that he would have been considered by the Battersea Labour Party as their standard bearer for the next election.

Notes

[1] Recollections of Mr Spittam Cama.
[2] Arthur Field, *Pages from my life*.
[3] *Labour Leader*, 26 April 1917.
[4] *Labour Leader*, 24 July 1918.
[5] Report of the 26th Annual Conference of the ILP, April 1918, p81.
[6] Report of the 26th Annual Conference of the ILP, *op cit,* p81.
[7] *Ibid*, p81.
[8] Report of the 27th Annual Conference of the ILP, April 1919, p76.
[9] Letter from Herbert Bryan to Arthur Field, 23 February 1937.
[10] *Labour Leader*, 4 December 1919.
[11] *Ibid*.
[12] *Labour Leader*, 1 January 1920.
[13] S V Bracher, *The Herald Book of Labour Members*, Labour Publishing Company 1923.
[14] *Labour Leader*, 31 October 1918.
[15] *Labour Leader*, 12 February 1920.
[16] *The ILP and the Third International*, leaflet issued January 1921 by the ILP Left Wing Group.

[17] *Labour Leader*, 28 August 1919.
[18] *Labour Leader*, 4 September 1919.
[19] Report of Communist Unity Convention, London, 1920.
[20] *Ibid.*
[21] Report of the 29th Annual Conference of the ILP, 1921.
[22] *Ibid.*
[23] *Ibid.*
[24] *Ibid.*
[25] *Ibid.*
[26] See reports in *Labour Leader* 1921.
[27] *Labour Leader*, 22 April 1921.
[28] City of London Branch ILP Minutes, and *Labour Leader*, 22 April 1921.
[29] City of London ILP Minutes, and *Labour Leader* 27 May 1921.
[30] City Of London ILP Minutes, and *Labour Leader* 10 June 1921.

Chapter Three

The Labour Party

Saklatvala was adopted as the Labour candidate for the London constituency of Battersea North in June 1921. He joined the Communist Party at about the same time as his selection. At two general elections, although a known Communist, he was officially endorsed by the Labour Party nationally as one of their candidates. For almost a year he sat as a Labour MP, until he lost his seat in 1923. He was a member of the Parliamentary Labour Group, and was involved in policy-making at the highest level. He was a delegate to Labour Party conferences, and during the period of the first Labour government he was consulted by that government about Indian affairs. To all intents and purposes Saklatvala was a trusted, loyal, and active Labour Party member. He was by no means unique. There were many Communists who were equally involved in the Labour Party. Not all had risen to such dizzy heights as parliamentary candidate or MP, but many, particularly at local level, held responsible positions within the party.

Saklatvala's active involvement in the Labour Party spanned the years 1918 to 1925. During that period Labour's early radical ideas began to mellow. In the aftermath of the first world war, in 1918, the annual conference of the Labour Party adopted the now famous Clause Four addition to its constitution, advocating the public ownership of the means of production, distribution and exchange. Labour's 1918 general election programme, *Labour and the New Social Order*, demanded the 'burial of capitalism'. However, by the time of the first Labour government in 1924, Labour's ideas had changed.

There was no longer any demand for the radical alteration of society. The short-lived Labour government, dependent as it was on Liberal support, initiated no significant reforming measures. The revolutionary and reforming passion that was widespread at the end of the war had subsided by the early 1920s, and Labour altered its programme accordingly. The party's socialist message was even more muted by a postwar influx into its ranks of ex-Liberals. These converts saw a more 'moderate' Labour Party as the only viable alternative to the Tories, the Liberal Party having lost considerable support. The consequence of these changes was that during the time of Saklatvala's Labour Party involvement, the party moved steadily to the right.

The period of Saklatvala's Labour Party membership was terminated by the carrying out of expulsions of Communists from the party. Saklatvala played a prominent role in the unsuccessful campaign by Communist Party members for the right of their party to win affiliation. However, the failure of this campaign, together with Labour's move to the right, led to a growing hostility to Labour, culminating in a change of Communist Party policy in 1929. For six years after this, the Labour Party was regarded as the main enemy of the working class by Communists. Saklatvala's political career reflects these changing attitudes.

Communist-Labour relations

From the time of the Communist Party's formation, in 1920, until 1924, Communists could be individual members of the Labour Party. They enjoyed the same rights as other members of the party. It was not until the 1924 Annual Labour Party Conference that this practice was challenged and Communists were barred from holding dual membership. Their expulsion, for procedural and other reasons, was not instantaneous, and it was not until after the general strike in 1926 that Communists were finally driven out of the party. It was during this earlier period that Saklatvala established himself as the candidate of a united Battersea labour movement. Throughout the first half of the 1920s, whether in

parliament or outside, Saklatvala was as active in the
Labour Party as the Communist Party. If it was the ILP
that developed his political awareness, then it was the
Labour Party that acted as the springboard by which he
achieved fame. To understand why he was involved in two
parties at the same time, it is necessary to look at events
prior to the establishment of the CPGB.

Saklatvala belonged to a number of different socialist
organisations. He was a member of the Independent
Labour Party, the Labour Party, and the British Socialist
Party. This was not unusual before the first world war.
Labour Party membership did not exclude people from
belonging to the BSP, the ILP, the Fabian Society, or any
other socialist or labour organisation. The decision by the
Labour Party to refuse affiliation to the newly formed
Communist Party in 1921 was unique in Labour Party
history, particularly as the majority of CPGB members had
previously been members of the BSP, which had been,
before its merger into the Communist Party, a Labour
Party affiliated organisation.

Although in the first year of its existence the CPGB
attracted many revolutionary socialists to its ranks, many
members of the new party continued to work in the
Labour Party. For Saklatvala, and for many other
Communists, it was a part of their political culture to
belong to the Labour Party but to give their energies and
devotion to a smaller and more revolutionary organisation. It was perfectly natural therefore, after the
Communist Party was formed, that Communists should
seek to be active in both parties. It was the continuation of
a tradition that stretched back over a number of years.

Even during Saklatvala's intense period of activity in the
ILP from 1917-1921 he did not neglect the Labour Party.
He had challenged on a number of occasions for a position
on the Executive of the London Labour Party, from his
new found base in the National Union of Clerks, which
he joined in October 1917. The union's Central Branch
nominated him as the London Labour Party's delegate to
the Annual Conference; they also nominated him for the
London Labour Party Executive Committee, as one of its
seven trade union representatives. Although he was

unsuccessful in both contests, the branch nominated him again in 1919 and 1920, with the same result. At the 1919 London Labour Party Conference, which he attended as a delegate from the City of London ILP, he successfully moved an amendment to a housing resolution which committed the London Party to state intervention in house building. This indicates his concern for public housing, which was to be a major issue in Battersea. In addition Saklatvala attended a number of London Labour Party Conferences and this shows that he was sufficiently active in his branch to be selected as a delegate. This Labour Party involvement was to continue after he joined the CPGB.

Saklatvala, as a Communist operating within the Labour Party, reflected the Communist Party's changing approach towards the larger organisation; but he was also instrumental in altering Communist opinion about the Labour Party. Saklatvala's Labour Party career gives an indication of the increasing hostility felt by the Communists towards those they initially regarded as their allies. This antagonism reached its height with the adoption of the so call 'New Line' policy in 1929.[1] This strategy saw the Labour Party as the bastion of the ruling class, and it became the duty of Communists to oppose Labour in every conceivable way. Unlike earlier times, Communists stood against Labour candidates and party supporters were told not to vote Labour under any circumstances. During the period of the 'New Line' doctrine, Labour Party affiliation was no longer the party's chief strategic aim. Instead the Communists sought to replace the Labour Party, and to assert themselves as the only party of the working class.

The 'New Line' period lasted for six years and was not finally jettisoned until 1935. Saklatvala's contribution towards the adoption of the strategy is significant. He wrote to the Executive Committee of the CPGB in 1925 urging a much more hostile approach towards the Labour Party. His letter indicates that a number of Communists, even those most associated with the Labour Party, were already unhappy with the policy of seeking a united front with Labour. Many of the arguments put forward by

Saklatvala in 1925 were later to become party policy with the acceptance of the 'New Line' strategy four years later. Saklatvala's often contradictory attitude towards the Labour Party typifies the mixture of feelings that were held by Communists at this time. And through Saklatvala's intimate association with the Labour Party, both as an active member and as an MP, the issues that were hardening Communist sentiments against Labour can be clearly seen: the experience of the first Labour government, the expulsion of Communists from the Labour Party, the betrayal of the general strike. All these factors influenced Saklatvala's thinking about the Labour Party, just as they influenced the thinking of many other communists.

The main strategic aim of the CPGB, from its formation until 1927, was to gain Labour Party affiliation. The party's electoral tactics corresponded with this objective. At the foundation conference of the Communist Party in 1920, Lenin had sent a letter advising the delegates that the new party should affiliate to the Labour Party, and should participate in elections. These were the two most controversial issues at the conference, but the delegates voted to heed Lenin's advice, and the newly elected leadership set about trying to fulfil both these aims.

The question of Labour Party affiliation was the most contentious of the two issues and the conference had only voted in favour by 100 votes to 85; however, soon afterwards, the Party Executive sent a short letter to the Labour Party National Executive Committee applying for affiliation. The letter made two points: it stressed the Communists' belief in the dictatorship of the proletariat and the party's right of control over its own MPs – not demands that were likely to be sympathetically received by the Labour leadership. The response from the Labour Party NEC was to reject the application for admission, and this rejection was supported overwhelmingly by the 1921 Annual Labour Party Conference. After this rebuff the Communist Party changed its tactics. In further requests for admission it placed greater emphasis on the federal structure of the Labour Party, and the rights of affiliated groups, however critical, to operate within it.

The issue of Communist Party affiliation was discussed at every Labour Party Conference from 1921 to 1925. Saklatvala participated prominently in these discussions and he was influential in arguing the Communists' case. At the 1923 Labour Party Conference, he stressed the Communist Party's new realism and maintained that there was little basic difference between the two parties. He told the delegates that it would be in everyone's interest if they all worked together:

> If the British Labour Party had misunderstood the purpose of the Communist Party, if it had misinterpreted the idea of the Communist Party, which was not, as Mr Frank Hodges had said, that they were opposed to political action, but that they possessed less faith in its success than other members of the Labour Party, then he put it to the delegates it was merely a difference of opinion on a political point and not of a fundamental character, and it was quite possible – he had found it so in his own case – to accept the Constitution of the Labour Party, to work and serve the Labour Movement in this country and to be at the service of the working class organisations from Trade Unions to Communist branches, if they only made up their minds to fight with sincerity. The Communist Party only desired to work with the Labour Party and he appealed to the conference to give them a chance.[2]

The delegates were not impressed, and Communist Party affiliation was decisively rejected by 2,880,000 votes to 366,000.

Saklatvala attended the conference as a delegate from the St Pancras Borough Labour Party and Trades Council. He lived in Parliament Hill Fields, and it was his local constituency party. In all, 38 of the delegates to the conference were also members of the Communist Party. Apart from Saklatvala, who attended three Annual Labour Party Conferences, Harry Pollitt was another well known Communist who was regularly elected as a delegate. This gives an indication of the integration and acceptance of Communists within the Labour Party during the first four years of the 1920s. This integration, of which Saklatvala was a part, did not just extend to annual conferences. In a whole number of Labour Parties and

Trades Councils, Communists were often a significant factor. Communists were Labour councillors, aldermen, and sometimes mayors. In the London Borough of Poplar, where in 1921 the Labour Council made a stand for the equalisation of the rates, two of the subsequently imprisoned Labour councillors were also members of the Communist Party.[3] Another councillor, A A Watts, who was not sent to prison, was also a communist and served on the party's first organisation committee. In neighbouring Bethnal Green, Joe Vaughan, ex-mayor of the borough, and parliamentary labour candidate, was also a member of the Communist Party. Before their expulsion the activity of communists in the Labour Party, at every level, was often greater than their participation in their own party. This situation did not change until after 1925.

Communists were sufficiently involved in the Labour Party to win, in a number of instances, the Labour parliamentary nomination. At two General Elections in 1922 and 1923, a number of Communists won endorsement as Labour candidates. Some received national Labour Party approval, while others were supported by their local Labour Party and Trades Council. Saklatvala was the official Labour candidate at both elections. He was the nominee of the Battersea Labour Party and Trades Council and was endorsed by the Labour Party nationally as one of their candidates. At the 1922 election, when he won the seat for the first time, there were three other Communists who were Labour candidates: J J Vaughan in South West Bethnal Green, W Windsor in North East Bethnal Green, and Alec Geddes, who contested Greenock. Vaughan, like Saklatvala, was an officially endorsed Labour candidate. The other two received local Labour Party support, but did not gain national Labour Party approval. In addition, J T Walton Newbold, supported by the local Labour Party and Trades Council, stood as a Communist in Motherwell and won the seat. He was the first elected Communist MP.

By the General Election of December 1923 the number of Communist Party members standing as Labour candidates and endorsed by the Labour Party nationally had increased to five. Apart from Vaughan and

Saklatvala, William Paul in Manchester, M Philips Price in Gloucester and Ellen Wilkinson in Ashton under Lyme, had all won Labour Party approval. Two other communists were the nominees of their local Labour Party and Trades Council, but did not gain national Labour Party endorsement. These were Alec Geddes, again in Greenock, and Aitken Ferguson in Glasgow.

The endorsement of some Communists as Labour candidates, while others were not endorsed, was as much due to the lack of a coherent policy on the part of the CPGB as to any opposition from within the Labour Party. The Communist Party had issued no clear instructions to its members who were adopted parliamentary Labour candidates. They were not told whether or not they should accept the Labour Party's terms for endorsement. That this was the case emerged from the discussions that took place at two Annual Labour Party Conferences. In one of these discussions Saklatvala figured very prominently.

His endorsement by the Battersea Labour Party and Trades Council was first raised at the 1922 Annual Labour Party Conference. In the debate that ensued, which involved the Labour Party almost as a bystander, it became apparent that the CPGB had no clear strategy towards party members who were also Labour parliamentary candidates. A delegate asked why the Labour Party NEC had turned down the candidature of a Mr Foulis, a Communist Party member in Leith, and yet had accepted that of Saklatvala in Battersea. Arthur Henderson, the Labour Party General Secretary, on behalf of the NEC, replied by reading a communication of 12 December 1921 to Mr Coltman, the Secretary of Battersea Labour Party, setting out the terms in which the Executive had agreed to endorse the candidature of Mr Saklatvala for Battersea North. The letter had stated that the candidate should appear before the constituency with the designation of 'Labour Candidate' only, independent of all other political parties, and if elected should join the Parliamentary Labour Party; and that at the General Election he should in his election address and in his campaign give prominence to the issues as defined by the National Executive from the general Party programme. In addition, if elected, he should act in harmony with the constitution and standing orders of the party.[4] Arthur Henderson pointed out that Saklatvala was prepared unconditionally to accept all these demands. At a special meeting of the Executive Committee of the Battersea Labour Party and Trades Council at which he was present, a resolution had been passed unanimously endorsing his candidature on the conditions laid down in the communication from the Labour Party, and Saklatvala had reaffirmed his adhesion to the conditions.

Henderson therefore considered that there was no difference between the NEC's endorsement of Saklatvala's candidature and that of any other Labour candidate. Saklatvala had given the undertakings asked for; if there was any problem it was due to the Communist Party's own inconsistency. He told the conference that:

> The delegates would now see the position that the Executive took up with regard to the Saklatvala candidature. If there was anything wrong with that candidate, in his judgement it was not from the standpoint of the Labour Party but from the standpoint of the Communist Party. Mr Saklatvala, who was a delegate sitting in that conference, knew full well that he was in exactly the same position as any one of the candidates, as any one of the 73 members of the House of Commons, or any of the 400 candidates whom the Executive had endorsed.[5]

The difference between Saklatvala in Battersea and Foulis in Leith was simply that Saklatvala was prepared to accept the conditions laid down by the Labour Party, but Foulis was not.

The different tactics adopted by the Communist Labour candidates were highlighted at the 1924 Labour Party conference. Aitken Ferguson, a Communist Party member, was the Labour candidate for the Kelvingrove (Glasgow) by-election of 23 May 1924. After first receiving national endorsement, Ferguson and the local Labour Party and Trades Council jeopardised that support by not campaigning for Labour Party policy. The conference report stated that the candidature of Mr Ferguson had been recommended by the Scottish Executive and endorsed by the National Executive, but, because of developments during the contest, it had been found impossible to render further official support.[6] When the withdrawal of support was challenged at the conference by Communist Party member J R Campbell, Egerton Wake, the National agent, replied that

> the labour government's policy was not being advocated by the candidate who was the chosen nominee of the Kelvingrove Labour Party. The matter was taken up with officials at Kelvingrove, and the replies received by the National Executive were not satisfactory. There were statements in the Election Address and many more statements on the platform, which were certainly not in accord with the programme of the Labour Party and eventually, as satisfaction could not be secured, the Executive decided that while endorsement had been given, and while they did not desire to do anything in the midst of the contest to create further confusion, it was impossible under the circumstances to render further official support to the candidate in question.[7]

Saklatvala, Labour MP

Accusations of this kind were never levelled against Saklatvala, or the Battersea Labour Party. At the two elections at which he was the nationally endorsed Labour candidate he strictly abided by the undertaking given that he would campaign for Labour Party policy. In marked contrast to the stand taken by Ferguson, at the 1923 general election Saklatvala told the electors of North Battersea that he was prepared to stand by Labour's election programme. His election address declared: 'I enclose herewith the Labour Party's official Manifesto which I am pledged to support with the only criticism that this is the least that one can demand under the present conditions of life all over the world'. The previous year, standing for the first time as the Labour candidate, he had gained the support of one of the most vociferous of anti-Communists within the Labour Party, J R Clynes. Clynes, as Chairman of the Parliamentary Labour Party, had sent Saklatvala a personal message of support,

Mr Saklatvala has for years worked hard in the people's cause and he is intensely in earnest in the service he has undertaken. In Parliament he will not only be an able and devoted servant of the workers in this country, but his special knowledge of the economic conditions of millions of our fellow subjects in India would compel attention to the neglected conditions of workers in that part of the empire.[8]

Clynes had known Saklatvala since his days in Matlock; he did not share his views, but he was prepared to support him because he was a Labour candidate.

Saklatvala was elected as the Labour MP for Battersea North at the general election of November 1922. His election and short period as a Labour MP was fraught with contradictions. Although elected on Labour's electoral programme and a member of the Labour parliamentary group, Saklatvala also owed allegiance to the Communist Party. For almost a year he walked a political tightrope: he was committed to arguing Labour's case both inside Parliament and outside, and yet at the same time his conviction lay with the revolutionary brand of socialism.

Although in many ways he was regarded as the same as any other member of the Labour Parliamentary Group, in some respects he was very much an outsider. He was treated suspiciously by the Labour leadership, but nevertheless was given some important responsibilities within the parliamentary party. Even when he was outside Parliament, during the nine months of the first labour government in 1924, his expertise on India was utilised by the administration. His advice was sought after, if not adhered to, by those within the party who were opposed to his ideology. It says something for Saklatvala's grasp of colonial affairs that this wealth of knowledge was recognised, even by his political opponents.

The difficulties of Saklatvala's position as a Labour MP and a Communist Party member became apparent immediately after his election. At this election no Communist stood against Labour, and CPGB members were urged, where there was no Communist standing, to work and vote for the Labour candidate. However, immediately after the election the party issued a statement that did not differentiate between Saklatvala, elected as a Labour MP, and J T Walton Newbold, elected as a Communist. They were both referred to as 'the Communist fraction in Parliament'. The Communist Party made clear that Saklatvala, in spite of his Labour Party commitments, should still operate under the control and guidance of the party:

> In the promoting of Labour candidates, we are not concerned so much with the candidate getting there because of personal influence and personal deportment. The basis must be the Party programme otherwise the victory is not for the Party at all. The points of the programme must be agreed upon by the Central Committee and operated under the jurisdiction and control of the Party Executive. Moreover, when a candidate is returned to the House of Commons, he should hold his position there as a member of the Communist Party, responsible to the Executive Committee of the Party.[9]

In line with the strategy of trying to gain affiliation, both the newly elected MPs were urged by the party leadership to co-operate with the Labour Parliamentary Group wherever possible: 'our fraction will co-operate with the Labour Party in every struggle against the capitalist parties and they will not hesitate, where the Labour Party fails to carry through the struggle, to stand and fight alone for the interests of the working class'.[10] Saklatvala did co-operate, and throughout his first period in Parliament he functioned primarily as a Labour MP. Had he attempted, in the House of Commons, to argue Communist Party policy when it was at variance with that of Labour, he would have been liable to expulsion from the Labour Parliamentary Group. That this never happened says something for Saklatvala's acceptance of Labour Party discipline.

The careers of the two communist MPs, after their defeat in 1923, went in totally different directions. Newbold left the Communist Party and became a Labour Party stalwart. He moved to the right of the party and

supported MacDonald's formation of a National Government in 1931. Saklatvala remained a loyal and active
Communist Party member until his death.

It was during his first term in parliament that Saklatvala
changed his mind both about the adequacy of the House
of Commons, and the ability of Labour MPs to offer
resistance to that body's all encroaching power. He had
entered parliament with a commitment to open debate, a
commitment that stayed with him all his life. He was also
convinced that Labour MPs in the debating chamber
would be markedly different to the Tories. In both
respects he was disappointed. Looking back on his first
entry into Westminster he commented:

> After a whirlwind campaign in the Election of 1922, I
> found myself ushered into the Assembly at Westminster.
> My critics who were jesting and jeering, and my friends
> who were smiling in doubt, confidently looked forward to
> my almost immediate conversion to the requisite mentality
> for the Mother of Parliaments. However, I had decided to
> give the benefit of the doubt to the House of Commons, to
> take it as an assembly where democratic voice, manners,
> expressions and actions would be permitted if only one
> tried and gave them a chance. I came fresh from a
> Constituency where most of the Irish electors were
> annoyed by the proposed Irish Settlement, and, as in duty
> bound, I attempted to act up to the expectations of my
> democratic voters. Ridicule, contempt, sneers, showered
> from all sides and a look of 'cut him out, he is no good to us
> in this assembly' seemed to be upon the faces of all my
> colleagues. The heavy frowns were not limited to
> reactionary capitalists, for MacDonald's and Henderson's
> frowns were even more severe.[11]

Saklatvala was shocked by the attitude of Labour MPs, and
particularly the Labour leadership's willingness to conform to parliamentary niceties. The same Saklatvala that
during the 1918 General Election had travelled up and
down to Leicester every day to help MacDonald's
campaign was now aggrieved at MacDonald's lack of
resistance to the 'parliamentary embrace'.

Saklatvala's first taste of the House of Commons had
undermined his trust in the ability of Labour MPs to

institute reforms. Soon after this experience, his dealings
with the first Labour government only exacerbated his
doubts about the Labour Party. He was consulted by that
government about a number of matters concerning India.
Along with Hugh Dalton and another Labour MP, Mr
Charleton, he was asked for advice on certain matters in
the new Subsidies and Tarif Bill on India. In a
confidential letter to the members of the Labour Party
Advisory Committee on Finance, Saklatvala pointed out
some of the attendant problems that could be posed by the
new Bill. However, when the proposals drawn up by him,
Dalton and Charleton were sent by Saklatvala to Lord
Oliver, the Secretary of State for India, they met with little
response. Lord Oliver, who had previously been the
Secretary of the Fabian Society, made it clear that he was
not prepared to heed his own party's advice on the
sub-continent.

Saklatvala was also responsible for a much more
comprehensive set of suggestions, *The British Labour
Government and India*. The document was written for the
Labour Party Advisory Committee on International
Questions, and published in July 1924.[12] It was also
submitted to the Joint International Department of the
Trades Union Congress and the Labour Party. It made
clear that despite Saklatvala's commitment to a free and
socialist India, he was still prepared to advocate reforms
that could be achieved within the context of India's
prevailing social and political system. He did not argue for
immediate independence, or for the revolutionary
transformation of Indian society. Instead he recognised
the problems that a Labour administration faced in
relation to India. He put forward a number of proposals
that would alleviate some of the hardship, and would
bring about a limited extension of the franchise, without in
either case upsetting the sub-continent's established order.
None of these suggestions was listened too, and Lord
Oliver was, in Saklatvala's view, even worse than previous
Tory administrators. In an article for *Workers Weekly*
Saklatvala described Lord Oliver as a 'Fabian Imperialist',
who, 'defends the heaven born right of the exploiter, as
did Lord Curzon before him', with the possible difference

that Oliver did it in a more pronounced anti-socialist manner than Curzon as a Tory Viceroy found it possible to do'.[13]

Saklatvala was bitterly disappointed that even a reformist government should be so conservative about India's independence. The failure of the Labour government to take marginal steps towards self-determination was a crucial factor in pushing Saklatvala into a hard line anti-Labour position. Added to this disappointment was his frustration at seeing the way that the first Labour Secretary of State for India operated. Saklatvala's expertise on India made him an obvious choice for a high colonial position in a Labour administration: his knowledge and background of Indian industrial matters were second to none, and there was no one in the Labour Party with such varied experience. However, Saklatvala's commitment to the Communist Party meant that even during the time that he was a Labour MP, there was little chance of political advancement. Reg Bishop, Saklatvala's secretary, explained the incentives that were held out to the newly elected MP:

> For the first year or two after his election as the MP for Battersea North there were many who tried to get him to break from the Communist Party. The Undersecretaryship of State for India was the smallest of inducements held out if only he would be more orthodox in his politics.[14]

It was further alleged that he was sent for by Arthur Henderson and offered the India Office if he would just modify his ideas. He declined both offers.

Saklatvala was kept under close scrutiny during his period as a Labour MP, and Ramsay MacDonald was particularly interested in his activities. It was evident that a careful watch was kept on all left wing groups. There were police spies operating in most of the organisations of the labour movement. MacDonald, when he first became prime minister, received the following communication from Sir Borlaise Childe at New Scotland Yard: 'In accordance with custom I enclose for the Prime Minister a copy of my weekly report on revolutionary movements in

Great Britain in which the more important passages are marked'.[15] These reports, compiled by the Special Branch, contained a wealth of information concerning the Communist Party, and other left and anti-imperialist organisations. MacDonald was especially keen that Saklatvala's movements should be closely observed, and he read meticulously Special Branch Reports on his activities.[16] Saklatvala was certainly aware that while a Labour MP he was a marked man. His house was raided on a number of occasions and his letters were opened. It must have been particularly vexing that such practices, common under Conservative rule, should have been continued even when his own party was in power.

His close personal knowledge of the workings of the Labour government led to a serious disillusionment. He expected little from such a government, but he was still surprised by its lack of reforming zeal. Giving a retrospective view in 1925, he was very bitter that the Labour government had given no leadership and passed no measures that could not have been passed by a Tory government:

> The Labour Party in the present House of Commons has failed to repudiate the actions of the late Labour government. We are in a quandary almost every day in Parliament because there is nothing that the Tory government does about which it is not in a position to say that the Labour Government would have endorsed its action, and in fact did the same itself. The Labour Party in the House has so far failed to repudiate the capitalist measures of the Labour Government. They ought to take an official step and announce that the Labour Movement, as represented by the Parliamentary Labour Party, has nothing whatsoever to do with the reactionary actions of the late so called Labour Government.[17]

The expulsion of communists

A turning point in Labour-Communist relations was the historic decision of the 1924 Annual Labour Party Conference to expel Communists as individual members of the party. Saklatvala attended the conference, again as a delegate from the St Pancras Borough Labour Party and

Trades Council, and during the debate on the Communist Party he wound up for the opposition. The Labour Party NEC were recommending to conference that once more the application for affiliation from the Communist Party be refused. They were further recommending that no member of the Communist Party should be eligible for endorsement as a Labour candidate either for parliament or any local authority.

In the discussion that followed Saklatvala employed the same arguments that he had used the year before. In line with Communist Party strategy he emphasised the federal nature of the Labour Party and claimed that:

> The object of the Constitution of the Labour Party ... was also in the main the object of the Communist Party, there was no difference. They might maintain, as many people did on many questions, that the line which the Labour Party was treading would bring them to their object, perhaps it might or perhaps it never would. Other people rightly or wrongly might maintain that they would reach that object in a reasonable period of time by treading another road. But there was no fundamental opposition between the two parties as there was between Capitalism and anti-Capitalism.[18]

Saklatvala argued that it was a question of degree and little else: the Communists thought that socialism could be achieved quickly, whereas their Labour colleagues were of the opinion that the process would be more drawn out. He went on to say that it was not justifiable to keep Communists out of the Labour Party because they held a different opinion from others as to the method of a limit of time within which they could reach their goal: 'They did not apply such a limitation to any other organisation, wise or unwise, stupid or prudent. It was admitted to be a great working class movement, and yet, it was proposed now to put up a cast iron bar against it'.[19]

When the two motions were put to the vote they were passed overwhelmingly. The Communist Party's application for affiliation was turned down by 3,185,000 votes to 193,000; the proposal that Communists should no longer be eligible as Labour candidates received a smaller but still decisive majority, 2,465,000 votes to 654,000. The third motion on the agenda concerning the Communist Party was to be the most controversial. This was a resolution submitted by the Sutton Divisional Labour Party, which said that no member of the Communist Party should be eligible for membership of the Labour Party. Over this issue there was greater division of opinion but it was still carried, by 1,804,000 votes to 1,540,000.

The result of the 1924 Conference was a major defeat for the Communist Party. It was one of a number of events that was to change Saklatvala's thinking about the Labour Party. He was already greatly disillusioned by his experience of the Labour government, and this only added to his disenchantment. He had been an active Labour Party member for years, and it came as a cruel shock to be faced with a purge. He was doubly resentful that such tactics were adopted by those in the Labour leadership, like Ramsay MacDonald, in whom previously he had placed such trust.

After the conference, the Labour Party NEC decided to establish a sub-committee to look at the implementation of the decisions concerning the Communists. The sub-committee met on a number of occasions and their recommendations were discussed and later accepted by the NEC; while these deliberations were taking place Communists remained members of the Labour Party. It was not until a year later, after further ratification by the 1925 conference, that the removal of Communists from the Labour Party was enforced. This conference was the final blow. In future any Labour Party branch refusing to expel known members of the Communist Party was liable to disaffiliation.

After the setback of the 1925 Labour Party Conference, Saklatvala was one of the most prominent communists to urge a change of policy within the Communist Party. Within a week of the conference closure he had written to the party's executive committee demanding a change of line. He urged the party leadership, in the wake of the conference defeat, to adopt a far more hostile attitude towards the Labour Party. He told the EC:

I feel that the extraordinary circumstances prevailing at the moment call for extraordinary measures to be taken by our party. There is not much doubt in my mind that without drastic measures to build up our Party we shall be submerged into insignificance in Britain. Parliamentary customs and traditions have still a very great attraction for the masses. In order to overcome this we must adopt merciless measures to fight the Labour Party. We shall not succeed to the point of actually wiping it out, but we do not require to do that. What we shall succeed in doing is to give a dangerous shaking to the Parliamentary position of all the Right Wingers and it would then be their turn to patch a peace with the Communist Party at any price and the Left Wing will be forced into an open fight against the Right.[20]

He argued, in what later was to become typical of the CPGB's position, that the Labour Party was no longer a workers' party and had abandoned the struggle for socialism. The Communist Party therefore had to establish itself as the only anti-capitalist party:

We must appeal to the Central Committee at Moscow to let us work temporarily along the lines I am suggesting. We should adopt the attitude that the Labour Party has now deserted its original function and turned itself into a Liberal Reformist Group, like the Irish Nationalist Party, and that the real political crusade for Socialism has been abandoned by the Labour Party, therefore the Communist Party must now set itself up as the only avowed anti-Capitalist party to take such action inside and outside Parliament as will lead to the taking over of the means of production and the abolition of imperialist exploitation.[21]

He further advocated that the trade union movement should be split from the Labour Party and that trade union branches should affiliate to the Communist Party instead; 'We should then in an open manner invite all Trade Union Branches that take this view to affiliate to the Communist Party for the purpose of assisting in the carrying out the political economic struggle of the workers'.[22] The intention of this was to be another feature of future communist policy, the standing of Communist candidates against Labour: 'This affiliation of Trade Union Branches would greatly weaken the position of Right Wing MPs and will increase the chances of rival candidates'.[23] In virtually

every respect the course of action recommended by
Saklatvala in 1925 was later to become communist party
policy, after the adoption of the 'New Line' in 1929.

His letter to the party's executive committee was not just
an isolated example of his growing hostility towards the
Labour Party. At a National Minority Movement
Conference in March 1926, (this was a trade union
grouping set up by the Communist Party in 1924, to
agitate for revolutionary action in the trade unions) he
urged all trade union branches to withhold their political
subscriptions. Saklatvala told the delegates that he hoped
the branches represented would withhold their political
levy and suspend their support to local members until the
leadership behaved more fairly.[24] His view of the
Parliamentary Labour Party was equally critical. He
maintained that Labour MPs were no different to the
Tories. He told the CPGB Executive that, 'the class
struggle is represented in the House of Commons by one
Communist, the policy of duping the working class is
represented by the 614 other members'.[25] With this
perspective he saw little difference between the election of
a Labour or a Tory MP. His criticisms were not just
confined to the Labour leadership: he now had little
confidence in the ability of the Labour left to fight for a
change of policy. He told the delegates to the CPGB's
Seventh Congress, in June 1925: 'Some comrades,
especially our Scottish left wing comrades, are quite honest
in their intentions. But they are not prepared for a clear
breakaway attitude from the front oppositional bench.
The left wing in fact serves very little use. On the whole it
does little more than scratch the surface of the right wing
reactionary attitude'.[26] Saklatvala's response to the
decisions of the Labour Party Conference was symptoma-
tic of a growing demand for change from amongst the
Communist Party membership.

One further influence on Saklatvala's increasingly hard
line attitude towards the Labour Party was the effect of the
1926 general strike. Saklatvala was one of the strike's first
victims, and he shared with many other Communists the
experience of a period in jail. He was arrested for a speech
he made on the eve of the strike to a May Day rally in

Hyde Park. He told the audience that troops should not be used to suppress the strikers:

> We tell the Government that young men in the forces, whether Joynson-Hicks likes it or not, whether he calls it sedition or not to suit the financers and his rich friends, we have a duty towards the men to say to them that they must lay down their arms.[27]

He was arrested three days later and sent to prison for two months. He was in Wormwood Scrubs for the duration of the dispute. Even after the strike's conclusion there was no let-up in the repression faced by the strikers, particularly those in the Communist Party. At Saklatvala's first intended public meeting after his release from prison, he was not allowed to speak and the meeting was banned.

Saklatvala's experiences of police harassment, before, during, and after the strike, was shared by many in the Communist Party. Although their pre-strike membership was less than six thousand, Communists were active in a wide range of activities in solidarity with the miners. For their efforts they were dealt with severely by the state. At its Eighth Congress, held not long after the finish of the strike, the Communist Party estimated that during the strike about 1000 party members were arrested. With subsequent arrests, by the time of the Congress, 1200 party members, between one quarter and one fifth of the entire pre-strike membership of the party, had suffered government repression in one way or another in the miners' cause. As the Congress Report claimed, this was a proportion which no other political body in the labour movement could remotely approach.[28]

The strike reinforced Saklatvala's belief in the inadaquacy of the Labour Party. While he languished in jail, the Labour leadership distanced itself from the miners and called for respect for law and order. The strike hardened his belief that when the capitalist class was challenged it was prepared to resort to force to maintain its rule. The notion cherished by many in the Labour Party of a constitutional advance to socialism was, in Saklatvala's view, dealt a severe blow by the events of May 1926.

Despite his growing criticism of the Labour Party, and

his demand for a change of policy by the Communist Party, he still continued to operate within the larger body. At the beginning of 1925, at the same time as he was writing to the executive committee of the CPGB, he successfully defeated an attempt to remove him from the St Pancras Trades and Labour Council. The Labour Party branch had decided to replace him as the delegate, because of the recent Labour Party Conference decision concerning Communists. However, a meeting of the Trades and Labour Council overturned that decision and ruled that Saklatvala should remain the delegate until such time as the Labour Party NEC made a final ruling on the issue of Communists within the party. He was evidently a popular figure on the council, and at the same meeting he was elected a delegate to a conference of the National Minority Movement. Another active communist on the St Pancras Trades Council was Reg Bishop, Saklatvala's secretary while he was an MP. Bishop was the delegate from St Pancras at the 1925 Labour Party Conference.

Saklatvala's feeling for the Labour Party epitomised the dilemma that the Communist Party as a whole faced. It was not until 1929 that the party finally decided on a qualitative break with its old strategy of unity and affiliation. In the intervening period Saklatvala, like many other Communists, held a mixture of views about the Labour Party. Although after 1925 he argued strongly that the Communist Party should change its policy, it took some time before he could break with his old love. Speaking in the House of Commons on the eve of the general strike, he paid tribute to the Labour Party and argued that the Communist Party was also trying to achieve Labour's aims:

> I myself am the child of the British Labour Party. I am the product of the teachings of the British Trade Unions. I am a member of the Communist Party because, rightly or wrongly, it honestly appears to me to be pointing the way through which the objects laid down by the Labour Party are to be achieved.[29]

Leaving the party

It was not until the end of 1928 that Saklatvala finally broke with the Labour Party. Throughout that year the Communist Party leadership had been involved in discussions with the Communist International about a change of line. The Comintern had expressed reservations about the party's attitude towards the Labour Party, and had urged the CPGB to adopt a more independent role. The membership too was unhappy about the strategy of Labour Party affiliation. These problems were not finally resolved until the 11th Congress of the CPGB in 1929. It was in the midst of this debate, during the transition year of 1928, that Saklatvala, within the space of a month, expressed two opposing views about the Labour Party. At a meeting organised by the District branch of the Communist Party at the Nine Elms Baths in Battersea in November 1928, he claimed he was still a Labour Party member. The local paper, the *South Western Star*, reported that Mr Saklatvala said his position was just the same as before, he was a member of the Communist Party, and also a member of the Labour Party'.[30] (In some cases Communists were still members of the Labour Party where expulsions had not yet been successfully applied. It is difficult to believe, though, that as prominent a Communist as Saklatvala could have escaped the notice of the Labour Party authorities.) If the report of the meeting is correct however, Saklatvala was still expressing a desire, as late as November 1928, and despite all that he had said, to belong to the Labour Party. A month later he seemed to have changed his mind. In reply to a question at a public meeting he repudiated the Labour Party and declared, 'Do you expect me, after the complete desertion of socialism, to belong to the Labour Party? Are you surprised that I belong to the Communist Party'.[31]

Despite his long association with the Labour Party, Saklatvala was no longer convinced that it could achieve any radical reforms. His experience over the previous few years had shaken his confidence in the Labour Party's socialist commitment. And by 1928 it was apparent that the expulsion of the Communists from the Labour Party was a permanent decision, with Communists successfully evicted from most constituency parties. Faced with this changed situation the Communists looked to a more independent role for their own party. Saklatvala's advice to the party's executive, first made in 1925, was now more acceptable; most of his suggestions concerning the Labour Party were incorporated into Communist Party policy with the adoption of the 'New Line' in 1929.

Notes

[1] For a full account of the 'New Line' strategy and its evolution, see appendix, p208.
[2] Report of the 23rd Annual Conference of the Labour Party, June 1923, p188.
[3] For a more detailed account of this incident, see Noreen Branson, *Poplarism*, Lawrence and Wishart 1979.
[4] Report of the 22nd Annual Conference of the Labour Party, June 1922, p174.
[5] *Ibid*, p175.
[6] Report of the 24th Annual Conference of the Labour Party, October 1924, p16.
[7] *Ibid*, p116.
[8] Saklatvala's 1922 General Election Address for Battersea North.
[9] Speeches and Documents of the Sixth Conference of the Communist Party of Great Britain, May 1924, p28.
[10] *Ibid*, p66.
[11] *Communist Review*, April 1926.
[12] See S Saklatvala, *The British Labour Government and India*, TUC and Labour Party, July 1924.
[13] *Workers Weekly*, 14 March 1924.
[14] *Daily Worker*, 20 January 1936.
[15] Report on Revolutionary Organisations in the UK. Letter to the Private Secretary of the Prime Minister from Sir Borlaise Childe, 24 January 1924, contained in the Ramsay MacDonald Private Papers at the Public Record Office.
[16] See P S Gupta, *Imperialism and the British Labour Movement 1914-1964*, MacMillan Press 1975, p109.
[17] Report of the Seventh National Congress of the Communist Party of Great Britain, May/June 1925, pp32-33.
[18] Report of the 24th Annual Conference of the Labour Party, *op cit*, p129.
[19] *Ibid*.
[20] *Communist Papers, Documents selected from those obtained on the arrest of the Communist leaders on the 14th and 31st October, 1925*, HMSO CMD2682, 1926.

[21] *Ibid*.

[22] *Ibid*.

[23] *Ibid*.

[24] *Daily Telegraph*, 22 March 1926.

[25] *Workers Weekly*, 16 January 1925.

[26] Report of the Seventh National Congress of the Communist Party of Great Britain, *op cit*, p33.

[27] *The Young Striker*, 6 May 1926.

[28] Report of the Eighth Congress of the Communist Party of Great Britain Oct 1926, p13.

[29] *Hansard*, Vol 194-1338, 21 April 1926.

[30] *South Western Star*, 16 November 1928.

[31] *South Western Star*, 14 December 1928.

Chapter Four

Candidate of the Battersea Labour Movement

Saklatvala was adopted as the Labour candidate for Battersea North in 1921, and contested the seat at three general elections as the nominee of the Battersea Labour Party and Trades Council. At two of these elections he was officially endorsed by the Labour Party nationally.

Until 1925 there were no restrictions placed on Communists, and they were able to play an active role in the Battersea Labour Party and Trades Council. Communists were elected as Labour members of the borough council, and were involved at all levels in the constituency. As long as this unity prevailed there was no serious challenge to Saklatvala's candidature. It was only after 1925, when the Labour Party conference decisions affecting Communists became fully operational, that Communist influence within the borough declined. Even then, it was only after a hard fought battle between the left and the right, a battle in which the Labour leadership had to resort to disaffiliation in order to win victory. Once the Communists had been expelled, Saklatvala's chances of success in retaining his Battersea seat disappeared. Although he did enjoy a large personal following, it became apparent that he had been successful not because he was a member of the Communist Party but because he had stood as the candidate of a united local labour movement. At the 1929 general election, when he was first opposed by an official Labour candidate, his vote slumped dramatically, and Sanders, the Labour candidate, won the seat.

The seeds of this eventual split were already in evidence between 1920 and 1924, when Battersea and Saklatvala received massive publicity, particularly at election time. This publicity sought to portray the Communists as enemies of free speech, outside the British political tradition, and unworthy of a place within the Labour Party. The newspapers, which were almost unanimously anti-Saklatvala, attacked the Battersea Labour Party for adopting a revolutionary candidate. Battersea was castigated as a 'red metropolis' in which 'foreign influences' were at work. The area was a threat to the establishment because of the militancy and unity of the local labour movement, who had had the cheek to adopt an Indian revolutionary as its standard bearer. Saklatvala was denounced not because of his racial origin, but because he was a Communist and against the constitution. In the short-term, and in Battersea, the attack on the Communists was not successful, but ultimately it achieved its objective. The rejection of Communists by the Labour Party in 1924 was in part due to the kind of anti-Communist publicity that constituencies like Battersea received.

The Battersea labour movement

No examination of communist influence in Battersea, or Saklatvala's success, can be explained without looking at the borough's radical past. It was this Battersea socialist and anti-imperialist tradition that laid the basis for Saklatvala's adoption as the labour candidate. He was the continuation of a radical tradition, of which revolutionary socialism was a part, that stretched back over a number of years, Saklatvala embodied many of the virtues that the local labour movement had come to call its own. Revolutionary socialists were an intrinsic part of the local labour movement, and at the time of the Communist Party's formation they were the backbone of the Battersea Labour Party and Trades Council. A number of Battersea Labour activists joined the Communist Party in the first months after its formation. Many did not stay long, but sympathy for the Communists remained. The decision to expel them from the Labour Party in 1924 was anathema to the Battersea labour movement. A number of Communists were active in the Battersea Labour Party and Trades Council and enjoyed wide support from that organisation. Saklatvala was a popular choice as candidate, and the Battersea Labour Party and Trades Council saw no reason why he should be dropped. Above all the local party, which had for some time united reformist and revolutionary socialists, was united in its opposition to any discrimination and splitting of the movement.

The key to the Communists' initial success in Battersea is to be found in the radicalisation of Battersea politics up to and during the first world war. It was one of the first areas in London where organised labour began to exert a political influence in local affairs. The Battersea Trades and Labour Council was formed in 1894, and was an amalgamation of different Trade Unions and Labour Groups, but it also included such organisations as the Battersea Street Traders Association, and, significantly, the Battersea Liberal and Radical Association. It established an election committee and this alliance of Liberals and Labour, calling themselves the Progressives, won control of the vestry, the forerunner of the borough council, in the local elections of that year. They retained control until 1909, when the newly formed Battersea Labour Party, established the year before, decided to field its own candidates. The split in the Liberal/Labour vote allowed the Tories to gain office, and they ran the council for the next three years. The re-formed alliance regained control in 1912 and retained it until after the war, by which time Labour was sufficiently powerful to bid for power in its own right. In the local elections of 1919, the Labour Party candidates, many of whom were ex-members of the Progressive Alliance, won a majority. In Battersea North they polled over 77 per cent of the vote.

The Liberal/Labour Alliance in local government also entended into the parliamentary arena. John Burns, supported by the Battersea Liberals, was returned as Labour MP for Battersea in 1892, and held the seat until his resignation in 1918. He was a local man who had first come to prominence as one of the leaders of the 1889 dock strike. His first step towards becoming the first ever working man to hold cabinet office was his election to the London County Council as Battersea's representative in 1889. This itself was a tribute to the strength of organised labour in the borough: the local Liberal Association, rather than stand its own candidate, had decided to support Burns. The electoral pact was not without its problems; for lending their support to Liberal candidates, the Battersea Trades and Labour Council was expelled from the newly formed Labour Representation Committee in 1906. The local alliance – apart from the temporary setback in 1909 – did not show any serious signs of strain until the outbreak of war, when under the impact of inflation, and the demand for sacrifices, it started to break up. In 1915, rather than make council employees redundant, the Progressive Group on the council decided to increase the rates. This was done despite the opposition of the leader of the group and six of his colleagues. At the instigation of a number of Labour councillors, they were expelled from the group, and this effectively brought to an end the Liberal/Labour alliance.

The domination of Battersea politics by the labour movement, from the 1890s onwards, was in part due to the growth of socialist organisations in the borough. The Social Democratic Federation had a branch in Battersea, and John Burns was for a brief period a member. It met in Sydney Hall in York Road, in North Battersea, and speakers such as George Bernard Shaw, H M Hyndman and Ramsay MacDonald addressed the branch's weekly lectures. The SDF had two members of the vestry and for a time it had a number of flourishing sections. These included a Women's Group, an Athletic Club, a Co-operative Store, and its own library. The Shaftesbury Estate, in the heart of the borough, built to 'help the working class become owners of the houses they occupy', and to 'raise their position in the social scale', did not have the desired effect. The estate became a stronghold of the SDF and Booth's Survey of London in 1902 said of it, 'It is chiefly inhabited by superior artisans and it is there that the intelligent portion of the socialism of the district is chiefly to be found, and the colony represents perhaps the high watermark of the life of the intelligent London artisan'.[1] The branch held regular public meetings every Sunday morning at the South East entrance to Battersea Park and there were usually more than a thousand people in attendance. Tom Mann and Will Thorne, as well as John Burns, were popular speakers with the crowd, and it was claimed that Battersea was the first area to promote the Gasworkers and General Labourers Union, the union that with these three at the helm, fought and won the fight for the 'Dockers Tanner'.[2]

It was the SDF that was instrumental in establishing in Battersea the first ever Socialist Sunday School in 1892. The school started with just two pupils but two years later the number had grown to 86. Regular treats and outings were organised for the children and they were instilled in the principles of 'honesty, truthfulness, cleanliness and love to one another'. There was an annual Christmas Party held at Sydney Hall. *Justice*, the SDF's paper, gave the following report of the event:

> At 5 o'clock proceedings started with a substantial tea, the table being tastefully decorated with flowers and fairy lamps. Games and dancing followed in the hall until 7.30, when after further refreshments, a Christmas Tree loaded with prizes was unveiled to the great surprise and delight of the children. After the distribution of the presents, and a few words to the youngsters from one of our comrades, the programme concluded with the singing of the 'Marseillaise' and cheers for the good time coming. Each child received a bag containing fruit and sweets before leaving the hall. The clean and tidy appearance and hearty good nature displayed by the children, the capital singing of socialist songs, the intelligent answers to a few questions put to them, are all evidence of the good work being done among these children. We may be proud of the results, especially when we realise that 75% in the school are children of strangers to the movement, and come, moreover, from some of the poorest homes in Battersea.[3]

The Social Democratic Federation was just one of a number of socialist and labour organisations that proliferated in Battersea during this period. In 1889

Burns helped establish the Battersea Labour League, whose main purpose was to secure Burns' election to Parliament. It remained in existence long after its originator's demise, and met regularly at Latchmere Baths, a municipal building built by the Council's direct labour department. Other left-wing groups in the borough before the first world war were the Battersea Socialist Council formed in 1907 and the Battersea Socialist Party which was active around the same time. During and immediately after the war, the Battersea Herald League, initially established to win support for the *Daily Herald*, carried out a wide range of activities. It held open-air meetings at least three times a week as well as weekly branch meetings; there were socials once a month and dances at less frequent intervals. In addition the League had an orchestra, a dramatic society, a cricket club and a rambling and cycling club. It also had time to publish its own paper, *The Standard*.

These groups, along with the more powerful Labour and Trades Council, helped popularise radical and socialist ideas in the borough. In addition the vestry, and after 1900 the borough council, carried out a number of measures that, although pioneering, gained widespread support. Significant among these was the setting up of a direct works department in 1895, a year after the Progressive won control. Its purpose was not so much the perpetuation of municipal socialism, but rather the elimination of exhorbitant charges by unscrupulous middle men, as well as the maintenance of good building standards and the regulation of employment for building workers. The council intervened in a number of areas apart from building: it had a municipal laundry, and later its own electricity supply; it was the first London borough to set up a health visiting service; and it provided free school milk for its school children. These were all measures that were popular, not only with the working class, but also amongst the middle class. The Liberals in the borough supported municipal intervention as a means of eliminating waste and keeping the rates low.

As well as a radical socialist tradition, there had also developed in Battersea an antipathy to imperialism. This first became evident with the outbreak of the Boer War. Almost immediately a Stop the War Committee was set up, in February 1900. It consisted of representatives of the Battersea Labour League, the Battersea Liberal and Radical Association, the Battersea Ethical Society, Battersea Spiritualist Society, Clapham Labour League, and local branches of the Municipal Employees Union and the Amalgamated Society of House Painters and Decorators. It was a broad organisation that enjoyed strong support from the vestry; its chairman, Matthews, was also the vestry's chairman. The committee organised a number of meetings in opposition to the war and at one of these, in Battersea Park, George Lansbury spoke to an estimated crowd of five thousand people. As a tribute to the Boers, the council decided to have one of the roads on the newly built Burns Estate named after a Boer general. General Joubert, and it named another road on the estate, built by the Council's Direct Labour Department, after Mathews. The high point of Battersea's resistance to the war was a meeting at the town hall addressed by two Afrikaners which attracted fourteen hundred people. Another action taken by the Stop the War Committee was taking over a pro-war meeting and organising amongst the audience a collection for the wives and children of the Boers. In another gesture of defiance, the council refused to fly the Union Jack after the relief of Mafeking.

This resistance to imperialism, and international solidarity, was to be a recurring theme in the Battersea labour movement. During the first Russian revolution, in 1905, the borough council passed a resolution protesting against the massacre of Russian workers. Two years later it refused to fly the Union Jack from Council buildings on Empire Day, and turned down a request that school children in the borough be given a half day off to celebrate the event. The influence of anti-imperialists on the council was strong, and this was reflected in the mayoralty elections of 1912 and 1913. In 1912, a Liberal Councillor, T Brogan, supported by the Labour Group, became Mayor. He was an Irish Nationalist and the President of the Battersea Branch of the Irish League. The following year a Labour councillor, J R Archer, took over the position. He was of mixed race, having a West Indian father and an Irish mother, and was a member and supporter of the Pan African Congress. He was to be prominent in Battersea politics for a considerable time. Both men were campaigners against colonialism at a time when support for imperialism was great; that they were elected to the highest position in Battersea's local government is an indication of the support that they received from the rest of their council colleagues.

During the first world war this tradition continued, although neither the borough council or the labour movement actively opposed the war. Feelings in the borough were mixed – they were neither fervently anti-war nor were they super-patriotic – and the consensus seems to have been a policy of peace by negotiation. However, this did not deter the Trades Council from protesting against what it saw as an affront to free speech, when the No Conscription Fellowship was refused the hiring of a hall in 1916. There was also much sympathy for Battersea resident Clifford Allen, when he was tried before a military tribunal in Battersea for refusing to be conscripted. When the war finished the council was not slow to protest at the outbreak of any new conflict, and this led them to condemn the military intervention in Russia.

The net result of these developments, stretching from the 1880s to the end of the war, was that Battersea had evolved as a borough where organised labour was a powerful political force, and which, as soon as it was strong enough, ended its reliance on the Liberals and governed in its own right. The council, dominated by the Labour Group, introduced a number of radical reforms that were popular with all classes. In order to consolidate and extend this basis of support the borough council was active in mobilising the electorate through demonstrations, pro-tests, town's meetings, and so on, so that in the borough there began to develop a political awareness. This was helped, and ran parallel with, the growth of a variety of socialist groups which, through their campaigning and recruiting activity, helped to spread socialist ideas. By the turn of the century socialism was well established in the borough and although the labour movement still needed the finances and support of its Liberal allies in elections, the Liberals were very much a junior partner.

In this alliance, Socialists and Liberals were both equally opposed to imperialism. The borough council, the trades council, and the Battersea Liberal and Radical Association, sometimes jointly, sometimes independently, carried out campaigns against government policy in this area. A strong anti-imperialist movement developed out of this alliance, and was continued after Labour had asserted its independence. Militant opposition to war and nationalism was not just confined to motions from the borough council: for example, during the Boer War, there were strenuous efforts made to rally the local inhabitants in support, and not without success. The labour movement, and the borough council which they dominated, organised meetings and rallies in which thousands participated. This was an important feature of the borough's political development. Over the years a wider and wider circle of Battersea people became involved in politics in one way or another. This was to be reflected in the immediate postwar years in the massive attendances at meetings held in Battersea addressed by labour movement figures.

Thus, at the time of the Communist Party's formation, there was in Battersea a politicised electorate with a degree of socialist understanding; and amongst the organised working class there was opposition to imperialism. Saklatvala combined these traditions. He was therefore not a surprising choice as Labour candidate.

Saklatvala in Battersea

The radicalisation of the labour movement in Battersea was one factor in Saklatvala's adoption as Labour candidate. Another was his friendship with a number of people who lived in the borough, or were active in the labour and trades council. He had made these friends during his years of activity in the Independent Labour Party and other organisations, notably the Workers Welfare League of India, for example. Arthur Field lived in Battersea – and he had been for a time the secretary of

Saklatvala's old ILP branch and also an activist in the Workers' Welfare League. Duncan Carmichael also knew Saklatvala through the Workers' Welfare League, and he was the treasurer of the Battersea Labour and Trades Council. J R Archer, already mentioned, the ex-Mayor of Battersea, and the first black mayor of any London borough, was also in close liaison with Saklatvala. At Saklatvala's funeral, it was claimed by an ex-Labour councillor that it was Archer who had first brought him into contact with Battersea and that Archer had, for some years, been Mr Saklatvala's most loyal and doughty champion.

One of Saklatvala's most consistent supporters was Charlotte Despard, the sister of General Sir John French. She had rejected her family background and decided to make Battersea her home, living for a number of years in the Nine Elms area and turning her house into a soup kitchen/school. She was an ardent feminist and her socialism, like Saklatvala's, was coupled with a hostility towards imperialism. In the Kharki election of 1918, she was the Labour candidate for Battersea North, John Burns having declined reselection because of differences with the local party. She was not successful, but received a respectable vote of 5634. Something of the radicalism of Battersea Labour politics can be gauged from her election address. The general election took place just after the conclusion of the war, when patriotic hysteria and support for the armed forces was at its height, yet Labour in Battersea called for an ending of military training in schools and an immediate termination of conscription. It further demanded justice for Ireland and India and the end of Empire. Its opposition to imperialism was coupled with the demand for sweeping social reforms: factory inspection, particularly of young children, a minimum wage based on the cost of living, increased old age pensions, equal pay for women, provision for disabled men and women, and the nationalisation of land, mines and transport.

Even before his adoption as the Labour candidate, Saklatvala was no newcomer to Battersea. For example in April 1921, he had addressed a meeting in the town hall

called by the Battersea Labour Party and Trades Council
in support of the miners. By all accounts the meeting was
an overwhelming success. The *South Western Star* reported
that 'the hall was crowded and an overflow meeting in
Town Hall Road gathered another three or four hundred
people'.[4] His speaking ability was further in evidence
when, some time after his adoption, the Battersea Labour
Party was congratulated on its choice of candidate by
South Wales miners in Aberdare. After hearing Saklatvala
speak, the miners unanimously carried a resolution, 'that
this meeting, after hearing such an excellent address,
congratulates the labour movement in Battersea on their
selection of comrade Saklatvala as their representative.
Further, that we ask him to come into the district to
organise the miners of the valley'.[5] Needless to say
Saklatvala declined the offer, but it is an indication of both
his national popularity as a speaker, and his potential as a
parliamentary candidate.

The influence of the Communists in Battersea, and
Saklatvala's selection as Labour candidate, was not due to
the strength of Communist organisation in the borough.
Until 1926, and the disaffiliation of the Battersea Labour
Party and Trades Council, the Communists exerted what
influence they did, not through their own party, but
through the local Labour Party. Independent communist
activity in the borough in the early 1920s was sporadic. At
the founding Congress of the Communist Party in 1920,
there were in attendance a number of delegates from
socialist organisations in Battersea. The Battersea Herald
League and Battersea Socialist Society were represented,
as was the Guild Communist Group. After the congress
there were quickly established two Communist Party
branches in the borough, based on the two newly created
constituencies of Battersea North and Battersea South.
But by November 1920 both branches had collapsed, and
the party's London Division Organiser, E W Cant,
pleaded in the party paper: 'Battersea is a district where
we have no branch but a great influence, will comrades
endeavour to form a branch'.[6] By March 1921 his appeal
had met with no response and a notice appeared in *The
Communist* saying 'wanted, Communists to form branches

in Lambeth, Lewisham and Battersea – names to E W Cant'.[7] It was not until September 1921 that a branch was re-established, so that at the time of Saklatvala's adoption as Labour candidate, in June 1921, there was no Communist Party branch in the constituency.

A Communist Party branch was functioning by the end of 1921 but it had some early teething problems as a notice in *The Communist* implied: 'The Battersea Branch of the Communist Party desires to warn all Labour organisations against its late Secretary, W J H Hunwick (NUR) who turned to his own use Branch funds of about £30 and has refunded nothing'.[8] The notice also gives an indication of the rapid turnover in personnel in the Communist Party during the first two years after its formation. Many joined after the inspiration of the Russian revolution, but did not remain long.

Although organisationally weak, the Communists in Battersea during the early 1920s did have some successes. They maintained a number of workplace branches and were influential among the railwaymen in the borough. The railways were one of the most important of Battersea's industries, and like the Communist Party nationally, the local Communists concentrated on their industrial organisation. Communist railwaymen in the borough produced two newspapers, *The Bystander* and the *Nine Elms Spark*. The *Nine Elms Spark* was the first Communist paper produced especially for railwaymen, and its front page was reproduced by *Inprecorr*, the journal of the Communist International, in 1926. Apart from the railway news-sheets, the Battersea Communists also produced a local paper especially for women, *The Battersea Woman Worker*, a novel venture at the time.

The overall impression of independent communist activity in Battersea in the early 1920s is of a branch which held fairly regular meetings, but had a fluctuating existence. There was some industrial organisation and a concentration on trade union work; and there were good sales of the party paper and regular distribution of leaflets. But the number of Communists in Battersea throughout this early period, according to contemporary evidence, was small, and at the time of Saklatvala's

selection, and in the months immediately following, there
was not even a Communist Party branch in existence. Why
then was Battersea considered a Communist stronghold,
and what was the reason for Saklatvala's triumph? The
answer lies not in the strength of the local Communist
Party organisation, but in the integration of the
Communists in the local labour movement. After 1926,
when the Communists were driven out of the Labour
Party, their influence diminished rapidly. In Battersea,
unlike other Communist citadels during the interwar
years, the Communists did not exert a hegemony in their
own right. They were only influential as long as they
remained a part of the Labour Party. Once this
relationship ended, so too did their power base in the
constituency.

A number of Labour Party activists in Battersea joined
the Communist Party at the time of its foundation. In his
election address for the 1922 general election, Saklatvala
made no secret of the involvement of Communist Party
members in local Labour politics:

> The scare cry of Communist which is sure to be raised by
> eleventh hour leaflets will fortunately not frighten the
> electors of North Battersea, as your two faithful servants
> on the London County Council, some half a dozen
> members of your Borough Council and your retiring
> Mayor, have not proved themselves false to you and have
> recently secured re-election as a token of your confidence.

The election address indicated just how intimately
involved the Communists were in the Battersea Labour
Party and Trades Council. The Communist Party was not
afraid of naming those party members who were also
Labour candidates, and in the local elections of 1922 there
were a fair number of them in Battersea. In the elections
for the London County Council both Labour candidates in
Battersea North, A A Watts and J Butler, were Communist Party members, as was Mrs Ganley in Battersea South.
In the borough council elections later in the year, *The
Communist* publicised those Communist Party members
who were standing as Labour candidates:

The following members of the Communist Party are candidates at the forthcoming Borough Council Elections, Battersea Kiloh (A.E.U.) endorsed by Trades Council
Edwards (A.E.U.) endorsed by Trades Council
Okines, Labour Party, endorsed by Trades Council
Harlin, Labour Party, endorsed by Trades Council
Mrs Ganley, Womens Co-Op, endorsed by Trades Council[9]

R C Kiloh was the Secretary of the Battersea Labour Party and Trades Council, and Joe Edwards was the Vice President.

Saklatvala was adopted as the Labour candidate for Battersea North in June 1921. Some time after his adoption, the local paper accused him of being unrepresentative of the local labour movement, and over the next few years this was to be a recurring theme. The *South Western Star*, a popular Battersea paper, claimed in an editorial in 1922:

> It is not at all certain that North Battersea wants to be nominally represented by him. If he is nominated he will probably be nominated by a Labour group, rather than by the Labour Party and that group is the one that has the least hold on public confidence or public sympathy. It calls itself the extreme wing and it is undisguisedly out for fundamental change. Some of its members do not hesitate to call it revolutionary. Now North Battersea is advanced, but it is a long way to giving countenance to revolutionary dogma. It is eager for progress but it is dead set against violent upheaval. At the Polling Stations its inherited constitutional sanity may triumphantly assert itself.[10]

The response by the Battersea Labour Party and Trades Council to the allegation was to emphasise Saklatvala's popularity in the constituency, R C Kiloh, the council's secretary, made the following reply:

> Saklatvala was chosen by a very full meeting of delegates representative of all sections of the Battersea Labour Party and Trades Council, properly and officially convened, and I am committing no breach of party orders when I say that the figures speak for themselves and that his selection was

definitely decided upon by an overwhelming majority. We in Battersea consider ourselves extremely fortunate that we have been able to place such an able exponent of economics at the service of the people of Battersea, particularly so when we remember that our candidate could probably have been chosen by other constituencies which would have been equally as favourable as Battersea.[11]

Kiloh's letter gives an indication of Saklatvala's widespread support amongst the Battersea labour movement. This support was to be maintained through three general elections – 1922, 1923, and 1924 – and only began to decline after the Communists were excluded from the Labour Party. The Battersea Labour Party and Trades Council required its parliamentary candidates to be reselected before each election. At all three general elections at which he was their candidate there was no challenge to Saklatvala's nomination from within the local Labour Party. Even at the general election of 1924, which took place three weeks after the decision of the Labour Party National Conference to expel the Communists, he was reselected almost unanimously. By this time the *South Western Star* had retracted its previous insistence on the Communists' lack of support in Battersea. Commenting on the Labour Party Conference decision, its editorial proclaimed:

> These decisions are awkward ones for the Party in North Battersea. Here the prospective candidate is Mr Saklatvala, and Mr Saklatvala has on several occasions declared himself a Communist. Officially the Labour Party can no longer support him. Locally this is sincerely regretted. It is unlikely that a candidate so popular with Labour as a whole and with so intimate a knowledge of the division, can be secured at such short notice.[12]

Any study of Saklatvala's two election campaigns reveals a great enthusiasm for his candidature from a united local labour movement, and the prominence of communist involvement in these campaigns. It must be stressed that Saklatvala was not a local candidate. From 1921 until his death he lived near Parliament Hill Fields in North London,

and all his local political involvement was there. In his
election material in Battersea he made little reference to
any local issues, and was more concerned to look at national
questions. He was not involved in any local campaigns and
was at no time a member of the Battersea Labour Party and
Trades Council. In addition North Battersea at this time
was a marginal constituency, and yet at no time did Saklatvala's racial origin or his revolutionary politics seem to
have been a disadvantage. Saklatvala was Labour's
standard-bearer in the constituency and this was the most
important factor in the eyes of the electorate. He was
elected not because he was a communist but because he was
the local labour movements's parliamentary candidate.

The 1922 election

The first of his electoral contests took place in November
1922. A large group of Tory back-bench MPs were
dissatisfied with the Liberal Lloyd George, and his
continued leadership of the National Coalition Government. They wanted to remove the Liberals from power
and to institute rule by the Conservative Party alone. As a
result the Tories withdrew support from the government
and the coalition collapsed. An election was called for 18
November. From the outset the press minimised
Saklatvala's chances of success, giving all their support to
his rival Mr Hogbin. Under the heading of 'Hogbin for
Battersea', the *Lloyd's Sunday News* declared:

> Mr H C Hogbin in Battersea is waging a strenuous fight
> with increasing chances of success in a constituency where
> the 'Die Hard' attempts to split the Conservative vote have
> proved unsuccessful. Ex-Servicemen have rallied to Mr
> Hogbin who is one of themselves and local betting is now
> on his return by a substantial majority.[13]

The *Daily Telegraph* was a little more apprehensive and
pointed to the danger of a split in the anti-Labour vote:

> Viscount Curzon has a straight fight with Labour in
> Battersea South, but in the Northern Division the vote will
> be split by the Independent Liberals. Fortunately the

Conservatives and National Liberals have joined forces
against what in this constituency is a very real socialist
menace.[14]

This closing of ranks by the anti-Saklatvala forces was
applauded and the article went on to give a useful potted
history of how this unity had been achieved:

> Co-operation between Conservatives and National Liberals
> being an indispensable condition to success against other
> parties in North Battersea it is well that it does exist in a
> very emphatic manner. Indeed 'the whole of the
> Conservative organisations in the division have given solid
> support to Mr Hogbin. There is not a Conservative
> Association in the constituency but there was a Conser-
> vative Club. This Club and the Constitutional and
> Democratic Association ... have now joined forces, forming
> together the North Battersea Constitutional Association,
> which is representative of Conservative and Unionist
> opinion in the division. The Association last Tuesday
> agreed to give unanimous support to Mr Hogbin's
> candidature.[15]

In the face of a concerted and unified opposition
campaign, Battersea Labour Party and Trades Council
responded by emphasising the unity that existed for
Saklatvala's candidature. His popularity amongst all
sections of the movement was given wide publicity. It
featured large in his election material and in adverts in the
local press. In his election address under the heading
'Labour's United Front' a number of labour movement
personalities and others expressed their support. Clifford
Allen, the treasurer of the ILP, wrote 'Dear Saklatvala –
Battersea must be won for Labour. I wish you all the
success in the world in your fight'. The Reverend Herbert
Dunnico, of the International Christian Peace Fellowship,
also expressed his solidarity:

> Dear Mr Saklatvala – Permit me to wish you every success
> in your great fight on behalf of the workers. The great and
> supreme need of the time is a 'Real Peace' and I earnestly
> appeal to the Christian men and women of your
> constituency to give you their wholehearted support for no

other party has a peace policy worthy of support, and I use the word Christian in no narrow theological sense.

Charlotte Despard, the previous Labour candidate, made a special appeal on Saklatvala's behalf, to women and to the Irish in the constituency:

> I appeal to you – to Labour which I have always honoured, to women, women workers and mothers who are the greatest workers of all – I appeal to my Irish fellow countrymen and women in North Battersea – support the Party and support the man, Saklatvala.

Saklatvala's 1922 election manifesto was in accordance with the pledge he had given to the Labour Party's National Executive Committee. It was moderate in tone, and put forward in an uncritical way Labour's policy. Its most radical demands were the prompt nationalisation of industries 'where grievous harm by private ownership has been clearly proved', and a levy on massed fortunes. The rest was a set of social and political demands that were liable to appeal to all sections of society. Some were aimed particularly at the middle class, like the call for 'a more just distribution of the Income Tax' which was coupled with a pledge to 'relieve the lower middle class earner from his income tax on unlivable incomes of £250 a year'. Much of the manifesto, though, was aimed directly at winning over the working class and concerned itself with bread and butter issues: 'better State Housing, the highest possible type of State Education, financial provision for aged people, mothers, widows, orphans, ex-service victims and locked out workers'.

There was a call in the address for full adult suffrage and Saklatvala declared his support not just for a woman's right to vote, but also for more far-reaching demands, which included, 'equal opportunity and equal moral standards'. He supported the introduction of women police, and was in favour of legislation that would provide a 'proper division of rights and responsibilities in regard to the guardianship of children'. He also favoured government measures to improve the position of the unmarried mother and her child.

Despite the predictions of the press, Saklatvala secured a little over 50 per cent of the poll: when the vote was announced, to the usual enthusiastic gathering outside the town hall, he had a comfortable majority over his opponent, with 11,311 votes, 50.5% of those cast, while Mr Hogbin received 9,290 votes, 41.6% of the poll. The turnout, of 56.5% of the electorate, was low by today's standards, but was comparable to other London constituencies. Saklatvala not only secured more votes than the combined opposition candidates, he also more than doubled the support that Charlotte Despard had received in the previous election. She had gained 5,674 votes for Labour, compared to 11,231 for her Coalition Liberal opponent.

The 1923 election

Saklatvala's short period as a Labour MP lasted for less than a year, and was brought to an abrupt halt by the calling of a general election for 6 December 1923. Baldwin, the prime minister, although enjoying a comfortable Tory majority, decided to make trade protection a national issue. He dissolved parliament and the country prepared itself for the second election within twelve months. In the event, the Tories lost control of parliament during this election: Labour increased its share sufficiently to be in a position to form a minority government supported by the Liberals.

Battersea Labour Party and Trades Council required its parliamentary candidates to be endorsed before every election but Saklatvala seems to have had little trouble in gaining reselection. The *South Western Star* reported that he was readopted at a full meeting of delegates in November 1923. His election address was published ten days before polling day and once again it emphasised the unity that still prevailed in the local labour movement. It called for unity, full support for the Labour Party, and international solidarity:

We want a solid, unbroken, united front at home, backing our Labour Party, as far as we are all prepared to go, and then planning our further onward march, till we bring ourselves into an international unity with our brethren in other countries of the world, through a joint organisation that operates on our behalf every day.

The manifesto, which was four pages long, was concerned with one or two national questions, primarily unemployment and a tax on capital, but there was no mention of how these problems affected Battersea nor again was there any reference to any local issues. Saklatvala's election address was, as before, wordy and difficult to read, and seemed more concerned with the theoretical attraction of socialism than with its immediate effect on workers' lives. The statement concluded with an appeal to the electors' morality, rather than to their revolutionary zeal:

> With this spirit, with this resolve, I ask you to vote for me, and I shall expect you after you have voted to work with me. Over-confidence on the Election day will bring defeat; out of forty thousand electors of North Battersea it would be a moral loss if at least twenty thousand did not solidly vote for us.

The campaign was to prove an exceptionally dirty one, with Saklatvala's opponent Hogbin making much use of the press in his attempt to win the seat. Saklatvala faced a much more difficult task in this second contest because there were only two candidates and thus no split in the anti-Saklatvala vote. Hogbin, now standing as a Liberal, had gained the support of the Battersea Conservative Association, and all Tories in the constituency were being advised to vote for him. The national press looked on Battersea as a 'little Moscow', and considered that the area was a launching pad for revolution. The *Daily Telegraph* claimed:

> The Borough has long been recognised as one of the nerve centres of the Communist Movement. By insidious propaganda, the unemployed – of whom, unfortunately there are many –have been ensnared into believing the spurious promises held out to them, and a determined effort is being waged to win over both divisions in support of the Red Revolution on which to bring in the millenium of the workers.[16]

(The reference to the southern division was an attempt to slur the name of Mr Albert Winfield, the Labour candidate for Battersea South, who was neither a member of the Communist Party, or for that matter very left wing.) Battersea's notoriety was further highlighted a few days later by an article in the London *Evening Standard*, alleging that it was 'one of the four Red Boroughs in the Metropolis' and that 'to call it a nerve centre of communism would be no exaggeration'.[17]

The attention that Battersea received in the newspapers during the election was staggering. It was to be expected that Saklatvala, as a well-known communist, would receive some criticism from the usually anti-socialist press; but what took place was a concerted publicity drive aimed at presenting Saklatvala and his supporters as opponents of free speech, who were quite prepared to bring armed gunmen into the constituency in order to secure his re-election.

A few days before the election, the national dailies carried stories of the breakup of Hogbin's meetings, allegedly by Saklatvala supporters. Both the *Daily Telegraph* and the *Daily Chronicle* accused the Labour candidate and his followers of terrorist tactics: 'Battersea Reds – Terrorist Tactics – Free Speech Denied'[18]; and 'Terrorism in North Battersea'.[19] The *Daily Mail* called the disrupters a 'Communist Gang' whose aim was to prevent Hogbin being allowed to address the electorate.[20] The London *Evening News* carried an editorial attacking the Labour Party and condemning rowdyism in Battersea:

> Rowdyism would hardly be condemned by the motley Statesmen of the International Socialist headquarters to whom the Labour leaders have harnessed themselves. After all, a party which proposes to help itself to 3000 million of other people's money is not likely to have enough sense of sportsmanship to denounce its adherents who break up other people's meetings. At North Battersea Mr Hogbin has been so badly treated by Communist gangs that he has had to abandon his meetings.[21]

These accusations of organised disruption were answered by both the Labour and the Communist press. The

Communist Party, through *Workers Weekly*, denounced such claims:

> The Communist Party has never approved of rowdy interruptions at opponent's meetings, and we believe that members of the Communist Party are less given to this sort of thing than are members and adherents of other organisations ... Our members understand that much more effective service can be rendered to the cause by steady work for the Labour and Communist candidates and by discussion and debate both on and off the platform.[22]

The *Daily Herald* was even more forthright in its condemnation of the accusations, and claimed that the alleged Labour rowdyism was 'the latest stunt of the millionaire press'. The paper gave publicity to Saklatvala's declaration in favour of broad meetings:

> I consider it wrong to hold only party meetings on such occasions to be addressed by candidates representing one side only. I invite all Conservatives and Liberals to attend meetings to be addressed by me, and I also invite the candidates who are opposing me to address my meetings, and to let me have a similar privilege at their meetings. This seems to me to be the only course for those who do not desire to hide the truth.[23]

This was no idle gesture, and on a number of occasions the Labour candidate allowed opposition speakers to address his meetings. This tolerance of his opponent's point of view did not go unnoticed. After one such meeting, addressed by Hogbin's representative Captain Godfrey, the *Daily Herald*, under the headline, 'Who Said Rowdyism', published the following letter which had been written to Saklatvala by Captain Godfrey:

> I write again to express my thanks for the hospitality you extended to me last night. I do not hesitate to say that, considering the pent up feelings of the electors of North Battersea at the present juncture, I have had a very fair and considerate hearing.[24]

To quell any more stories about organised disruption of meetings, Saklatvala issued an appeal to his supporters:

> Battersea Comrades making a noise or causing distur-
> bances at meetings of our political opponents is not in
> keeping with the traditions of Battersea, where the people
> are ever ready to listen to all kinds of opinion. Many
> elections have been won by candidates in the past by unfair
> treatment given to them at public meetings ... I strongly
> advocate a fair hearing and a calm discussion with
> everybody who wishes to explain his opinions. I strongly
> urge upon you all to preserve the fair name of Battersea
> and to be calm and well conducted at all meetings. Do not
> let me appeal to you in vain.[25]

There were also accusations at the 1923 election that the Communists in Battersea had armed gunmen in the constituency and that they were out to eliminate the Liberal candidate. The story first appeared in the *London Evening Standard*. The 'Gang' – twenty in all – included 'Irish Rebels' and was, according to Hogbin, 'sworn to get me by polling night'. Three days before the election many of the national dailies carried stories of the allegations. The *Daily Graphic* had a photograph of Hogbin, with a headline '20 gunmen are threatening him'[26]. The *Daily Sketch* had a similar headline: 'Sleeps with a gun at his bedside'[27]. The *Daily News* also carried a story of the threat to the candidate's life. The *Daily Express*, publishing the same day, must have had favoured treatment – Hogbin revealed to them that the number of gangs had increased, and he now claimed to have 'positive knowledge that there are two gangs operating in the division – one of Irish Republican Gunmen and another of Continental and Russian Communists'[24]. Such was the press build-up that the *Daily Mirror* advised its women readers living in districts in which rowdyism has occurred, 'to record their votes early on Thursday and thus avoid the mobs'[29]. But when polling day arrived an almost disappointed *Daily Telegraph* correspondent in Battersea reported:

> The only incident in fact which had occurred before dark
> was when someone threw a lump of coal at a Liberal
> Official's head. Otherwise there was not the slightest sign

of feeling exhibited anywhere. At Battersea South, also, everything was calm, and one official said that it was more like a Sunday school treat than an election.[30]

When the result was announced Saklatvala had increased his vote by 9.1% adding over a thousand to his previous total. But it was not enough. Hogbin had done even better, and had won the seat with a majority of 186. Hogbin received 12,527 votes, while Saklatvala received 12,341. The turnout was 61.9%, an increase of 5.4% on the previous election, and was once again comparable with other London constituencies.

After his defeat, Saklatvala, although no longer an MP, continued his association with the constituency. His offer of open meetings made during the election was taken up again, when, at his suggestion, a debate took place between himself, H C Hogbin and Viscount Curzon, the Conservative MP for Battersea South. They met at the town hall and the subject for discussion was 'The Socialist Government in Theory and Practice'. Saklatvala, when asked about the value of such meetings, emphasised once again his commitment to equal representation for all points of view: 'If he had his way he would not allow a single political meeting to be held in a lop-sided manner ... He would always have allocated seats for members of all parties'.[31] And during the period of less than a year between the loss of the seat and his re-election in 1924, Saklatvala continued to close contact with the Battersea Labour Party and Trades Council.

Despite the attention Battersea received from the press, it had little effect on Saklatvala's fortunes in the constituency. At the two elections at which he was the official Labour candidate his vote increased. Labour supporters in Battersea seemed to have been immune to the press barrage. Saklatvala's vote climbed from 11,311 in 1922, to 12,341 in 1923. He never polled less than 49 per cent of the vote, and when he was defeated it was by less than 200 votes.

Notes

[1] C Booth, *Life and Labour of the People in London 1892-97*, 1907, Vol 1, p280.
[2] W Stephen Sanders, *Early Socialist Days*, Hogarth Press 1927, pp51-52.
[3] *Justice*, 12 Jan 1895.
[4] *South Western Star*, 15 April 1921.
[5] *South Western Star*, 3 Feb 1922.
[6] *The Communist*, 18 Nov 1920.
[7] *The Communist*, 26 March 1921.
[8] *The Communist*, 23 Dec 1922.
[9] *The Communist*, 28 Oct 1922.
[10] *South Western Star*, 17 March 1922.
[11] *South Western Star*, 24 March 1922.
[12] *South Western Star*, 10 October 1924.
[13] *Lloyds Sunday News*, 12 Nov 1922.
[14] *Daily Telegraph*, 8 Nov 1922.
[15] *Ibid.*
[16] *Daily Telegraph*, 19 Nov 1923.
[17] *Evening Standard*, 26 Nov 1923.
[18] *Daily Telegraph*, 1 Dec 1923.
[19] *Daily Chronicle*, 1 Dec 1923.
[20] *Daily Mail*, 1 Dec 1923.
[21] *London Evening News*, 1 Dec 1923.
[22] *Workers Weekly*, 30 Nov 1923.
[23] First published in *South Western Star*, 23 Nov 1923. Also reported in *Daily Herald*.
[24] *Daily Herald*, 4 Dec 1923.
[25] *South Western Star*, 30 Nov 1923.
[26] *Daily Graphic*, 4 Dec 1923.
[27] *Daily Sketch*, 4 Dec 1923.
[28] *Daily Express*, 4 Dec 1923.
[29] *Daily Mirror*, 4 Dec 1923.
[30] *Daily Telegraph*, 7 Dec 1923.
[31] *Clapham Observer*, 23 May 1924.

Chapter Five

Battersea 1924–29

During the 1924 Annual Labour Party Conference the decision was taken to call the third general election in less than two years. Ramsay MacDonald's decision to dissolve parliament on 9 October, was due to the lack of support from his Liberal partners in the coalition. The minority Labour government was challenged over an article in the communist party's *Workers Weekly*. The article, entitled, 'Don't Shoot', called on the armed forces not to fire on workers who were involved in strikes. The government was urged to prosecute J R Campbell, the paper's editor, but, partly because of labour movement pressure, decided against this course of action. Tory and Liberal MPs then joined together and defeated the government over the issue. Soon after the election campaign had begun, the *Daily Mail* added to the already growing anti-communist hysteria, by publishing what was allegedly a letter from Zinoviev, the Chairman of the Communist International, which instructed the Communist Party on how it could control the Labour Party. When it was published without his permission by his own Foreign Office, MacDonald, instead of repudiating the letter as an obvious forgery, said nothing. It was in this climate of opinion that the 1924 General Election took place, and the result of the election was a defeat for Labour.

The Labour Party conference decision to expel Communists was taken just three weeks before the election took place, and as a consequence it had little effect on Battersea Labour Party's choice of a candidate. Even if the local party had been dissatisfied with Saklatvala there was little time available to find an alternative choice. As it transpired, his reselection was by an overwhelming majority, in spite of the Labour Party conference ruling. He was readopted as the candidate by 104 votes to 14.

The Labour Party conference decision prevented Communists from standing as Labour candidates, but it did not prevent local Labour Party branches from supporting Communist candidates, as long as they stood as Communists. Saklatvala contested the election as a Communist, but nominated by the Battersea Labour Party and Trades Council. The local party even tried to gain national Labour Party endorsement for his candidature, but, not surprisingly, this was turned down. At this election, for the first time, Saklatvala stood as a Communist, supported by the local Labour Party and Trades Council, but without the endorsement of the Labour Party nationally.

As at previous elections the newspapers took a particular interest in Battersea and were solidly anti-Saklatvala. The *Daily Mail* was first into the attack and once again claimed that free speech was being denied to Saklatvala's opponent, and that sinister 'foreign' influences were at work in the Constituency:

> The Communist Party and the Young Communist League have sent their emissaries, and there are even more mysterious agents at work in the back streets and at open air meetings. Attempts are being made to make free speech impossible. Mr Hogbin is denied the right of speaking at open air meetings by bands of interrupters in which a foreign element is distinctly noticeable. Canvassers on his behalf have been threatened with personal violence, and women warned that if they go to certain streets in the constituency to urge his claims their necks will be wrung.[1]

This theme of electoral violence was taken up by *The Times* and the *Daily Graphic* and both papers published photographs of Hogbin standing by his car, which had a shattered windscreen. It was left to the *Daily Herald* to give an explanation of how the incident had occurred:

While Mr Hogbin was making a canvassing tour of the division, stones were showered upon his car by a number of noisy children. One of the missiles came with sufficient force to pass through the mica windscreen. A boy who is said to have thrown the stone ran away. Mr Hogbin jumped out of the car, caught him and brought him back. According to the urchin's mother, the affair was accidental.[2]

In spite of this explanation, the newspapers continued in the same vein the next day. Under the headline of 'Battersea Elections under Police Protection', the *Daily Graphic* carried a photograph of a crowd outside one of Hogbin's election meetings, and told its readers that the meeting needed police protection because 'extremist ruffianism has been rife'. Towards the end of the election however, this newspaper admitted, albeit in racist terms, that Saklatvala did enjoy widespread support

If Saklatvala returns to the House across the river it won't be because North Battersea is seething with communism. The Parsee might be Svengali, or an Indian fakir with a knowledge of black magic. He wields a magnetic influence over his audience that verges on hypnotism. I met a Battersea charwoman yesterday who was almost in tears because she lived on the wrong side of the street and couldn't vote for Saklatvala. And I saw excited women waving his handbills and actually kissing his portrait painted on them.[3]

Saklatvala's popularity as a speaker was acknowledged by all sides, and as at previous elections he continued to draw large crowds. At one meeting in the town hall the number of people turning up was so great that an overflow meeting was organised in a neighbouring hall and even then there were crowds left milling about in the street. The *South Western Star* reported the size of the meeting, noting that

All were spoken to, there being no lack of strenuous orators – members of the Borough Council and other well known units of the Labour Party. Mr Saklatvala was given an enthusiastic reception and his speech was punctuated with applause.[4]

The campaign was organised by the Battersea Labour Party and Trades Council and Saklatvala's election meetings were addressed by a cross-section of speakers from the local labour movement. At a meeting for railwaymen, who formed a fair proportion of the electorate in Battersea, the supporting speakers were J Butler and A Watts, who were Battersea's representatives on the London County Council. The meeting was chaired by J Archer, the ex-Mayor of Battersea. At all Saklatvala's election meetings he was supported by prominent Labour figures in the Borough, including many councillors.

The attack on Saklatvala in the press also focused on Battersea Labour Party's continued support for him, despite the Labour Party conference resolution to expel the Communists. The *Daily Telegraph* characterised Battersea as a communist stronghold, and one of the most important contests in the election:

> The contest in North Battersea promises to be one of the stiffest fights in the campaign, resolving itself in fact into a grim struggle, as at the last election, between constitutional government and Communism. Battersea is known as the Mecca of Communism, an unusually large number of whose supporters live in the division. It is the starting point of most of the Communist processions which are to be seen from time to time parading the streets of London.[5]

The paper attacked the Battersea Labour Party and Trades Council for its refusal to drop Saklatvala. Other papers took up the same theme. The *Morning Post* accused the Labour Party of dishonesty in its refusal to reject Saklatvala, arguing that 'the Labour Party dare not disown Mr Saklatvala, which shows how thoroughly dishonest was the resolution of their conference excluding the Communists'.[6]

The idea that the Communist Party was particularly large in Battersea was without much substance. Although there are no surviving branch records, at this time the party nationally was about 4,000 strong, which means that, even with an above average membership, the Battersea branch could not have been very big. The influence held by the Communists in Battersea was not because of their numbers but because they could operate openly within the Labour Party and were an accepted part of the local labour movement. The Communists' efforts and involvement in the Battersea Labour Party and Trades Council were documented in a Special Branch report on revolutionary organisations sent to the Prime Minister. The report stated that there had been evidence of great activity by the Communists in connection with the election and included the text of a report sent to a Communist official by the party organiser in Battersea. This report which had obviously been opened and read by the Special Branch gives an insight into just how well integrated and active the Communists were in the local Labour Party:

> The work at present being done is as follows – 'Workers Weekly' normal sale 20 quire. This week 48 quire and we have not finished yet, the 20,000 election manifestos (received by me on Monday night) are just on all distributed. A start is being made on the 20,000 leaflets which only reached me last night. Canvassing is being done consistently in the more promising areas. Those members known to the Labour Party as Communists are working in the Labour Committee Rooms. Five members are engaged officially directing election work for the Labour Party and seeing that it is kept on Communist lines.[7]

The Communist Party regarded Battersea as a key area and spared no efforts in sending in personnel. It seems that the party, at least during election time, was the dominating force in Saklatvala's campaign.

The election result was something of a personal triumph for Saklatvala. Despite his lack of support from the Labour Party nationally, he managed to win back the seat. He increased his vote from 12,341 in 1923 to 15,096, beating his opponent Hogbin by a margin of 542 votes. The electorate was 40,586, a slight increase on the previous election, and the turn-out was 73.1% comparing favourably with the previous 61.9%. Saklatvala polled 50.9% of the vote.

Disaffiliation and the General Strike

For mainly administrative reasons, the Labour Party did
not implement the 1924 conference decisions for over a
year. In Battersea the constitutional changes went almost
unnoticed: immediately after the general election the
Battersea Labour Party ignored the annual conference
resolution when it decided to allow the affiliation of the
local branch of the Communist Party to continue; and
Communist Party members continued to be members of
the Battersea Labour Party and Trades Council and to
hold positions in that body; in addition five communists
stood for Labour in the 1925 local elections. In fact 22
Communists ran as candidates for Labour in the
municipal elections, and Saklatvala was himself a
municipal candidate, contesting unsuccessfully one of the
wards in St Pancras where he was a delegate to the Labour
Party and Trades Council.

The period of indecision by the Labour Party NEC was
however coming to an end. The 1925 annual conference
ratified the constitutional changes, and gave the leadership a mandate to act against the Communists. Battersea
was one of the first local parties to be disaffiliated, at a
meeting of the Executive Committee of the London
Labour Party in February 1926. At the same meeting
Bethnal Green Trades Council and Labour Party, and
South West Bethnal Green Labour Party were also
expelled. Saklatvala commented that it was 'the usual trick
of the Labour Party to leave their logic and their
consistency aside when it comes to working socialism'.[8]

Battersea Labour Party was disaffiliated on the eve of
the general strike, but it was not until some time after the
events of the Nine Days had subsided that the Labour
Party NEC decided on further action against the
constituency party; nor, during this interim period, did
the NEC take any further measures against any of the
other parties that had disregarded the constitutional
changes. The Communist Party claimed that the Labour
leadership's slowness in carrying out the expulsion order
was due to the militancy of the working class, which made

it impossible for the expulsion policy to be carried out. This interpretation was to some extent supported by events in Battersea. The Battersea Labour Party and Trades Council, in spite of its disaffiliation, was the driving force behind local support for the strike. And within the Trades Council the Communists remained an influential force, dominating the Battersea Council of Action set up to mobilise support for the strike. The popularity of the local communists, although they were few in number, meant that the Labour Party NEC was reluctant to take any further action until the revolutionary feeling generated by the strike had abated.

Saklatvala was one of the first victims of the general strike and was arrested for a speech he made in Hyde Park on the eve of the stoppage. He was initially released on £200 bail, which was provided by George Lansbury, but then a few days later he was tried at Bow Street magistrate's court, found guilty, and sentenced to two month's imprisonment at Wormwood Scrubs.

Despite being deprived of one of its most capable orators, the Battersea labour movement was solid in its support of the strike. Even before the strike began, the Battersea Trades Council and Labour Party had participated in a march to nearby Wandsworth Prison, where a number of imprisoned communist leaders were held. (These communists had been arrested in 1925 and given sentences of between six months and a year, as part of the government's persecution of the Communist Party.) When the strike actually began Battersea Labour Party and Trades Council established a local Council of Action almost immediately. This met in more or less permanent session at the Lower Town Hall, permission having been granted by the Borough Council; there was close co-operation between both bodies throughout the dispute. Despite the Trades Council's disaffiliation, the Council of Action was a very representative body. It consisted of over 120 people representing 70 local labour and trade union organisations, including the Battersea Labour League, the Minority Movement, and, towards the end of the strike, the Independent Labour Party. The influence of the Communists on the leadership was in excess of their very small numbers. Of the 124 representatives on the Council of Action, 10 were Communist Party members, but of the Executive of seven people, four were Communists.

The Council of Action's strategy was twofold: to close down all the major works in Battersea; and to ensure maximum support for the stoppage from amongst the Battersea working class. After some initial vacillation picketing became more intense, and on 7 May the Clapham Tram Depot was closed by mass pickets, in spite of a number of police baton charges. The next day thousands of trade unionists were out on all the major roads in Battersea, to prevent the passage of food lorries through the borough. They were particularly successful at the Dogs Home Bridge, in the eastern part of Battersea, where all the lorries were turned back. At the same time the Council of Action organised daily marches that took in every major factory in Battersea. Meetings were held outside, and those that were still working were asked to stop. After a few days all the large factories in Battersea were at a standstill.

The local labour movement remained united in its support of the miners throughout the dispute. The Borough Council also helped in a variety of ways. Many of the activists on the Council of Action were also councillors. C J Powell, who was a Labour Alderman, was also the President of the Battersea Trades Council and Labour Party's Political Section and acted as a liaison betwen the two bodies. Duncan Carmichael, a newly elected Battersea councillor, was also the Secretary of the London Trades Council, and this also gives an indication of the close relationship that there was between the two wings of the organised labour movement. In addition, the labour movement managed to influence other bodies: some of the churches in Battersea were sympathetic to the strikers, and Reverend Pritchard, a local vicar, was also an active Labour councillor. At the instigation of the mayor some of the churches allowed their halls to be used for meetings, and some gave permission for the Sunday Collections to be contributed to the strike fund. During the whole of the nine days of the strike Battersea was a hive of activity. Apart from picketing there were meetings every night at the Princes Head, a popular local meeting spot, and the local branch of the Unemployed Workers Committee Movement also held daily meetings. Because of the problems in communication there was little contact with the movement outside the borough, or even with the TUC, whose headquarters were just across the river in Eccleston Square. The TUC's daily strike bulletin *The British Worker* was difficult to get hold of in Battersea, so the Council of Action published its own, with a daily circulation of 2500.

Because there had been little contact with the leadership, it was with disbelief that the local labour movement heard the news that the strike had been called off: at first the radio announcement was treated as just another government trick. When it became clear that this was not the case, disillusionment set in. Local railwaymen tried to maintain their dignity by marching back to work in unison, and a march back to Victoria Station, where many worked, set out from the railwaymens' Headquarters, Unity Hall, in Battersea. Even the right-wing Battersea Number One branch of the NUR, which had not been represented on the Council of Action, was so incensed at the TUC's terms for a return to work that they, along with the Number Two branch, passed a resolution urging that all transport workers should only resume work at the same level of pay and conditions as existed prior to the strike. The left in the movement tried in vain to stop the drift back to work: Alf Loughton, a railwayman and a local communist, was arrested for shouting out at a railwaymens' meeting, urging the crowd not to go back to work. He was sentenced to two months in gaol and sent to Wormwood Scrubs, where Saklatvala was also imprisoned.

It was not until after the strike's conclusion that any further action was taken against the disaffilitated Battersea Labour Party and Trades Council. A reconstituted Trades and Labour Council was set up at a conference held in Battersea Lower Town Hall on 5 July 1926. It was a very representative gathering, but from the report of the meeting it is apparent that organised resistance to the expulsion of the communists had collapsed. In his address, the London Labour Party

Organiser, Mr R T Windle, gave an outline of the events leading up to the conference, stating that he had invited all eligible branches affiliated to the old party to take part in the formation of the new organisation. This invitation had been conditional upon the branches' accepting the constitution and rules of the party and its conference decisions. Sixteen branches had accepted the invitation and appointed delegates, three branches had refused, and one branch had wanted to send delegates on unacceptable conditions. This gives an indication of the weakness of any opposition to the re-organisation.

At the same time two new Divisional Labour Parties were established, one in Battersea North and the other in Battersea South. The newly elected Secretary in North Battersea was J Archer, who had previously been a Saklatvala supporter and now found himself in opposition to the Communists. The falling out of formerly close comrades in arms was also evident in South Battersea. E Fineran, the newly elected secretary of the South Battersea Party, had been the Secretary of the Council of Action during the General Strike; but his former comrade Jack Clancy, who had been the Council's Chairman, later stood for the post of councillor as the candidate of the disaffiliated Trades Council and Labour Party, causing great consternation to the new organisation (see p96).

The Communist Party was not slow to point out that Battersea was the only constituency where a new official Labour Party had been established. It was unusual for the Labour Party NEC to attempt to set up a rival party once a local Labour Party had been disaffiliated. Saklatvala, who had been in prison while much of the preparation for the new organisation was being made, commented that it was 'the latest development of the Liberalising Campaign of the Right Wing Officials of the Labour Party'.[9] Referring to the banning of meetings in Battersea under the Emergency Powers Act, he even hinted at collusion between the state and the right wing in the Battersea Labour Party: 'It is worth noting too, that this happened at a time when the police are refusing to allow me to address meetings of my constituents.'[10]

Last days of the Trades Council

There were now two Labour Parties and Trades Councils in existence in Battersea. The Communists continued to work in the disaffiliated body, and it was still the main source of their influence. As part of the organised resistance to the ban on communists, the *Sunday Worker* gave publicity to the activities of disaffiliated trades and labour councils. The paper reported that in Battersea over one hundred recruits had been made by the old trades council during the summer period of 1926.

In the months immediately following the establishment of the official Labour Party, there was keen competition between the two organisations, and both sides could claim some success. The conflict was at its sharpest on the borough council, which was Labour controlled, and included a number of councillors who supported the disaffiliated Trades Council and Labour Party. The differences between the Labour Councillors were finally resolved at a meeting that took place at the end of September 1926. Those who supported the constitutional changes in the Labour Party were successful, passing a resolution refusing membership of the Labour group to any member of the council who was a member of the Communist Party or Minority Movement or who did not adhere to National Labour Party decisions. This confirms that there were still a number of Communist Party members who were also Labour Councillors; but the effect of the resolution was the isolation of the pro-Communist Labour Group on the Council, and it was a major set-back for the Communists, who fought against it fiercely. They argued that the meeting was unrepresentative, and that left wingers as well as communists were being denied membership of the Labour Group – it was part of communist strategy to emphasise the unity of purpose that existed between Communists and Labour left wingers.

The growing antagonism between the Communists and their supporters and the official Trades Council was also evident in the electoral arena. Although the communists had suffered a defeat on the council, almost immediately

afterwards they were given a tremendous boost by the
Winstanley Ward By-election which was caused by the
death of Duncan Carmichael, who was one of the
councillors for that ward.

The disaffiliated Battersea Labour Party and Trades
Council put forward a candidate, and so too did the newly
established South Battersea Divisional Labour Party. The
contest aroused a great deal of animosity, and it was an
indication of the deep division that had now emerged in
the Battersea labour movement. Something of this
antagonism was recorded by the Secretary of the South
Battersea Divisional Labour Party in his report of the
result:

> It was highly gratifying that in spite of the difficulties put
> in our path by the disaffiliated party's candidate
> supporters, who made it nearly impossible for electors to
> hear our candidate at our meetings, and even went to the
> extent of pulling our double crown posters off the
> holdings, and those they could not pull off they defaced,
> which compelled us to placard more posters than
> necessary, we polled nearly a 1000 votes.[11]

Jack Clancy, the candidate of the disaffiliated Labour
Party and Trades Council, won the by-election by a narrow
majority, polling 1,113 votes; the official Labour candidate
received 988 votes. Communist supporters were jubilant,
and the result does indicate, at this stage, a certain amount
of local electoral support for the communists' continued
membership of the Labour Party. However, there were a
number of factors giving an indication that this would not
be a lasting victory of the left over the right: the
by-election took place not long after the termination of the
General Strike; Clancy was a respected and long standing
militant, and had been the Chairman of the Battersea
Council of Action; and the contest came about because of
the death of a popular left wing councillor; finally, the
newly established Labour and Trades Council had not
fully established itself, and this was its first electoral
contest.

The enmity of the Communists and their supporters for
their former allies was enhanced by the further actions of

the Labour Group on the borough council. Clancy and five other pro-communist Labour councillors were kept off of all the council committees. This was often achieved by an alliance of Official Labour and Municipal Reform councillors voting together.

It was almost a year after the setting up of an official Trades Council and Labour Party before moves were made to secure an official Labour candidate to oppose Saklatvala. The *South Western Star* seemed rather surprised at the announcement: 'Yesterday a morning paper came out with the startling news that the Socialists of North Battersea are going to oppose Mr Saklatvala at the next election'.[12] However, to most people in the Battersea labour movement the news came as no surprise. One active member of the disaffiliated Trades Council saw it as a further example of the Labour Party's retreat from socialism:

> 'I should smile', said a leading member of the Labour Party to whom we mentioned the matter. 'Of course the Labour Party will oppose Mr Saklatvala. That was inevitable from the moment the National Labour Party decided to disassociate itself from socialism. Labour is not out for revolution and it cannot ally itself with atheism. The decision to oppose the re-election of a Communist for North Battersea has not been arrived at suddenly. It is the natural consequence of political developments.[13]

An official Labour candidate was not finally adopted until November 1927, when William Stephen Sanders was selected. It marked the final severing of links between the old and the new trades council. Saklatvala, in an article for the *Sunday Worker*, called Sanders a 'Jingo Labour war monger', and after that there was little love lost between the two candidates.[14] Saklatvala's comments summed up the feelings of one side in the now deeply divided Battersea labour movement.

Up until 1928, Battersea was fairly typical of what was happening in the labour movement generally. The communists, although officially expelled from the Labour Party, still retained their membership in some cases. Many Constituency Labour Parties who opposed the ban

were actively fighting it, supported by the Communist
Party. They set up a national organisation to campaign
against the ban, the National Left Wing Movement. 1928
was to change all that, and in that year can be seen the
beginnings of a decisive change of policy by the
Communist Party. This change was to have a disastrous
effect nationally, and also on what little remained of
Labour-Communist unity in Battersea.

For the first two or three years after the ban on
communists there was still a good deal of harmony in the
disaffiliated Battersea Trades Council and Labour Party.
Communists and Labour left wingers worked together
and there was no sign of discord. The importance of
working with disaffiliated Trades and Labour Councils
was emphasised at the Communist Party's ninth congress
in 1927, and Battersea was singled out as of particular
strategic importance. The report to congress of the
'Parliamentary Department' stated its concern to place
party members as parliamentary candidates. It noted that
party members had been adopted as prospective
parliamentary candidates by disaffiliated Labour Parties in
North Battersea, Bethnal Green, North and South
Hackney and Westminster, while special attention had
been paid to Battersea. Even in the London County
Council elections of March 1928 the party maintained
these efforts, with the *Sunday Worker* giving publicity to left
wing candidates during the election. There were four of
these in Battersea – Joe Knock, Jimmy Lane, Mary Parran
JP and Jack Clancy. They were all defeated.

This was to be the last concerted electoral challenge by
the communists in unison with the old disaffiliated trades
and labour council. As 1928 developed communists
became increasingly exasperated with the Labour Party,
both at local and national level, and by 1929 they had
adopted their anti-Labour 'New Line' policy. Something of
this antagonism can be seen in the final break-up of the
trades council. Battersea Communists, with Saklatvala very
much to the fore, were operating a policy of hostility
towards the Labour Party a year before it became
communist party policy. Saklatvala was a fervent advocate
of such a change of strategy from 1925 onwards, but other

Communists in the constituency had not committed themselves. But by early 1928 they had changed their minds, and they too favoured a clean break by the Communist Party with the Labour Party. Battersea Communists, who had been such an integral part of the local labour movement, now saw no hope of winning the Labour Party for a left position. Their strategy therefore changed to a position of jettisoning the Labour Party, and asserting the independent and leading role of the Communist Party in the local labour movement. This new policy was not without its victims, and principal among these was the disaffiliated Labour Party and Trades Council.

The new tactics of the Battersea Communists came in for considerable criticism from their old allies. It is worth reprinting in full the letter of resignation from the disaffiliated Trades Council from a number of its stalwarts. This letter, which was sent in June 1928, shows the extent to which the local Communists had already developed their strategy of antagonism to Labour. It also shows the depth of hostility that this new policy encountered from amongst the Labour Left in the constituency:

> Mature consideration of the proceedings of the Annual General Meeting of the Battersea T.C. and L.P. convinces us that the most important question facing the party, viz – the new policy of the Communist Party towards the Labour Party – was not given the consideration its importance justifies to a disaffiliated Labour Party. The importance of this issue is to our minds emphasised by the significant silence of Mr Saklatvala and the members of the Communist party generally on the matter. It would seem that Mr Saklatvala preferred to make violent attacks upon active and consistent members of the party, not so much because he had any grounds for the attacks but rather for the purpose of avoiding the main issues involved.
>
> We are satisfied that with Comrade Saklatvala, the C.P. must, and does come first, the Battersea T.C. and L.P. only serving for the furthering of the C.P. objectives.
>
> It is interesting to note that, not withstanding the repudiation of Communist wire pulling, with one exception all those who voted in favour of the scheme of

re-organisation suggested by Mr Saklatvala, were members of the Communist Party.

We feel that the position has become farcical when a demonstration is advocated as under the auspices of the Communist Party and the Labour Party, for the purpose of explaining to the public why the former body had decided to fight the latter organisation. It is easy to see that the name of the Labour Party was only used to give a degree of prestige to a Communist recruiting campaign it otherwise would not have had.

We feel sure all will agree that we the undersigned have taken our full share in the fight against reactionary officialism (perhaps more so than many of those who talk so loudly of fighting to the bitter end). But we are as strongly opposed to being used as tools by an organisation, with which, in spite of the support we have extended to it in the past, we have always had considerable differences which have never been hidden.

The statement previously repudiated by us, that there was no middle course between membership of the Communist Party and the National Labour Party now becomes a truism in face of the new policy of the Communist Party, which entirely removes any arguments in favour of C.P. affiliation.

In our opinion the only course open to those wishing to support the C.P. is inside that organisation. We however, have differences with that body too considerable to make it possible to take that step. Consequently we have no alternative but to submit with regret our resignation from the Battersea Trades Council and Labour Party.[15]

This letter was signed by A P Raynor, Mrs Raynor, Alderman Chesterman, Mrs Chesterman, Cllr. J G Clancy, A Richardson, and J Knock.

Those that had resigned had been active in the Battersea labour movement for a number of years. Jack Clancy, the winner of the Winstanley ward by-election, had, along with Joe Knock, attended the first foundation conference of the Communist Party. They, along with the others, had been pushing for Communist participation in the Labour Party since that time. They did not take lightly the decision to resign from the disaffiliated body, and with their resignation the organisation virtually ceased to function. In the following November at the borough council elections there were no left wing candidates sponsored by the old Battersea Labour Party, and neither did Clancy seek re-election in Winstanley Ward.

The response of the Battersea Communists to these criticisms of their strategy was to imply that their former allies had now deserted socialism. By the end of 1928, the Communists 'New Line' policy can be seen in full flow in the borough. Labour left-wingers were now considered by the Communists to be as bad as the Tories. Saklatvala claimed that those who had left the disaffiliated Trades Council and Labour Party had done so for personal gain. He told a Communist Party meeting in the constituency:

> Temptations of Councillorship had proved too strong for some of those who professed loyalty to the workers. Others saw that they must run away from the labour movement otherwise they would not be accepted as candidates elsewhere.[16]

This was the kind of attack on the Labour left that was common during the Communist Party's 'New Line' period, but in Battersea, due in part to Saklatvala's influence, such attacks found a ready response at a much earlier date.

The tenth congress of the CPGB, in January 1929, decided to dump the Left Wing Movement, and to reappraise the party's strategy towards the Labour Party. In Battersea, even before the congress took place, moves were well underway by the local Communists to cease working with the disaffiliated Labour Party and Trades Council. Saklatvala, at a public meeting in the borough, was full of praise for the old Trades Council, but he now claimed that it had outlived its usefulness. The *South Western Star* reported his speech very fully:

> [The Trades Council] was only a shadow of its former self, it did not represent the 15,000 electors who had voted for him at the last election. In 1924, it had 185 delegates representing 55 Trade Union Branches but matters had changed. In the last 4 years there had been many changes. It had been a bitter struggle but he had the backing of his party ... Battersea Trades Council could be a help still and he hoped they would keep up their work, he had thought it would be necessary to form another body. They had

therefore formed the Workers' Electoral Committee, as they had done everywhere else. He was going to stick to them.[17]

The decision to establish a Workers' Electoral Committee was clearly a unilateral decision by Saklatvala and the Battersea Communists. It caused such consternation amongst the left in the local labour movement that the Battersea Labour League decided to call a meeting to discuss the future of the disaffiliated Trades and Labour Council. From the discussion that took place it was obvious that little or no consultation, had taken place between the local Communist Party branch and the disaffiliated trades council. Saklatvala was criticised at the meeting by a number of his former Labour Party allies. Chesterman, who was one of those who had resigned from the old Trades Council in 1928, in protest at the Communist Party's new strategy, claimed that Battersea Trades Council and Labour Party had been kept in existence with the one specific purpose of furthering Saklatvala's candidature. He argued that the Communist Party had thrown the left wing movement overboard and that setting up an electoral committee was another nail in the coffin of the Trades Council.[18]

W Powell, a Battersea Labour councillor and communist supporter, also criticised the communists for their treatment of the old Trades Council. Saklatvala defended the Communist Party, and claimed that it was only the communists that kept the disaffiliated council going. His view of the role of the old Trades Council seemed to be just what Chesterman implied – that it was there solely to secure Saklatvala's re-election. This seemed to be Saklatvala's idea of the role of disaffiliated Labour Parties everywhere:

> Dissaffiliated parties all over the country were shadows. A general election could not be run like that. The Communist Party who were outcast and cut away from the Labour official machinery, could do nothing but form an electoral committee of men and women who were once a part of the Labour movement. In Battersea, it did not cut out the Trades Council.[19]

At the meeting there was a good deal of animosity and this was mostly directed at Saklatvala and the Communist Party; however it did not prevent a joint social being organised by both parties in March 1929, at which Saklatvala presided. This was to be the last public function of the disaffiliated Trades and Labour Council: without the support of the Communist Party the organisation collapsed.

The 1929 Election

Parliament held its last session on 10 May 1929, and a general election was announced for 30 May. In Battersea the new organisation, the Workers' Electoral Committee, started to organise its first activities. These were to be a series of outdoor meetings addressed by Saklatvala, at the Princes Head and Battersea Square. There were also to be a number of indoor meetings.

This election contest was the first time that Saklatvala stood as a Communist without the support of the local Labour Party and Trades Council, and against an official Labour candidate. Yet despite that he still managed to secure a number of influential backers. Charlotte Despard, at the age of 83, came over from Ireland to help in the campaign, and spoke at some of his meetings. Notwithstanding the Communist Party's attacks on the Indian National Congress, Pundit Nehru sent Saklatvala a cablegram from India, wishing him every success and donating £100 to his election fund, Saklatvala received other messages of support from the subcontinent, including one from his hometown of Navasari, with a further donation of £200. There was a letter of solidarity from the Madras Branch of the Indian National Congress, with a donation of £100.

Saklatvala's election address, as in previous contests, made little reference to specific issues in Battersea. Instead the demand was for 'a Revolutionary Workers' Government, not as an alternative change of political parties but as a final step for socialisation of the land, mines, railways and transport, banks, factories, houses etc., and to place them permanently under working class control and administration'. Even reforms of a general kind were kept to a minimum in a statement that dealt mainly with the need for the revolutionary overthrow of capitalism. Saklatvala told the electors of Battersea that 'the workers of Great Britain at General Elections do not require only a nominal change of party but a complete revolutionary change of the system of life'.

Even though his election address, in line with the Communist Party's new thinking, contained many attacks on the Labour Party, he still made much of his local Labour support and emphasised his past success as a Labour candidate:

> I am coming once again as a member of the Communist Party and one of their National Parliamentary Candidates, adopted locally by the Battersea Trades Council and Labour Party (with which is also affiliated the old Battersea Labour League) and the North Battersea Workers' Electoral Committee. I practically repeat the same anti-capitalist and anti-imperialist out and out Socialist program as in my election addresses of 1922, 1923, and 1924, which you substantially approved of by your votes. At the last General Election of 1924, when the Labour Party, which was rapidly drifting toward capitalism, disowned me and made me stand solely upon the merits of my Communist programme, you showed increased confidence in me by giving me over 15,000 votes or 3,000 more than when I had been officially endorsed by the National Labour Party.

Saklatvala was optimistic about the result of the forthcoming general election, and at a meeting in Nine Elms Baths, Battersea, called early on in the campaign, he claimed that it was his firm belief that if the Communist Party could put 200 candidates in the field they would win more seats than the Labour Party.[20] He was optimistic too about his own chances of success, and thought that if he was defeated it would be by the Tory candidate. After the election he told a reporter from the *South Western Star*, that the result, a Labour win, had been something of a shock. That a Tory victory in Battersea would be the most likely outcome was the view held by Sanders, the Labour candidate, although his main concern was Saklatvala's defeat. He told the press that he would have been content if the result of the election had been to oust Saklatvala, and was quite prepared for the return of Commander Marsden (the Tory candidate).[21] There was personal as well as political animosity between Sanders and Saklatvala, so much so that Sanders refused to shake Saklatvala's hand at the nominations. He alleged that this was because Saklatvala had referred to him as a murderer for enlisting in the army during the war. By contrast, Saklatvala and Commander Marsden were, on a personal level, fairly friendly, and according to local reports, 'bowed to each other and shook hands with the utmost politeness and apparent cordiality'.[22]

The organisation of Saklatvala's campaign was carried out entirely by the North Battersea Workers' Electoral Committee, and all meetings were held under its auspices. There is little surviving material on the committee but it probably consisted almost entirely of Communist Party members: the election agent was E R Pountney, a CP member. The campaign had committee rooms in each of the wards that made up the constituency, but it is difficult to say how many were involved in the campaign. Saklatvala, during one of his optimistic speeches at the end of 1928, had said that it was possible to recruit 200 supporters onto the new committee, but it seems very unlikely that this ever happened.

As at previous elections, Saklatvala spoke at a large number of meetings. On some occasions he would speak at three or four indoor or outdoor meetings a night, but it is unlikely that these meetings were as well attended as in the past. The campaign, unlike that of previous contests, was not marred by accusations of denial of free speech, and generally speaking seems to have been a fairly mild affair. Although the electorate had increased by 25 per cent, from 40,586 in 1924 to 50,460 in 1929, there was none of the enthusiasm that had been the hallmark of previous elections. However, ten thousand people gathered outside the town hall on election night to await the result. When it was announced, Sanders had won a comfortable victory, and Saklatvala had been pushed into third place. Despite the increase in the electorate Saklatvala's vote had been cut in half, and his percentage of the poll was down from 50% to 18.6%. The turnout was 67.7%. Sanders polled 13,265 votes, 37.8% of the voters, Marsden received 10,833, 30.8%, while Saklatvala received 6,544 votes.

A disappointed Saklatvala told his supporters from the town hall steps that one phase of the election may have been lost but that through all the vicissitudes the peoples' struggle would go forward to victory.[23]

Saklatvala's parliamentary career was at an end. Although he fought other electoral contests, in Battersea and elsewhere, he never again came remotely close to winning a seat in parliament.

The general election of 1929 marked the end of an era for Saklatvala. The result showed conclusively that his success in Battersea relied solely on the Communist's involvement in the Labour Party. Saklatvala had been successful in Battersea because he was the candidate of a united local labour movement, of which the Communists were an integral part. This movement was sufficiently powerful to ensure that its parliamentary candidate would get elected. Even in the 1924 general election, when Saklatvala did not receive national Labour Party endorsement, he still won the seat because of this local support. However, after the establishment of a new trades and labour council in 1926, the labour movement in Battersea was irreconcilably split. Although in many respects it was a split between the left and the right, over the next couple of years the increasing antagonism of the Communists towards the Labour Party alienated many of the Communists' supporters in the borough. The Battersea Communists, with Saklatvala very much in the lead, made sure that the Communist Party's new hard line approach towards the Labour Party was implemented locally, some time before it was applied nationally. Saklatvala, an enthusiastic supporter of the 'New Line', even before it became party policy, was in the forefront of those in the area who wished to turn the old Battersea Labour Party and Trades Council into an addendum of the Communist Party. And eventually, it was reduced from a once powerful organisation that united the left and the right in the Battersea labour movement to a mere handful of individuals.

The developments in the borough from 1929 to 1935 confirm that Saklatvala's success, and the Communists' influence, was due to their involvement in the local Labour Party. After 1929 there was a rapid decline in Communist support as expressed in electoral terms. By the time of Saklatvala's death in 1936, the Communists in Battersea were faring no better than in any other London consti- tuency. This confirms that there was not a communist base in the area, despite Saklatvala's electoral appeal. The *South Western Star's* analysis of 1926 had been proved correct:

> The votes of communists alone would never have brought Mr Saklatvala within sight of the House of Commons. Cut off from the Labour Party the Communists would be as impotent as the little band of red flaggers who used to plot at Sydney Hall.[24]

Notes

[1] *Daily Mail*, 13 Oct 1924.
[2] *Daily Herald*, 27 Oct 1924.
[3] *Daily Graphic*, 20 Oct 1924.
[4] *South Western Star*, 24 Oct 1924.
[5] *Daily Telegraph*, 18 Oct 1924.
[6] *Morning Post*, 20 Oct 1924.
[7] Report on Revolutionary Organisations in the U.K. Report No 278 dated 30 October 1924, Special Branch, New Scotland Yard. Contained in MacDonald Papers. Public Record Office.
[8] *The Star*, 3 Feb 1926.
[9] *Sunday Worker*, 11 July 1926.
[10] *Ibid.*
[11] South Battersea Divisional Labour Party, Minutes of Meeting held on 25 November 1926, Battersea Labour Party.
[12] *South Western Star*, 8 July 1927.
[13] *Ibid.*
[14] *Sunday Worker*, 4 Dec 1927.
[15] Photocopy of this letter is in author's possession.
[16] *South Western Star*, 16 Nov 1928.
[17] *South Western Star*, 14 Dec 1928.
[18] *South Western Star*, 1 Feb 1929.

[19] *Ibid.*
[20] *South Western Star*, 1 March 1929.
[21] *South Western Star*, 31 May 1929.
[22] *Ibid.*
[23] *South Western Star*, 31 May 1929.
[24] *South Western Star*, 5 Feb 1926.

Chapter Six

A Revolutionary in Parliament

In this chapter I shall look specifically at Saklatvala's years in parliament. Saklatvala's five year term of office was the Communist Party's first sustained experience of parliamentary representation. To Saklatvala fell the onerous task of pioneering the role of a revolutionary in parliament. His experience at the House of Commons gave the Communist Party an insight into how that institution operated. His period as an MP is also important because it contributed towards his reassessment of the Labour Party, and helped set him on the path towards the 'new line' policy of communist hostility to social democracy.

Saklatvala was elected as a Labour MP in 1922. He was re-elected as a Communist in 1924, and retained the seat until 1929. He did not have the distinction of being the first elected Communist MP; that privilege went to J T Walton Newbold in Motherwell. But Newbold was in parliament for less than a year, from 1922 to 1923, whereas Saklatvala was an MP for a full term.

The Communist Party had mixed views about the usefulness of parliamentary representation. Although officially it was party policy to take part in elections, there were many Communists who were opposed to this strategy. Many on the revolutionary left felt that participation in parliament would lead to corruption, and the betrayal of socialist principles. Saklatvala's experiences illustrate that pressures can be brought to bear on a militant MP, pressures of an overt and not so overt nature. His ability to resist these pressures was, in part, because of

the close ties that were maintained between Saklatvala and
the Communist Party.

The Communist Party had a unique view of the role of
an MP, quite different from that of the Labour Party. The
Communists believed that a revolutionary in parliament
should have a close relationship with the movement
outside. The party did not believe that parliament could
bring about socialism, but that it was useful to win
representation in that body in order that the demands of
the masses could be raised at the highest level. In turn,
Communists argued, elected representatives would be
given encouragement by the mass movement outside
parliament. Although Saklatvala, in the party's view, made
mistakes, and his parliamentary role was criticised, even by
the Communist International, his accomplishments at
Westminster gave the Communist Party, despite its very
small numbers, a national presence that it would not have
achieved had it not been for its MP. It was partly because
of his success in this field that even during the years of the
Communist Party's greatest hostility to the Labour Party,
and parliamentary socialism, it never relinquished its
commitment to electoral intervention.

Saklatvala's attitude towards the power of parliament
was well within the mainstream of Communist Party
thinking. Like most Communist Party members he did not
view parliament as an instrument that could achieve
revolutionary change. When in 1928 he was asked for his
opinions about parliament and the use of force, Saklatvala
made the following observation.

> The Communists are intent in pointing out ... that the
> capitalist class will resist the workers and that the workers
> instead of fooling themselves with dreams of an easy
> victory over capitalism must prepare to break the capitalist
> resistance by mass action. This does not mean that the
> Communist Party is not prepared to utilise Parliament and
> the local governing bodies to the full extent of their
> possibilities. It is not prepared to say that a Labour
> Parliamentary majority is impossible, on the contrary it
> believes that the workers should regard it as possible, and
> strive to get a Labour majority returned ... It is prepared
> to argue from experience of the class struggle that the

capitalist class which is prepared to suppress a Board of Governors* for carrying out a policy which is in a small way hostile to capitalism, would be prepared to resist a Parliament which challenged capitalism in a fundamental fashion. Holding these views, the Communist Party, while prepared to use Parliament, lays the chief emphasis on the organisation of the workers outside Parliament, for the mass struggle which it regards as inevitable.[1]

This early view on the use of parliament did not fundamentally alter. What did change was his notion that a parliamentary Labour majority was desirable. In this respect his first period in the House of Commons had a profound effect on his political perspective. His close proximity to parliamentary power changed his views both about the commitment of Labour MPs to change and about the ability of a Labour government to introduce even moderate reforms. These doubts, based on his parliamentary experience, had a radical affect on his thinking.

Participation in elections had been one of the two most contentious issues at the foundation congress of the Communist Party. (The other one, as mentioned earlier, had been Labour Party affiliation.) Although the vote in favour of electoral intervention had been quite over-whelming, almost ten to one, it was not an accurate reflection of the anti-parliamentarian and syndicalist tradition within the British labour movement which was strongly represented in the Communist Party. Party members were sceptical about the worth of participating in parliament. Gallacher, the leader of the Clydeside shop stewards, was hostile to Westminster at the time of the party's formation, and it was only after personal discussions with Lenin that he came to recognise the usefulness of electoral contests. Lenin had no hesitation in proclaiming his own support for electoral intervention, and in a letter to the party's first conference, he urged the assembled delegates to 'utilise the Parliamentary struggle.[2]

The Communist Party, throughout Saklatvala's life, adhered to Lenin's advice. Its own assessment of

---

* Saklatvala is referring here to the Poplar councillors, see page 41.

parliament's uses was most succinctly put at the party's
sixth congress in 1924. The party leadership argued,

> It [the CP] enters Parliament not in order to delude the
> workers that they can achieve their emancipation by its
> means, but to use Parliament as a tribune whence to issue
> rallying calls and watchwords to the masses.[3]

These were the party's objectives, and it was within this
overall perspective that Saklatvala operated during the
time that he was a Communist MP.

From the outset there were a number of obvious
disadvantages for Saklatvala. During his second full term
in parliament he was the only Communist in the House of
Commons; there was no one of his own party to whom he
could turn for support. His five year term of office
spanned both an upturn in working class militancy leading
to the 1926 general strike, and a downturn following its
failure. Soon after his election, a united working class
movement forced the government to concede a subsidy to
the coal industry, and for nine months this meant that the
miners did not suffer a wage cut. When that period
finished, the leadership of the labour movement was
prepared, albeit reluctantly, to call a general strike on
behalf of the mine workers. For nine days an increasingly
confident working class showed their solidarity. Then, to
the amazement of all except the TUC leaders, the
government and the coal owners, the strike was called off
and the miners were left to fight on alone. After this the
labour movement went on the defensive. Trade unions
came under attack and there was legislation to curtail their
rights.

Unemployment never dropped below one million
throughout the period that Saklatvala was in parliament.
One of the consequences of this was a falling off of trade
union membership, and many working class and socialist
organisations showed a drop in numbers at this time. Thus
for much of the time that Saklatvala was in parliament
there was no mass movement, to which he could turn for
support. The Communist Party's notion – of a revolutionary MP being given aid and encouragement by a
militant working class movement, and of that movement's

demands being voiced in parliament by its elected representatives – was difficult to accomplish in Saklatvala's second term of office: for most of this time the working class was on the defensive.

Despite its misgivings about parliament, the Communist Party had early on recognised the practical advantages of having Communist MPs. Even during Saklatvala's first term, when he was elected as a Labour MP, the party had noted the upsurge of interest in communist ideas that had come about because of its elected representatives, with Saklatvala and Newbold receiving many invitations to speak from non-communist organisations. Their election also had the added advantage of enhancing the CPGB in the eyes of the Communist International. The special importance of Saklatvala to the Communist Party, because of his work as an MP, was emphasised at the first meeting of the new Central Committee, after the party's Seventh Congress in 1925. Although Saklatvala had not been elected to the Central Committee at the congress, the meeting decided to make him a full member during his term of office as a member of parliament.

Part of Saklatvala's function as a revolutionary in parliament was to maintain close contact with the local labour movement. From the beginning he had promised regular consultation with the workers in his constituency: his 1922 election address had declared, 'to meet the changing positions which will arise I promise to present myself to my Labour electors about once a month to ascertain their wishes on all fresh issues'. He held frequent report-back meetings, and in addition regular canvassing took place to uncover the grievances of the voters. Saklatvala continued with this practice throughout his time as an MP and there were a number of mass meetings at the town hall at which he explained his parliamentary actions.

Saklatvala's early work in parliament reflected the unity that existed within the local labour movement. He was in regular consultation with the Labour-controlled borough council, and at their instigation he raised the important issue of housing in the constituency. The borough council had been spending money to repair property owned by private landlords, and was facing difficulty in getting the money back. Saklatvala, in the House of Commons, pleaded the Council's case. A little later, in the same parliamentary session, he again intervened on the Council's behalf, when Viscount Curzon, the Tory MP for Battersea South, asked the Minister of Health whether he had the power to stop Battersea Borough Council from purchasing a plot of land in the borough for the purposes of erecting a showroom for the sale of electrical appliances. Saklatvala countered by pointing out that the Battersea Borough Council was running its own power station and selling electricity more cheaply than in the neighbouring borough where a private company was the supplier.[4] This co-operation between Saklatvala and the borough council came to an end after the arguments in the Battersea labour movement over communist membership. Saklatvala was less inclined to defend the actions of the council, and to raise borough council issues, after the Communists had been expelled from that body. In fact, for much of the period that he was a Communist MP, in keeping with his anti-Labour thinking, he ignored the grievances of the Labour local authority.

The same cannot be said for Saklatvala's endeavours on behalf of the Communist party. He made a number of direct interventions at the Communist Party's request, and they are a good illustration of the unity that the party was trying to build between its parliamentary representative and the mass movement outside. During the campaign against the arrest of the Communist leaders in October 1925 (see p91) Saklatvala sought to combine both Parliamentary and extra parliamentary struggle. The Communist Party had launched a petition in protest at the arrests, and in the space of less than four months it had collected over 300,000 signatures, including those of 100 MPs. Saklatvala got a good deal of publicity when he presented the petition to parliament.[5] At the same time, he unsuccessfully raised the issue within the chamber, as well as the government's unauthorised opening of letters addressed to the Communist Party.[6] This attempt to combine two aspects of struggle was to be a hallmark of Saklatvala' work in parliament. In many of the parliamentary issues in which he was involved there was a constant reference back to and an attempt to involve, the movement outside. The Communist Party had made it clear from the outset that this was what it expected of its MPs. When Saklatvala and Newbold were first elected, the Party leadership had recognised that they had 'a lonely fight to fight at present', but had argued that

> even one good fighter can be enough to expose the working of the system and to show up the intrigues of the Government, and, where necessary, the failure of the present Leaders of the Labour Party. Our comrades can feel strong in the confidence that they are there to voice the feelings and wishes of the masses outside .... The Executive Committee calls on the workers to back them in their efforts, to follow closely their activities, and to see that they are not left isolated in the struggle in the enemy camp.[7]

After 1924, when Saklatvala was the only communist MP, there was an even greater need to rely on support from outside.

This relationship of mutual support took on many and unusual forms. In 1925, at the direct request of the Communist Party's seventh congress, Saklatvala agreed to ask questions in the House of Commons about the treatment of the Greenock Young Pioneers, who had been denied the right to demonstrate in their own city. Greenock, in Scotland, was far removed from Battersea, and the Young Pioneers were small in number, but Saklatvala took up the case, and in so doing gave some publicity to the Communist Party's Children's Organisation. As Saklatvala explained to the congress, which included a delegation from the Young Pioneers, there were particular difficulties of operating as a Communist MP:

> I think our Young Pioneers have placed upon us a very onerous duty because they do not know the system of questioning in the House. Out of about twenty questions we wish to ask, generally about 19 are refused, and one is allowed. In the present mood of Joynson-Hicks, who hates all Communists and is sure to have a greater hatred of the

Young Pioneers, we have a difficult task, but still I shall try
and I promise my young comrades that we shall not rest
quiet until we have put that question.[8]

A month later Saklatvala managed to raise the banning in
a question to the Secretary of State for Scotland. In what
was to be an almost standard response to questions of this
nature raised by the Communist MP, Saklatvala was told it
was in 'the public interest' to maintain the ban[9] He
persisted, raising the question again a week later, and
receiving a similar response.

Incidents of this sort, although unsuccessful, showed the
importance the Communist Party attached to developing
the two aspects of the struggle. Saklatvala emphasised this
point when speaking at a conference organised by the
Battersea Trades Council and Labour Party in June 1925.
He warned the delegates not to simply rely on parliament
to bring about the necessary changes, and that they should
also depend on their own militancy. *Workers Weekly*
reported:

> Comrade Saklatvala emphasised the great danger of
> looking only to Parliament and expecting to find
> ready-made legislative happiness. What is absolutely
> necessary is unity and action among the fighting forces of
> the working class ...[10]

Apart from this side of his work, the Communist Party also
put to good use Saklatvala's parliamentary orations.
Workers Weekly regularly carried extracts from his
contributions in the House of Commons. In 1924, a
pamphlet entitled *The Class Struggle in Parliament* was
produced, which consisted entirely of extracts from
Saklatvala's speeches. The pamphlet sold 10,000 copies
and had to be reprinted. In 1928 two more pamphlets
were produced and sold at 1d each. These were called
With the Communist Party in Parliament and *Socialism and
Labourism*. Both pamphlets, like their predecessor,
consisted of extracts from Saklatvala's speeches in
parliament. They were both published at the time of the
transition to the 'New Line' policy, and were an indication
of a changing attitude towards the Labour Party by both

Saklatvala and the Communist Party. In the introduction to *Socialism and Labourism*, the Parliamentary Labour Party was accused by the Communists of collaborating with capitalism and deserting socialism:

> Obsessed with the responsibility of being His Majesty's opposition, preferring the role of advisers to His Majesty King George, and demonstrating their bourgeois conscience and respectability, and exercising themselves for another term in office, the Labour Party has ceased to concern itself with the propaganda of Socialism[11]

In the Communist Party's estimation, Saklatvala was now the sole representative of socialist thought in parliament. Commenting on his intervention in a debate the party proclaimed,

> Saklatvala seized the occasion to rescue Socialism and Communism from the dishonourable hands of the Labour Party and to be its standard bearer. The result is a speech giving a clear exposition of the elementary things the socialist movement stands for, in such simple language as will be understood by every worker. Bearing in mind that Saklatvala stands alone in the House, hated and detested by the entire block of Labour Members, from whom he got nothing but jeers during his speech – limited as it was to 40 minutes – it was a great achievement.[12]

The speech in question showed just how far Saklatvala had moved along the path of the 'New Line' policy during his time in parliament. Gone was his idea of four years earlier, of making common cause with the parliamentary left. Now any semblance of reform was rejected out of hand. Saklatvala dismissed suggestions by Labour MPs that socialist measures could be introduced under capitalism:

> It is a mistaken notion to argue for a moment that Socialism can be introduced alongside Capitalism, side by side, and gradually. Such a thing would never happen, such a thing cannot happen[13]

The international dimension

The Communist Party used its parliamentary representation to raise issues in the House of Commons, to
popularise its ideas in the labour movement, and, in the
later part of the period, to make attacks on the Labour
Party. A further important dimension was Saklatvala's
international work. He made use of his position in
parliament to develop anti-imperialist solidarity, particularly with the nationalist movement in India. In the days
before the 'New Line' policy, he suggested to Parliament,
unsuccessfully, that Pundit Nehru be invited to the House
of Commons to explain the situation in India.[14] The idea
was rejected, but sections of Saklatvala's speech were
reproduced in *Workers Life*, the communist party's weekly
paper, and used as propaganda. Throughout his
parliamentary career Saklatvala raised at every conceivable occasion the condition of India, to such an extent
that the press referred to him as the 'Member for India'.[15]
He was widely recognised in the subcontinent as the
champion of independence, and many in the nationalist
movement who did not share his views applauded his
actions in keeping Indian issues before the House of
Commons. In recognition of this stand Saklatvala received
donations from the subcontinent towards his election
expenses. Even at the 1929 general election, when he was
standing as a Communist, not backed by the Labour Party,
he received messages of support from a number of
provincial branches of the Indian National Congress.[16]

Saklatvala also made use of his trips abroad on
parliamentary business to liaise for the British party with
the Communist International. On a visit to Copenhagen in
1923, with a British Parliamentary delegation, he used the
opportunity to collect money for the CPGB from the
Communist International. A Special Branch report
claimed that,

> Saklatvala stated recently that he received £500 from the
> Communist International when he went to Copenhagen in
> connection with the International Conference of MPs in
> August 1923. It will be remembered that after visiting
> Copenhagen Saklatvala went to Moscow.[17]

Saklatvala was certainly invited to Moscow at this time to attend a private conference organised by the Executive Committee of the Comintern on propaganda, so there seems no reason to doubt the report's accuracy. (There is some controversy though about whether or not the British Party took money from the Communist International: R Palme Dutt later claimed there was opposition from within the British Party to such financial assistance.)[18]

In September 1928 Saklatvala went to Berlin with a group of MPs for a conference of the Interparliamentary Union. It is probable that while he was there he carried out work for the Communist Party. Two months after his return Ernst Thaelman, the Leader of the Communist Party of Germany, made a speaking tour of Britain, speaking with Saklatvala, Arthur Horner and J R Campbell at a Communist Party meeting in Battersea town hall. It is highly probably that much of the preparation for this tour was made by Saklatvala while he was in Germany. (This trip also caused some controversy (see p126))

Pressure to conform

Although the Communist Party recognised the value of having Communist representation in Parliament, and Saklatvala's services were put to good use by the party in the ways outlined many in the Communist Party at that time contended that it was inevitable that a revolutionary would be corrupted by the parliamentary system. And in fact there was pressure to conform brought to bear on Saklatvala, both of a direct and indirect nature. These pressures are worth examining, as are the reasons for Saklatvala's ability to resist.

In many respects Saklatvala was untypical of the prescribed view of a revolutionary in parliament. He was from an extremely wealthy background and had attended an exclusive private school in Bombay. He had little work experience in Britain, and that which he did have was as a departmental manager for Tatas. He had no direct comprehension of class struggle and had been involved in no industrial disputes. He lived in a large house overlooking Parliament Hill Fields and there is no evidence that he, his wife, or his five children were ever in want. His credentials for understanding of the working class were far worse than that of many Labour MPs. His family background and upbringing made him socially much closer to the Tories in Parliament than to the left.

In other ways too his approach to parliament was not in keeping with that generally ascribed to the revolutionary left. He admired the insitution of the House of Commons; he enjoyed debate, and was prepared to abide by parliamentary rules and procedures. He was always polite, even to his most vociferous opponents, and was always at pains to separate personal feelings from political views. His friendship with George Lansbury, the Labour leader, survived even the harshest years of the 'New Line' policy.[19]

Newbold's defeat in 1923, and his resignation from the Communist Party a year later, gave weight to those in the party who argued that parliament corrupts. However it is not clear whether or not pressure was brought to bear on Newbold to get him to break with the Communist Party. What is certain is that there were definite inducements held out to Saklatvala if he would just temper his ideas. Saklatvala's secretary, Reg Bishop, later gave an account to the *Daily Worker* of the incentives that were held out to the new MP during his first year in Parliament. Many tried to get him to break from the Communist Party, and, according to Bishop, the Under-secretaryship of State for India was only one of many inducements held out if only he would drop his revolutionary politics.[20] Even later on, when Saklatvala had been re-elected as a Communist, his loyalty was put to many a severe test. Bishop, who was working with him all the time, saw the pressure that was brought to bear on him, pressure of a personal as well as of a political character. Saklatvala did manage to resist these personal persuasions, but they were only part of the pressure to make a militant MP conform. Another side of the 'parliamentary embrace' was the more overt form of pressure which ensured that Saklatvala would be treated very differently from other MPs. He had experience of this kind of pressure early on in his parliamentary career.

In the summer of 1925 he decided to join a group of

other MPs who were planning to visit the United States. To be eligible to join the group's trip, an MP had to have paid five shillings subscription to the Interparliamentary Union and to be prepared to pay their own fare and Saklatvala fulfilled both of these conditions. The first hint that there might be trouble was raised by the *Daily Graphic*.[21] The paper printed a suggestion that Saklatvala might not be allowed to land in America, although it also quoted Mr Madison, the Secretary of the Interparliamentary Union who pointed out that Saklatvala already had his visa, and that an MP from any political party was eligible to join the delegation if they were willing to sign the declaration of adherence to the principles of arbitration in the countries they were visiting. Saklatvala had signed this declaration and thus demonstrated his fitness to travel. Mr Madison acknowledged that, 'America does not want anarchists', but asserted that 'all men in this party have proved that they do not come within this category'.[22]

Once the story had been floated however, there followed an attempt by the media and some members of the House of Commons to discredit Saklatvala, and to turn him into a parliamentary leper. A number of Tory MPs, with a good deal of publicity, decided not to go on the trip. One of these, Captain Peter MacDonald, Unionist MP for the Isle of Wight, issued a statement to the press and claimed he had withdrawn his name from the list of British delegates because of Saklatvala's inclusion in the delegation. A few days later, Mr Madison, in a letter to Captain MacDonald which was reported in the press, made it clear that this had not initially been Captain Macdonald's stated reason for withdrawal from the trip. The *Daily Chronicle* printed the text of Mr Madison's letter:

> In your letter to me of 18 August, asking to have your name removed from the list of delegates, you gave not the slightest hint of this reason ... On the contrary you wrote, 'I very much regret that business arrangements will not permit me to attend this Conference after all.'. This certainly did not reveal the motive you speak of. Further you wrote, 'I understand Mr Lougher MP wishes to go, and perhaps he can take my cabin accommodation'. It seems difficult to believe that when you wrote this you were

retiring from the delegation on account of Mr Saklatvala's presence on it, for in that case I should have thought you would not have treated this matter in such an easy fashion and taken it for granted that one of your colleagues would do what you now regard with such horror.[28]

However, the damage had been done. The US government, which had issued a visa to Saklatvala, now revoked it. Kellogg, the American Secretary of State, claimed that his revocation was due to Saklatvala's recent revolutionary speeches in the House of Commons, Saklatvala denied that the purpose of the intended visit was to preach anarchy but in spite of his protestations no visa was forthcoming and the parliamentary group left without him. This was the first example of the penalties he was likely to face if he remained committed to revolutionary politics. The Communist Party, pursuing its strategy of not allowing its parliamentary representative to become isolated, organised a number of protest events. In Battersea a packed meeting at the town hall gave its MP a rousing reception. The *South Western Star* estimated that there were five hundred people in attendance,[24] and the *Daily Herald* reported that Saklatvala was received with ringing cheers and the singing of 'For he's a jolly good fellow' when he appeared on the platform.[25] George Lansbury was due to speak at the meeting but arrived too late to take part. Protests were also made from the trade union movement, with the Annual Conference of the National Federation of Building Trades Operatives condemning the ban. Saklatvala even received a message of support from his home town of Navasari.

The American visit was not the only time that restrictions were placed on Saklatvala's right to travel. Before his much publicised trip to India in 1927 there was speculation that his right of entry would be refused. Saklatvala wrote to Stanley Baldwin, the prime minister, who reluctantly agreed to grant him a visa; however that did not prevent the Egyptian authorities from refusing him entry, after he had planned to spend a few weeks in that country on his way back from the subcontinent. Several months after his return the government took steps to ensure that he would never again return to the country of his birth. News of this action was conveyed to Saklatvala in a letter from the Foreign Office, which was reprinted in *Workers Life*:

> With reference to the endorsement of your passport granted on 21 December 1926. I am directed by Secretary Sir Austen Chamberlain to inform you that the validity of your passport for India has been cancelled. The fee for the endorsement can be refunded to you on your returning the passport to this Office for cancellation of the endorsement[26]

Saklatvala issued a press statement which, in a mild tone pointed out that in addition to being a member of the British parliament he was also an Indian-born subject of Indian parents. However this had no effect, and the ban on Saklatvala remained in force for the rest of his life. Even towards the end of 1929, when he was no longer an MP and at the time of a Labour government, he was again refused entry, after having been elected a delegate to the Indian National Congress from its London branch.

Apart from serving a term of imprisonment during the general strike (see pp54-55), having restrictions placed on his right to travel, being kept under surveillance, and having his mail opened, Saklatvala also suffered other indignities while he was an MP. He explained some of these in a speech at a public meeting in Battersea towards the end of his term in Parliament, which was reported in the *South Western Star*:

> In the last four years there had been many changes. It had been a bitter struggle but he had the backing of his Party. His house had been raided. There had been telephone calls at all hours of the night. There had been a plot against him and for days he had never moved without being accompanied by some of the comrades of the Minority Movement.[27]

In another incident in 1928 the *Sunday Worker* recounted the following threat to Saklatvala's well being:

> A crowd of Fascists attempted to mob S. Saklatvala MP
> after an International Class War Prisoners Aid Meeting at
> the Workmen's Hall, Clerkenwell Road, London, but were
> glad to leave well alone when workers came to Saklatvala's
> support.[28]

There were other challenges to Saklatvala's personal, as
well as political, courage during his years in parliament.
One such challenge came soon after his re-election. In
June 1925 he was invited by the Secretary of the Ranker
Officers' Association to address a meeting in Central Hall
Westminster. The meeting was called to decide what
action to take in view of the government's refusal to grant
Ranker Officers (those who had risen up through the
ranks in the first world war) the same rate of retirement
pay as those of commissioned rank. Saklatvala had
expressed support for the officers' demands, and had
agreed to speak at the meeting. The *Daily Telegraph* gave a
full report of what happened:

> When Mr Saklatvala ascended the platform, Lieutenant
> J Needham rose in the body of the Hall, and called out, 'Mr
> Chairman, is it right that we should have a man who is
> saying everything against our Flag in a meeting like this?
> He is a Red Flag man, he is not a Union Jack Man'. ...The
> President [Sir Arthur Holbook MP] then rose and left the
> platform and was followed by several of the audience. A
> Member on the platform asked the audience if it wanted to
> hear Mr Saklatvala or Sir Arthur Holbrook. A mighty
> shout of 'Sir Arthur' rang out from the audience. Mr
> Saklatvala then left the platform, and Sir Arthur Holbrook
> returned to it, the audience rising and singing, 'For He's a
> Jolly Good Fellow' and 'God Save the King'.[29]

Undeterred, the next day Saklatvala informed the
secretary of the Association that he was still prepared to
argue the officers' case in parliament.

Saklatvala was one of Britain's best known communists
and anti-imperialists. He must have known what kind of
reception he would receive from an audience of this type.
That he was prepared to address such a meeting was a test
of his political conviction. Some three years later, when he
was due to take part in a debate at Grays Inn, a similar

bitter experience was avoided , only because some members forced the invitation to be withdrawn before the event took place.[30] Incidents of this sort all contributed to the pressure to tone down his communist ideas, not just in the House of Commons, but outside as well; and they all had the aim of weakening the resolve of a revolutionary MP.

Saklatvala's commitment to communism while in parliament remained firm. But that did not mean that, in the Communist Party's view, he was above reproach. He was criticised by the party on a number of occasions, for personal as well as political reasons. On one occasion the criticism received wide publicity, and was reported in the British and Indian press. His duties as an MP were even discussed by the Communist International, who had some reservations about his work. These criticisms showed that Saklatvala was not, in the party's view, untainted by the parliamentary system; but it nevertheless felt that he still operated as a loyal communist.

Party discipline

Two incidents that occurred in close proximity during the summer of 1928 indicate that Saklatvala, in his parliamentary work, sometimes operated a little too independently for either the British party or the Communist International. The first of these concerned a speech that Saklatvala made on the occasion of the retirement of the Speaker of the House of Commons. He told his fellow MPs:

> I sincerely join in the expression of opinion which we have heard, for not only have I enjoyed perfect and impartial protection at your hands, but on all those occasions when you have had to turn me down, your informative advice to me was of even greater value than the opportunity of speaking ... I say without exaggeration and with complete sincerity that my guests and countrymen from India who have come here and came in contact with you through the Parliamentary Association and your leadership of it, have invariably gone away with the impression, however unfair it may appear to others, that in you they have met the first gentleman of Britain.[31]

It was felt by some party members that Saklatvala's remarks were far too flattering of someone who was nothing more than a trapping of capitalist democracy. The Political Bureau received a letter of complaint condemning Saklatvala's speech and calling for his expulsion from the party. The issue was discussed at the Political Bureau, in June and July 1928, and it was decided that in future the party should exercise even greater control over Saklatvala's activities.

No sooner had this criticism subsided than Saklatvala found himself in hot water again, and this time his indiscretion had international repercussions. When he attended the meeting in Berlin in September 1928 Saklatvala had not obtained prior approval from the Central Committee, and for this he was criticised by the party leadership. His participation was also condemned by the German Communist Party, who objected to a speech he made while at the meeting. The KPD raised the issue with the Communist International, and the question of Saklatvala's expulsion from the Communist Party was discussed. The Executive Committee of the Comintern were opposed to this course of action, but agreed to relay their criticisms of Saklatvala to the British party. The matter was discussed by the Central Committee of the CPGB and they passed a resolution approving of the decision not to expel Saklatvala; however the committee decided that it needed to exercise firmer control over Saklatvala's parliamentary and political activities.

Thus, the Central Committee of the CPGB, had found it necessary to criticise Saklatvala in connection with his parliamentary work twice within the space of three months. The only other time Saklatvala came in for public criticism was when he had his children initiated into the Parsee religion at a ceremony at Caxton Hall in Westminster. The ceremony took place only a few months after his return from India in 1927. The ceremony had only ever been performed in Britain once before, and was a very elaborate affair. It involved all five of the Saklatvala children, whose ages ranged from eight to nineteen. The event was covered extensively by newspapers both in Britain and in India. The *South Western Star* outlined the proceedings that were to take place.

> The ceremony lasts an hour. After being bathed the
> children are clothed in white trousers, black sandals, and
> velvet scull caps. They then don the 'Sudra' or sacred vest,
> which is never again discarded. Throughout the rite the
> novitiates continually chew betel nut. They are fed with
> milk almonds and pomegranate leaves. Afterwards they
> are branded on the forehead with a brick-red paste.[32]

The many hundreds of guests included a number of
Labour MPs, and it was reported that even Viscount
Curzon, the Tory MP for Battersea South, was present.

In a letter to an Indian merchant, Mr Dessai, reprinted
in the *Daily Chronicle*, Mrs Saklatvala explained that the
ceremony was being performed for purely personal
reasons,

> I thank you and your friends for your valuable assistance
> today with all the pride of a mother at seeing her children
> take their place in the society in which they are born. I feel
> particularly happy that despite the peculiar and difficult
> circumstances of my case, it has been possible for me to
> redeem my pledge to my late lamented father-in-law that
> his grandchildren be brought up within the fold of their
> fathers and remain a part of his family and his country.[33]

Although the ceremony was a personal affair, this did not
prevent the Communist Party from issuing a statement
condemning Saklatvala's action, as being likely to
encourage 'religious prejudices', particularly in India. The
Resolution was reprinted in full in *Workers Life*:

> The Communist Party of Great Britain recognises that in
> capitalist society many revolutionary workers, who are
> sincere enemies of capitalism, have not yet succeeded in
> fully shaking off the religious prejudices and traditions in
> which they were brought up. It therefore does not require
> of its members that they should be atheists as a condition
> for joining the Party. However, the Communist Party
> insists that they shall not actively participate in religious
> propaganda.
> As a responsible Party worker, Comrade Saklatvala is
> bound, not only to be familiar with this essential rule of the

Communist Party and of the Communist International, but to set an example to other members. He knows the particularly disastrous effect of religious prejudices and quarrels amongst the masses of India, and the unscrupulous and successful use made of religion by British Imperialism to perpetrate the enslavement and exploitation of the Indian people.

An infringement of Communist principles in this respect by a leading Party member may have undesirable repercussions in other sections of the Communist International, where religious issues divide the working class more sharply than in Great Britain.

Despite these considerations Comrade Saklatvala found it possible last week to take a leading part in a public religious ceremony associated with his name and given extensive publicity.

The Political Bureau considers it necessary, in the interests of the Party, publicly to express its disapproval and censure of Comrade Saklatvala's action.[34]

Saklatvala, in a response which was published in *Workers Life*, reinforced what his wife had said in her letter, that the ceremony was carried out for family reasons. He further argued that he was in complete agreement with the sentiments expressed in the party statement, but that the affair was completely outside his control:

> To the above resolution Comrade Saklatvala writes to say that he is in entire agreement with the attitude of the Political Bureau, and only wishes to add that the circumstances were outside his control and due entirely to the peculiar position of his people and of a purely domestic character.[35]

The condemnation of Saklatvala, although both public and forthright, had little effect on his standing in the Communist Party. This was despite later allegations by both the *Birmingham Post*, and the *Manchester Guardian*, that the ceremony led to him being banned from the party's executive committee. The *Manchester Guardian* claimed that his banning was at the instigation of the Communist International in Moscow 'as no member of the

Third International must belong to a religious community'.[36] However, Saklatvala remained an EC member until his defeat in Battersea in 1929.

Saklatvala's period as an MP came to an end at the general election of November 1929. Throughout his term in parliament he had tried to fulfil the expectations of the Communist Party in utilising the parliamentary arena for the furtherance of the class struggle, and it had been a pioneering role. The party might theorise about how to build links between parliament and the mass movement, but it was left to Saklatvala, as a lone Communist MP, to put those ideas into practice. It had not been an easy five years. The political and personal pressures that had been placed on Saklatvala were a salutary lesson, demonstrating the problems that all revolutionaries would face in a similar situation. Given the Communist Party's lack of experience in this area, it was almost inevitable that its first long serving MP would make mistakes. This did happen, and on occasion Saklatvala was criticised by the party leadership although they were, on the whole, pleased with his achievements in the parliamentary field.

Two years after Saklatvala's defeat the *Daily Worker*, in an article entitled 'The Importance of Communist MPs', paid tribute to Saklatvala's pioneering efforts. The article urged that no worker should underestimate the importance of securing the return of Communist MPs. Although the securing of revolutionary representation in the House of Commons did not enable the securing of vital changes for the workers, it did give an opportunity for 'the most widespread and effective exposure of the Capitalist State, its methods, and the policies of its parties from a forum wider and more far-reaching than any other ... a forum from which to rally the masses for action'.[37] The record of Saklatvala during the period that he was in parliament was cited as evidence for this view.

This was not the first time that Saklatvala had received praise from the Communist Party. At the first Congress after Saklatvala's re-election as a Communist, J R Campbell had singled him out for a special mention. These sentiments were endorsed by the Central Committee and it too recognised Saklatvala's achievements in a difficult situation, noting his speeches on communism, the Egyptian Indemnity, the Supplementary Reserve, the Princes Tour, the Air Force, the Party's Programme For Sailors, Profit-Sharing and the Budget. The party was gratified by the efforts which Saklatvala made 'to keep its policy before the workers'.[38] In 1925 *Workers Weekly* praised Saklatvala's oratorical skill, which was even recognised by his political opponents:

> The effect of Comrade Saklatvala's speech on the House of Commons was very obvious. After he had been speaking for a few minutes a previously almost empty House began to fill, until eventually the Government Front Bench was crammed, even the Prime Minister having come in to listen to the authentic note of the class struggle, which is so seldom heard in these surroundings.[39]

The paper also gave publicity to a tribute from John Bromley, the railwaymen's leader, in an article for the union journal. This was reprinted in *Workers Weekly*.

> I feel I must mention a very great speech by Saklatvala, the Communist Member for Battersea, during the discussion on the Co-Partnership Bill. In spite of the taunts and jeers which he always receives from the Tory crowd, Saklatvala made what to me was really a fine speech. His economics were great, covering as they did, capitalist activities throughout the world, and although he is not a member of the Party, I feel that the least which I can do is to pay a tribute to what was a real contribution to working class argument.[40]

Numerous compliments were paid to Saklatvala's work as an MP throughout his period of office. He managed to prove to the satisfaction of most party members that it was possible to enter parliament and yet retain socialist principles. Thus, as well as meeting the parliamentary challenge, he played an important role in reinforcing opinion within the communist party that electoral intervention was worthwhile.

Why did Saklatvala remain a loyal Communist? Newbold had left the party soon after his election defeat. Other revolutionaries, not members of the communist party, had entered parliament at the same time as Saklatvala, and, for all their rhetoric had been effortlessly absorbed by the establishment. What was it that stiffened Saklatvala's resolve? There were certainly temptations, and he must have known that had he resigned his membership of the Communist Party he could have chosen from any number of safe Labour seats, as well as almost certainly being retained by the official Battersea Labour Party as their candidate. Yet Saklatvala chose none of these options, and decided instead to retain his allegiance to the Communist Party. To a certain extent this is explained by the strength of the relationship between the Communist Party and its elected representatives. Of the four elected Communist MPs in Britain, three have continued to be active party members after their election defeat. On this rather small sample, the claims of the anti-parliamentary trend, both inside and outside the Communist Party, have not been ratified by experience.

Ralph Miliband, in *Parliamentary Socialism* maintains that, apart from the pressures of parliamentary life itself, the resilience of Left MPs has often been muted by their own lack of a socialist ideology. He argues that although the Clydeside left MPs elected in 1922 were affected by the atmosphere of the House of Commons and by the 'aristocratic embrace', such influences would not have been nearly as effective had those MPs brought with them to Westminster 'not only social indignation, but a clearly defined Socialist ideology'.[41] However, it was not simply a commitment to socialist ideas that separated Saklatvala from other militant though non-Communist MPs, important though that was. The Communist Party had a carefully worked out strategy for the relationship between a revolutionary in parliament, and the revolutionary party. And this was vital to Saklatvala's success as a Communist MP. His work was constantly supervised by the leadership of the party, and he kept the party closely informed of what he was doing. Saklatvala did not work in isolation from the party, and his strategy in the House of Commons was always discussed with the Party leadership. Sometimes the most minute details of his parliamentary interventions would be worked out in consultation with

the Central Committee. For example it was reported at the
ninth congress of the CPGB that during the discussion of a
trade union bill in the House of Commons, 'Comrade
Saklatvala tabled on behalf of the Party a number of
amendments designed, not merely to neutralise the Bill,
but to show up its class character.[42] It was to help in this
consultation process that Saklatvala was brought onto the
Central Committee at the beginning of his parliamentary
term. Even in 1928, when his work was being criticised it
was decided to overcome these deficiencies not through
condemnation, but by a greater supervision of his activities
by the Central Committee.

In this, the Communist Party's approach towards its
elective representatives was fundamentally different to
that of the Labour Party. No matter how left a Labour MP
might have been, they were not subjected to the same
scrutiny and control as their Communist counterparts.
The Labour Party was committed to the transformation of
society by parliamentary means, whereas the Communist
Party believed that parliament, although useful, could
never be an instrument for social revolution. This meant
that the Communist Party and the Labour Party had
different conceptions of what should be the function of a
parliamentary representative. The Labour left in the
1920s had committed itself to a party with a parliamentary
strategy, and even though they did not necessarily believe
in this strategy, they were forced to operate within the
confines of agreed party policy. The Communist Party,
rightly or wrongly, demanded rigid control over its
parliamentary representatives. It also held that they
should be a part, but only a part, of the overall struggle to
overthrow capitalism. Thus it was not socialist ideology
alone that made Saklatvala resistant to pressure; it was the
fact that he belonged to a political party that had a
coherent policy towards parliamentary struggle.

Saklatvala's experiences as an MP were also important
because of the effect that they had on the development of
his thinking about the Labour Party. His two periods in
parliament brought him closer to the parliamentary
Labour Party than any other Communist. From the
beginning he was discouraged by the performance of

Labour MPs. This disillusionment was accelerated by his involvement with the Labour government in 1924. Soon after that government's collapse Saklatvala began to urge on the Communist Party leadership the need for a new strategy towards the Labour Party. The performance of Labour in parliament and in government had not inspired him to believe that the Labour would institute any major changes. His years in the House of Commons had the effect of consolidating and strengthening his already growing reservations about the Labour Party.

Notes

[1] H B Lees-Smith, *The Encyclopaedia of the Labour Movement*, Vol 1, Caxton Publishing Company, London 1928, p153.

[2] Report of Communist Unity Convention 1920, CPGB 1920.

[3] *Speeches and Documents of the Sixth Conference of the CPGB*, CPGB 1924, p33.

[4] *Hansard*, Vol 162-506, 28 March 1923.

[5] See *Daily Herald*, 25 Feb 1926. Many other national dailies also carried the story.

[6] See *Hansard*, Vol 189-1230, 15 Dec 1925, and *Hansard* Vol 192-487, 24 Feb 1926.

[7] *Speeches and Documents of the Sixth Conference of the CPGB, op cit*, p66.

[8] Report of the Seventh National Congress, Communist Party of Great Britain, CPGB 1925, p22.

[9] *Hansard*, Vol 185-2044, 29 June 1925.

[10] *Workers Weekly*, 12 June 1925.

[11] Introduction, *Socialism and Labourism. A speech in the House of Commons by S Saklatvala*, CPGB 1928.

[12] *Socialism and Labourism, op cit*.

[13] *Ibid*.

[14] *Sunday Worker*, 27 Nov 1927.

[15] *Daily Graphic*, 11 Aug 1925.

[16] *South Western Star*, 24 May 1929.

[17] Report of Revolutionary Organisations in the U.K. Special Branch Weekly Report No 253, 1 May 1924. Contained in MacDonald Papers, PRO 30/69/1/221,*op cit*.

[18] See *Times Literary Supplement*, 6 May 1966.

[19] See The Lansbury Collection, Vol 8, Vol 9 and Vol 11. Collection of George Lansbury's papers and letters at London School of Economics.

[20] *Daily Worker*, 20 Jan 1936.

[21] *Daily Graphic*, 11 Aug 1925.

[22] *Ibid*.

[23] *Daily Chronicle*, 12 Sept 1925.

[24] *South Western Star*, 25 Sept 1925.

[25] *Daily Herald*, 21 Sept 1925.
[26] *Workers Life*, 9 Sept 1927.
[27] *South Western Star*, 14 Dec 1928.
[28] *Sunday Worker*, 12 Feb 1928.
[29] *Daily Telegraph*, 15 June 1925.
[30] *Daily Sketch*, 23 Nov 1928.
[31] *Hansard*, Vol 218-1601, 19 June 1928.
[32] *South Western Star*, 22 July 1927.
[33] *Daily Chronicle*, 23 July 1927.
[34] *Workers Life*, 5 August 1927.
[35] *Ibid*.
[36] *Manchester Guardian*, 17 January 1936.
[37] *Daily Worker*, 23 Oct 1931.
[38] Report of the Seventh National Congress CPGB, *op cit*, p137.
[39] *Workers Weekly*, 27 March 1925.
[40] *Workers Weekly* 9 May 1925.
[41] Ralph Miliband, *Parliamentary Socialism*, Merlin Press 1961, p96.
[42] Report of the Ninth Congress CPGB, *op cit*, p50.

Chapter Seven

Saklatvala the Anti-Imperialist

Saklatvala's life sheds light on the way the labour movement in the 1920s and 1930s conducted the fight against imperialism and racism. It must be said at the outset that throughout his political career, he was subjected to very little racial abuse. Racism directed against black people was, in Saklatvala's day, not an important political weapon. Such organised racism as there was, was directed against Jews. And even this, throughout much of the period, was sporadic. It was only towards the end of Saklatvala's life that political anti-semitism began to make progress. Mosley's British Union of Fascists did not emerge as a political force until after the conquest of power by the Nazis in 1933. For most of the time that Saklatvala was politically active there was no major party that used racism as a political lever. This is not to say that racism did not exist. However the black population was small and thus there was no political mileage to be gained from harnessing hostility to a black immigrant community. At the turn of the century, in Whitechapel in the East End of London, the British Brothers League, one of the first overtly racist organisations, had managed to incite local feeling against the 'influx' of Jewish immigrants. But by the first world war this was no longer an issue, and anti-semitism as a political force lay dormant.

Although there was no organised political party of racism with which Saklatvala had to contend, racist ideas were widespread. The British empire, although past its heyday, was widely recognised as a vital asset. The

Conservative Party were the traditional guardians of the empire, and it was the Tories who governed throughout most of the 1920s and 1930s. However, when Labour ruled for a brief interlude in 1924 and again in 1929, they did nothing to dismantle the colonial system. As we have seen, part of Saklatvala's disillusionment with the Labour Party was because of its lack of commitment, when in office, to any shred of colonial reform. As long as there was an empire racism would be an intrinsic part of the political scene. The defence of colonialism after the first world war could no longer rely simply on brute force; there was now a greater emphasis on ideological support.

That part of the left to which at various times Saklatvala belonged, the ILP, the Labour Party, and the Communist Party, were all opponents of imperialism. Their degree of opposition, however, varied enormously. The response to racism amongst the left was also mixed. While it is true to say that racism was not widely used by that part of the left with which Saklatvala was associated, it is a fact that racial prejudice also permeated sections of the revolutionary left. One obvious case in point is the 'Horror On the Rhine' incident.

Racism in the labour movement

After Germany's defeat in the first world war, the area along the River Rhine between France and Germany was garrisoned by French troops. Between 1920 and 1921, German socialists began agitating against the use of soldiers for this purpose, from France's African colonies. Their plea was taken up by socialists in Britain and France. E D Morel, wrote a pamphlet in August 1920 entitled, *The Horror on the Rhine*. He attacked the use of French colonial troops to patrol Germany's border with France. The language he used was racist in the extreme. Calling upon all the prejudices that had been instilled over the years, Morel used both sex and race in order to incite hatred and opposition to France's actions. Morel claimed to be both scientific and reasonable:

Will anyone who knows anything of tropical and

sub-tropical Africa, whose tribes the French have been conscripting for the past eight years, contend that sex does not play an immensely important part – and rightly – in the sociology of that part of the world. The admission that it does implies no reproach to the African negro in Africa. Nature opposed such obstacles to man in Tropical Africa that a strong sex instinct is essential to racial survival. If that strong sex instinct were non-existent, what between nature and the abominations of the old and the modern slave trades, the negro race would long ago have vanished from the face of the earth.

Again, and speaking generally, will it be denied that among the more primitive – or the more natural, if that word is preferred – races inhabiting the tropical and sub-tropical areas of Africa, the sex impulse is a more instinctive impulse, and precisely because it is so, a more spontaneous, fiercer, less controllable impulse than among European peoples hedged in by the complicated paraphernalia of convention and laws.[1]

Morel claimed that the, 'sexual urges of the African' must 'in the absence of their own women be *satisfied upon the bodies of white women*' (his emphasis).[2] He then went on to detail cases of rape and attempted rape by French colonial troops upon German women.

It would be nice to think that this was a transgression, an isolated example of racism on the left – but it was not the case. *Labour Leader*, in an article in February 1921, applauded Morel's pamphlet, and claimed that, 'public meetings are being held in the United States to draw attention to the unspeakable crime against humanity which is being committed'.[3] It was ironic that *Labour Leader*, with its fine record of anti-imperialism, could use racism and then claim that it was doing so for anti-colonial ends:

> The root of the wrong is the tearing of these black soldiers away from their homes utterly against their will for the sordid ends of their imperialist rulers.[4]

The incident showed all too clearly that even convinced and dedicated anti-imperialists were not immune from the undercurrent of racism that permeated all sections of society. *Labour Leader's* comments came at a time when Saklatvala was still a member of the ILP.

The Communist Party also, a party whose establishment was a direct result of the Second International's failure to confront imperialism, was not untainted by racism. The party's weekly paper, *The Communist*, just over a year after *Labour Leader*'s article, carried an appeal by some German socialists against the use of black troops in Europe. The appeal was headed 'Outcry Against the Black Horror' – 'Urgent Appeal to Englishmen'. Its language and message was similar in tone to that of Morel two years before:

> An awful crime against the white race, against our German women, maidens and children is being perpetuated by the French in using black and coloured troops for the occupation of German territory in an ever increasing number without our being able to prevent it.
>
> In the Wild West when a coloured man outrages a white woman, he is lynched without more ado. But what have our German women, girls and children to suffer from the African troops in the occupied districts. What says the world to hundreds of thousands of white people being enslaved by black and coloured savages? What says the world to the ever increasing assaults and crimes committed by these wild beasts on German women and children? Do the other white nations of the world know about this? It must really be doubted, for it can hardly be believed that they should have no fellow-feeling for this disgrace which is being perpetuated on us and thus on all white people. Therefore the crime committed by the French must be shouted all over the world and the other white nations must be made aware of that this disgrace hits them as well as us.[5]

The appeal ended with a plea for racial solidarity:

> You members of the white race help us to free our women, girls and children from the hell in the occupied districts into which they have been cast by the black and coloured hordes of Africa.
>
> Englishmen – Help us if you have any feeling for the awful disgrace which is being done to our white women on the Rhine by the eager lust of African savages – put a stop to the darkest crime ever committed in the world's history: The Black Horror.[6]

The Communist's response was very similar to that of *Labour Leader*. The paper maintained that what it was doing was in the interests of anti-imperialist solidarity.

> We have received the following appeal and reprint it in verbatum believing it to be true in substance and in fact. It is part of the normal brutality of Imperialism to ignore things like those set out herein on the grounds that the protest comes 'from Germany'. Such a pretence only adds to the inequity.[7]

In subsequent editions of the paper there was no outcry against the use of racism. Not a single letter was published attacking the Communist Party's implicit support for the appeal.

Apart from these examples of overt racism, the ILP and the Labour Party, in their support for colonial freedom, distinguished between the African colonies and other parts of the empire. The White Dominions – Australia, Canada, and New Zealand – had already gained a large measure of independence. Much of the focus of anti-colonial activity centred on India. Other parts of the British Empire were forgotten by the left. Two other countries were often cited in calls for national liberation, Egypt and Ireland. Saklatvala, speaking in support of a resolution dealing with colonialism at the 1919 Annual ILP conference, expressed this limited view of colonial freedom:

> This Conference demands the withdrawal of British troops from Ireland, and the recognition of that form of government which is desired by the Irish people. It further regards the claims of the Indian and Egyptian peoples to self government as essentially just and demands that they be granted at the earliest opportunity.[8]

This view of colonial freedom, concentrating attention on Ireland, Egypt, and India, predominated in the ILP throughout Saklatvala's years of membership. There was a distinction drawn between the black races of Africa, and those of a paler skin who lived in India, Egypt, or Ireland. There was a racist approach by the ILP at this stage, which

distinguished between those colonies that were deemed
suitable or unsuitable for independence. The 'Horror on
the Rhine' episode illustrates all too clearly that there were
prejudices amongst ILP members, and this was reflected
in the party's approach towards colonial liberation.

In the Labour Party too during Saklatvala's active years
of membership there was a distinction drawn between the
African colonies and others. Once again Egypt, India and
Ireland were mentioned by name as those parts of the
empire which should be granted self government. At
annual conferences a number of resolutions were passed
which called for blanket independence, but they never
mentioned any of the African colonies by name. Even
when there was a demand for wholesale national liberation
on a world scale, it was hedged around with the
supposition that it could only be applicable to those
colonies that 'showed themselves capable of expressing a
common will'. In other words, in the African colonies,
where there was as yet no developed independence
movement on a scale comparable with the Indian National
Congress, freedom could not yet be contemplated. This
seems to be the reasoning behind the resolution passed by
the 1920 Labour Party Annual Conference:

> This Conference reaffirms its conviction that only on the
> basis of democratic self determination, with adequate
> protection for minorities, can any stable or satisfactory
> settlement of the world be arrived at: and that this
> principle is applicable to all peoples that show themselves
> capable of expressing a common will.[9]

It was because of Saklatvala's impeccable record of
opposition to colonialism that he was chosen by the
Battersea Labour Party to be their parliamentary
candidate. Throughout his ten years of active involvement
in the constituency there are few examples of personal
racial abuse. The numerous attacks that were made on
him in the press, always referred to his revolutionary
beliefs, and his opposition to the constitution. There was
little mention, in an offensive way, of his racial origin. In
anticipation of any reference to his ethnicity, Saklatvala, in
his first election address, in 1922, pointed out that both

the Conservatives and Liberals had previously elected MPs who were Indian. His apprehension was over-hasty: the press, throughout his campaigns, ignored his colour and concentrated their attack on his revolutionary views. The *Daily Telegraph* summed up the press's approach towards Saklatvala, in a comment on his 1924 election campaign in Battersea, when it characterised the election as 'a grim struggle ... between Constitutional Government and Communism'.[10]

In Battersea Saklatvala's Indian origin was a help rather than a hindrance. The local labour movement prided itself on choosing a candidate who combined anti-imperialism with a proven radical record. Until the expulsion of the Communists from the Labour Party, the Battersea Labour Party and Trades Council remained staunchly loyal to Saklatvala. His ethnic origin was neither an impediment to his selection, nor an obstacle to his electoral fortunes. When, on one occasion, Hogbin, his principle opponent, attempted to use Saklatvala's nationality as a smear, it only succeeded in uniting Saklatvala's supporters.

The incident occurred during the 1923 election campaign. Hogbin had accused Saklatvala of organising disruption at his meetings and in response Saklatvala had invited Hogbin to speak at one of his meetings. The offer was declined, and instead Hogbin sent Captain Godfrey to address the meeting in his place. According to the *Daily Herald* Godfrey opened by stating that 'as a representative he had an instinctive preference for an Englishman'.[11] Given the hostility of the Battersea labour movement to imperialism it was a very foolish opening remark, and what happened next was fairly predictable. The paper reported that 'reaction was sharp and noisy. Saklatvala's supporters were on their feet in protest and for a while the whole meeting was in uproar'.[12] In the end Saklatvala had to intervene to calm the situation in order that Godfrey could be heard. The incident showed that many Labour activists in Battersea were not prepared to tolerate the use of racism to slur their candidate.

Soon after the disaffiliation of the Battersea Labour Party and Trades Council in 1926, an interesting incident occured which highlighted some of the problems

connected with race and class. J R Archer, the black ex-
Mayor of the borough, was involved in a fight at a Guardians meeting with another Labour Guardian, West. During
the meeting a disagreement erupted between the two, and
West, in a derogatory way, called Arthur a 'black man'. In
the ensuing fracas, West was knocked out by Archer, in full
view of the other Guardians.[13] Afterwards West claimed
that what he had called Archer was said in the heat of the
moment. West, a left-winger, and supporter of Communist
participation in the Labour Party, was not averse to using
racist taunts in order to combat an opponent.

Incidentally, Archer, after the split in the Battersea
labour movement did not side with Saklatvala. He became
an opponent and fought against him in the Battersea
labour movement. Archer was the first secretary, in 1927, of
the newly established Battersea Labour Party and Trades
Council. He supported Saklatvala's Labour opponent and
was influential in Sander's successful 1929 campaign:
clearly racial solidarity was not a determining factor in
political alliances.

International liaison

Although always concerned with racism, Saklatvala did not
see the fight against racial prejudice as his main priority.
Instead he directed all his campaigning skills to the
struggle against imperialism. Even when he had the ear of
the Parliamentary Labour Party, during the period of the
first Labour government, his major efforts were chan-
nelled towards achieving a measure of Indian self-
government. The proposals contained in the *British Labour
Government and India* were directed along these lines. He
only once referred to the need to curb obvious examples
of racism. He suggested that the term 'coolie labour' no
longer be used in government reports. This would not
radically alter the situation, but at least it would show that
there was some difference between a Labour and a
Conservative government.

Certain other sentimental suggestions, for instance,
abolishing the words 'coolie labour' from the Government

Reports, should certainly be respected as a matter of self respect demanded for the Indian Working Classes. Of course the right cure is to abolish the coolie system instead of letting them go on as they are and calling them by a more ambitious nomenclature. However, these little attentions are bound to show the people of India the difference of a Labour Government from other Governments.[14]

The Communist Party, too, during its early years, spent little time on the direct fight against racism. Its energies in this area were devoted to exposing the injustices of British imperialism in the colonies. As we have seen with the 'Black Horror on the Rhine' incident, the party was not immune from the prejudices that abounded at the time. However, by the mid-1920s the Communist Party was prepared to recognise that racial prejudice did exist amongst wide sections of the working class. To combat this prejudice was now one of the Party's major concerns. A motion passed by the Seventh Congress in 1925 declared:

> Hitherto the Trade Union and political Labour Movements of Great Britain has been criminal in its neglect of the colonial masses; its foremost leaders actually sharing the prejudices and ideology of the British Bourgeoisie on colonial exploitation and rule. The Communist Party of Great Britain is determined to reverse this role of the British Labour Movement. With this end in view every Party member must actively take up the fight against the imperialist prejudices still existing amongst large sections of the working class in Britain.[15]

The way this prejudice was to be overcome was by a united fight of the workers of the empire and the British labour movement, and this strategy of anti-imperialism remained at the heart of British communist thinking about colonialism throughout the period.

For Saklatvala there was no separate fight against racism. The enemy was always imperialism. In this approach he was at one with the rest of the revolutionary left. And, in the fight against colonialism, he waged a struggle on two fronts. He was involved in the anti-imperialist movement in Britain, and at the same

time, at an international level, he acted as a liaison between
the developing nationalist and communist movement in
India and the British labour movement. He was not simply
concerned with India however; his activities in this sphere
brought him into contact with revolutionary movements
throughout the world.

In his position as an intermediary between India and the
British Party, Saklatvala played an important role in
helping to establish the Communist Party of India.
Throughout the 1920s he encouraged and helped
organise the small number of Communists that there were
in India at this time. Eventually the Communist Party of
India was set up at a conference in Cawnpore in 1925, and
was recognised by the Comintern in 1926. Saklatvala's own
work reached its peak with his highly publicised tour of
India in 1927. During the tour, with the help of some
British Party members who were working clandestinely in
India, Saklatvala helped create communist nuclei in all the
cities that he visited.

Much of his work as an international liaison was under
the direction of the Communist International. The
Communist Party of Great Britain had been given
responsibility for work within the British empire, and this
necessitated regular consultation with the Executive
Committee of the Communist International. Contrary to
what many historians have said about communism during
the interwar years, there was not total unifomity in the
international communist movement. Over the issue of
imperialism there were striking disagreements between
the CPGB and the CI. The CI, under the influence of
M N Roy, looked upon the native bourgeoisie as the allies
of imperialism, and as counter-revolutionary, whereas
Saklatvala and the CPGB, thought that the national
bourgeoisie could play an important part in the struggle
for liberation. Roy, for a time, was a member of the
Executive Committee of the Communist International,
and his ideas about colonialism were dominant in the
Communist International until his expulsion in 1928.
There was a deep animosity between Roy and Saklatvala,
which was political as well as personal. They fundamentally disagreed over anti-imperialist strategy, and in this

struggle Roy was supported by the Communist International, and Saklatvala by the CPGB. In Roy's view the national bourgeoisie, particularly in India, could not be won as allies in the struggle for national liberation. The Communist International accepted Roy's analysis.

In contrast to this stand, the British Party, because of Saklatvala's influence, adopted a far less sectarian approach. British Communists did not accept the view of the Communist International that the national bourgeoisie in the colonial countries was the ally of imperialism. The CFGB argued that the way forward for colonial liberation was by a united front of workers and peasants and the national bourgeoisie. And, in line with this perspective, the CPGB paid particular attention to the Indian National Congress, and its leader, Gandhi. The British Party had been given responsibility for developing the revolutionary movement in India, and it was Saklatvala who played the major role in this sphere. He made his own position clear in a message to the founding Congress of the Communist Party of India, in 1925. He told the delegates of the importance of working within the nationalist movement:

> I must ask you to remember that although the economic independence of the workers and peasants of India is your main task, that you must still remain friendly to the national organisation of the Indian Peoples, as National Independence is the birthright of all peoples.[16]

He also pointed out the danger of allowing the communists to be separated from the nationalist movement:

> I would ask you to notice the cunning remarks in the English papers in India trying to drive a wedge between you and the Swarajists [Indian nationalists]. You must not fall into their trap as our Swarajist friends must ultimately realise that Communism is the only way that will bring real freedom to the people.[17]

Saklatvala's assessment of Gandhi was quite different from that of M N Roy and others influential in the Communist International, and it was also at variance with some in the

British party who took an interest in colonial affairs. Roy, when writing his memoirs some years later, outlined the differences between himself and Lenin over this issue:

> The role of Gandhi was the crucial point of difference. Lenin believed that, as the inspirer and leader of a mass movement, he was revolutionary. I maintained that as a religious and cultural revivalist, he was bound to be reactionary socially, however revolutionary he might appear politically.[18]

Roy had his supporters within the British Party, and *Labour Monthly*, edited by R Palme Dutt, carried articles that attacked the CPGB's position.

Although Saklatvala's talents as an organiser and orator were widely respected, he was never viewed by the Communist International as a prominent theoretician on colonial matters. For this reason he was often overlooked, and never considered for a high ranking party position. The work of the Communist International in the colonies was directed by others, particularly Roy, and what contribution Saklatvala made was often at the instigation and discretion of the British Party. When the Communist International decided to establish a Colonial Bureau in 1924, Roy informed the CPGB that Clemens Dutt had been selected as the British Representative, after consultation with Arthur MacManus in Moscow.[19]

The British Party established its own colonial department in 1924, with Tom Bell in charge, replaced a year later by Arthur MacManus who had returned from Moscow. The early work of this department again points to the Communist International's dismissal of Saklatvala as a major theoretician on colonialism. In 1925, the CI requested the CPGB's colonial department to submit a number of articles on all aspects of imperialism. These articles were to be written by British Party members for inclusion in the journal *Communist International*. Saklatvala, in spite of his acknowledged understanding of India, was not asked for a single contribution.

The Communist International also used Saklatvala as an International courier. In his capacity as an MP he made a number of trips abroad, and these proved useful in relaying back information to the CPGB from the ECCI. In turn there is little doubt that Saklatvala used these trips to help organise joint work by the Communist Party of Great Britain and the Communist Party in the country concerned.

In his international work he also visited the Soviet Union and was impressed by the progresss that had been made. While in Moscow, in 1927, he made contact with Nehru, and they discussed the work of the League Against Imperialism, an organisation set up in Britain to combat colonialism. In a subsequent visit, seven years later, Saklatvala made a special study of the Far Eastern Soviet Republics, and compared their progress with that of India. On his return he addressed a number of meetings eulogising the advances made by the Moslem Republics in the USSR.

Even before he broke with the Independent Labour Party and joined the Communist Party Saklatvala was contacted by Roy, in 1920. Roy, on behalf of the CI, asked for his assistance in helping to organise a group of Indian Communists. This was first of a number of attempts to establish a Communist Party in India in which Saklatvala was involved, and the beginning of a long involvement in the CPGB's anti-colonial work.

Saklatvala's antagonism towards Roy first became apparent in 1923. The Communist International had decided to establish an Indian Labour Bureau, and wanted Saklatvala to help in the project. From the discussion that took place it was evident that Saklatvala, even at this stage, was dubious about Roy's involvement in the scheme.

> The English Communists Newbold, Donovan, Inkpen, and Fred Peat took part in January in the consultation at Berlin which led to the formation of the Indian Labour Bureau. Efforts are being made to secure Mr Saklatvala's co-operation but he appears to be very cautious with regard to Roy's activities. This caution evidently springs from mistrust not from timidity.[20]

Roy was the instigator of the scheme, and it was at his request that Saklatvala was asked to co-operate. The idea of the Bureau was to establish a legal connection beween

Indian and European labour organisations. Saklatvala's suspicion of Roy was not mutual, and Roy recognised that Saklatvala's contacts in India would be useful if the scheme was to succeed:

> He pressed for the cooperation of Saklatvala, the Communist MP for Battersea on the grounds that the latter was in touch with Charman Lal, the Secretary of the All India Trade Union Congress.[21]

The CI, through the Red International of Labour Unions, also sought Saklatvala's co-operation in the establishment of an Indian Seaman's Association. It is unclear why Saklatvala was chosen for this task, as he had no connection with the sea whatsoever. He became President of the organisation, which, from what information remains, appeared little more than a communist front. Soon after its formation the name was changed to the more auspicious sounding International Oriental Seafarers Union, and Saklatvala was ordered by the RILU to use the organisation for party propaganda. Although he did not appear to have any objections to the way the association was established, Saklatvala did not wish it to be too closely identified with the RILU. In the discussions that took place, it was apparent that Saklatvala favoured a much broader approach, and in this he was at variance with the representatives of the CI:

> Ajoy Banerji, Pubin Dinda, and J C Sen, had a discussion with Saklatvala at a meeting held on the 25th Feb., 1923, at which the speakers were George Lansbury and N Watkins of the Red International of Labour Unions. Shortly afterwards a constitution was drawn up with the help of Potter of the RILU for an Indian Seaman's Association. Apparently as a compromise, affiliation to the RILU was not insisted on, but a clause was inserted containing a declaration of identity of principal with the RILU. This nominal moderation is probably due to Saklatvala's influence and he evidently did not wish the association to be entirely dominated by the RILU through which he is working. It did not please Ajoy Banerji, but he accepted a place on the Executive Committee with Saklatvala as President, and two Lascar lodging house keepers as Assistant Secretaries.[22]

Saklatvala was also consulted about Indian trade union matters by those outside the Communist International. His knowledge of Indian labour conditions, and his activity in the Workers' Welfare League of India, earned him respect from a cross-section of Indian labour opinion. He was in fairly close contact with the trade unionists responsible for the establishment of the All India Trade Union Congress, and one of these, B P Wadia, a leader of the Mill Workers Union, visited Britain in 1920.[23] He met Saklatvala and they agreed on a joint campaign. Wadia, on his return to India, would concentrate on improving the trade union organisation there, with a view to forming an Indian TUC. Saklatvala, through the Workers' Welfare League, would mobilise support for the project in Britain. Saklatvala was also in contact with another prominent Indian trade union leader. Charman Lal, who regularly kept him informed on Indian labour matters. It is difficult to assess what part Saklatvala played in the formation of the All India TUC, but he was certainly involved in the discussions that led to the formation of that body.

Saklatvala was also used by the British Party to make contact with Indian nationals who were temporarily resident in Britain. A number of letters make clear that it was Saklatvala who was largely responsible for work amongst Indian students at British Universities. His task was to ascertain their political reliability, and to make contact with them after their return to India. In 1925, Arthur MacManus, in charge of the CPGB's colonial work, sent the following letter to Saklatvala regarding Indian students at Oxford:

With further reference to our letter of a few days ago, concerning Indian students at Oxford and the desirability of your arranging an appointment with certain of these who will be returning to India in the course of a few weeks, we have received a memo dealing with the political composition of the Majlis and we enclose herewith a copy of same for your information and desire to draw your attention particularly to the request on Page 2 of the memo that you should meet a number of these Indians during the course of the next few weeks.[24]

It was evident that the CPGB, although small, was well
organised and thorough about its colonial work. From
other correspondence it is apparent that a list had been
drawn up of Indian students studying at Oxford. Two
non-Indian graduates had drafted a report and sent a
letter to the colonial department outlining their opinions
about the political reliability of each of the Indian
students. The letter also requested that Saklatvala
interview the students before their return to India. As a
result of these interviews, the CPGB, in line with a
Comintern instruction, was able to draw up a list of
representative Indians who could be invited to an Oriental
Congress. Charman Lal, G Goswarmi, and J Joshi, all
prominent figures in the emerging Indian labour
movement, assisted Saklatvala in organising the British
side of the conference. The CPGB, and Saklatvala in
particular, were also asked to organise Indian peasants.
Krestintern, the Comintern's International Peasant Council, sent the following letter to Arthur Macmanus:

> We beg to inform you that in accordance with the decision
> of the Praesidium of Krestintern a special section has been
> formed for the purpose of carrying on work among the
> Hindu Peasants. It is understood, as a matter of course,
> that all this activity among the Hindu Peasants will be
> carried on through you and Comrade Saklatvala. We feel
> confident that we may count on your utmost co-operation
> in advance.[25]

The letter also showed the lack of cadres there were in this
area. Saklatvala had no experience whatsoever of peasant
organisation, and very few contacts in the agrarian
movement.

The disagreements between those concerned with the
colonial work of the Communist International were
highlighted at colonial conference held in Holland in
1925. The report of the conference revealed differing
assessments of who could be relied upon to support the
struggle for colonial freedom. Saklatvala and the British
Party, in line with their broad alliance policy, were
prepared to trust, and involve, non-communist members
of the national liberation movements. But from the

discussions that took place at the conference, it was apparent that Roy and the Communist International would only work with those they considered to be genuine revolutionaries. The conference was a fairly small affair with eight people present. The detailed report illustrates not only the differences between Roy and Saklatvala, but also the fact that Saklatvala, who was absent from the conference, was supported in his stand by representatives of the CPGB. Saklatvala was doubtful about some of Roy's followers, suspecting them of being spies. Evidently Robson, one of the British representatives, believed Saklatvala, and he too aired his doubts about some of Roy's contacts. Roy then attacked Saklatvala's recommendation that Charman Lal, G Goswami, and J Joshi be invited to the forthcoming Oriental Congress, claiming that they were 'untrustworthy' and 'not in contact with the masses'. Speaking on behalf of the Communist International, of which he was a representative at the conference, he stated that the International did not consider it necessary to get in touch with these people, but with 'the real revolutionaries'.[26]

The sharp political differences over colonial strategy between Saklatvala and the CPGB, and Roy and the Communist International, were sufficiently great for Saklatvala and his contacts to be opposed to even working with Roy and his supporters. This was revealed when Roy's wife, Evelyn, had tried to make contact with Charman Lal in Paris:

> Evelyn Roy has stated that she had met Joshi in Paris and informed him that she would like to meet Charman Lal and that Joshi had said that Charman Lal did not wish to meet her, as he was a friend of Saklatvala's, and that Saklatvala and Lal were opposed to her or having anything to do with her.[27]

The India Tour

Probably Saklatvala's greatest achievement in international solidarity was his highly publicised and immensely successful tour of India in 1927, which included a meeting with Gandhi. He arrived in Bombay in January 1927, and his reception in the city was a foretaste of things to come. The *Bombay Chronicle* likened his welcome to that received by Mahatma Gandhi some time earlier:

> Never before had the C J Hall of Bombay presented such an awaited appearance (except at the reception of Mahatma Gandhi) as it did on Saturday evening when Mr Saklatvala captured the imagination of his audience and kept them tense and spellbound for well nigh two hours. Although the meeting was called at 5:30 pm, the auditorium and galleries were packed to the utmost capacity long before 5:00 and the passages and approaches were thronged by crowds of humanity eager to hear the Parsi communist of whom they had heard so much through the press and the platform. When he made his appearance on the stage he was received with tremendous and continued cheers which were prolonged for a couple of minutes.[28]

When he visited Calcutta a while later the enthusiasm of the crowds was undiminished:

> The train arrived at 10:40 Calcutta time but long before his arrival a large number of people consisting of many Congress workers began to assemble on the platform … as soon as Mr Saklatvala got down from the train he was profusely garlanded by the members of several Labour unions.[29]

Many Indian cities agreed to give Saklatvala an official welcome and reception. These included Madras, Surat, and Ahmedabad. The Calcutta Corporation also agreed by 29 votes to 12 to hold a reception at the Town Hall, which went ahead despite a boycott by the European Councillors. In his home town of Navasari he was given the freedom of the city. He addressed meetings there in his native tongue of Gujerati, and he wore Parsi dress.

An indication of the intensity of the tour was given by a report of his programme in Gujerat in the *Bombay Chronicle*:

> Navasari, Wednesday 19th January – Public Procession – Municipal Welcome – Public Meetings.
>
> Surat – Thursday 20th January – Public Reception at 10:30am – Public Meeting in the evening.

Ahmedabad – Friday 21st January – Arrival 6:30am – Reception at Station immediately goes to Mahatma Gandhi's Ashrin.

Visit to Mill Quarters at Noon – Visit to Labour Union Public Meeting in the evening.

Ahmedabad – Saturday 22nd January – Visit to Mill Labourers' houses, hospitals and schools.

Public lecture in the evening.

Ahmedabad – Sunday 23rd January – Labour meeting in the morning.

Noon – talk with Mill Owners.

Evening – Lecture and Tea Party.[30]

The tour lasted for three months, during which time Saklatvala travelled throughout most of India. The open side of his activities was a whole series of public meetings, and his dialogue with Gandhi. However, there were other, more covert reasons for his visit, one of which was to attend the convention of the newly established, and temporarily legal, Communist Party of India. He was also to meet two British Party members, Phil Spratt and George Allison, who had been sent by the CPGB to help organise the Indian labour movement. The source for much of this information is from police files: a report by Jamark Prased Barjerhatta, a leading Indian Communist who had become a police informer, reported that Saklatvala had come to India with a preconceived plan of organising Communist groups in each of the cities that he visited.[31] The report named Allison and Spratt, although Allison was referred to by his code name, Campbell. Allison was in fact deported in 1928.

Two years after the tour ended, Spratt and Bradley, Allison's replacement, and thirty one others active in the Indian trade union movement were arrested. They were tried at Meerut in front of an English civil servant, and, after four years of deliberation, the prisoners received sentences of from three years vigorous imprisonment to transportation for life. The trial and the sentences received wide publicity, and, because of the deep indignation aroused, the sentences were later reduced, and some of the prisoners were released. That the trial was thought necessary at all was in large measure due to the active involvement of Saklatvala in helping to develop the Indian labour movement.

A public dialogue with Gandhi took place during the tour, which raised the role of India's workers and peasants within the nationalist movement. Saklatvala's pronouncements on this subject while on tour were widely reported in the Indian press. He implored Gandhi to recognise the importance of the trade union movement, and to use his influence to help organise the workers and peasants:

> Whilst Indian labour is illiterate, underpaid, underfed, mercilessly exploited and legislatively outplayed, it needs the help and assistance of outside people like yourself and those who are valiantly struggling to build up a Trade Union Congress.[32]

Gandhi offered little comfort to Saklatvala. There was no convincing him that India's way forward lay in a socialist direction. Saklatvala made a final appeal to Gandhi in September 1927, some months after his return, in a letter written from Dublin, where he was helping James Larkin Junior in his election campaign. He urged Gandhi to make a decisive break with imperialism:

> My thoughts again turn to you to lead our country on the right path to break with imperialism for the sake of the prosperity and happiness of millions of British workers, and in the cause of world humanitarianism ... Comrade Gandhi, let me appeal to you to do your duty in a political manner and as quickly as possible before the last lingering vestige of opportunity wafts away.[33]

Gandhi did not respond, and within a matter of months Saklatvala's assessment of him had changed. Like the Comintern, he came to the conclusion that Gandhi and the leadership of the Indian National Congress were accomplices of colonialism.

Saklatvala's change of heart is apparent in the Communist Party pamphlet, *Is India Different?*, published in December 1927. This was a compilation of the correspondence that had taken place between Gandhi and Saklatvala during the latter's visit to India. The CPGB, under Saklatvala's influence, was also moving into a much more uncompromising approach towards Gandhi and the Congress; fast disappearing was the previous CPGB idea of a popular front in India of all those oppressed by colonialism, to be replaced by strong criticism of the leadership of the Indian National Congress. In the foreword to the pamphlet, Clemens Dutt outlined the new thinking:

> In practice Gandhi's teaching has shown itself more and more clearly as socially reactionary and Gandhi himself is soon to be the ally of class exploitation ... Gandhism as a political force has proved itself bankrupt and impotent. As a social philosophy it is opposed to the needs of a growing working class in India, and in proportion as the latter develops in strength and class consciousness it is compelled to come out more and more decisively against it.[34]

Evidence of Saklatvala's own conversion from the idea of a broad colonial alliance can be seen in an article he wrote for *The Communist* in March 1928. He was now no longer convinced of the wisdom of uniting with the colonial bourgeoisie in order to achieve national liberation. In line with the more sectarian views which were influencing the CPGB, he argued that the national leaders in India must either side with the social revolution or become allies of imperialism:

> The Indian leaders, like the German Social Democrats and British Labour leaders, whom they criticise now so freely, must make up their minds on their future course. World events and world politics leave to them also the same choice as the others. They must imperialise themselves and share with their erstwhile opponents what spoils are received from exploiting and governing the masses, or they must Bolshevise themselves and lead the masses to a programme of common ownership and control, and administration of all land, industries and state departments. There is no middle course.[35]

The tour's success was undoubtedly due to the fact that Saklatvala was an MP. He would not have received the support he did, nor would he have been able to speak with the same authority, had he not been a parliamentary representative. During his five years as an MP, the tour of India was undoubtedly one of the CPGB's biggest propaganda successes, and showed the importance of Communist participation in parliament. The Foreign Office also recognised the success of the tour, and on Saklatvala's return took steps to ensure that nothing like it would be repeated, when it withdrew the validity of his passport for India. This ban on his return to India was upheld even during the period of the second labour government from 1929 to 1931.

Three months after his return he visited the Soviet Union as a member of the British Workers' delegation which went to celebrate the tenth anniversary of the Russian revolution. One of his travelling companions was Mary McCarthy, who was a member of a youth delegation. From her account of the voyage, Saklatvala seemed to have thoroughly enjoyed himself:

> On board with us was the Indian Communist Member of Parliament for North Battersea, Shapurji Saklatvala, a kind humorous man, delighted to be among the young revolutionaries. He spent a lot of time with us, and when our vessel was held up in the Kiel Canal he translated little notes containing revolutionary messages into German for me, and together we threw them down to the river workers in the passing boats and barges.[36]

Saklatvala was enthusiastic about the trip. After travelling on the Russian ship 'Soviet', he told *Sunday Worker* readers that, the comradeship and co-operation between crew and passengers was 'delightful'. He had never seen anything like it before.[37]

There was a serious side to the visit: on his arrival in Moscow he addressed an international gathering of supporters of the Russian revolution. He also met Nehru, and had discussions with him about the political situation in India.

After 1928 Saklatvala's international role began to diminish. There were a number of reasons for this. The British Government had banned his return to India and there was therefore no opportunity for a repeat of the

1927 tour. And since the CPI was now firmly established, there was no longer the same urgency that he be kept in close contact with developments in the subcontinent. In addition, in 1929 he lost his parliamentary seat in Battersea, and this deprived him of his opportunities to travel abroad as an MP. However, the most significant factor was undoubtedly Saklatvala's (and the CPGB's) change of colonial strategy. Until 1928 he favoured working with Indian nationalists. But by the beginning of that year, he was moving away from his old broad alliance strategy. And after 1928, the adoption of the Comintern's 'Class Against Class' strategy (see appendix) meant that all non-communist nationalist leaders were viewed with suspicion. Like their Social Democrat equivalents in capitalist countries, they were seen as agents of imperialism. With this perspective Communist contact and involvement with 'non-revolutionary' movements declined, particularly in India. The Communist Party of India, from 1928 to 1935, refused to involve itself in the work of the Congress. This meant that there was no longer the need to maintain such close contact with the Indian nationalist movement.

The labour movement and India

For the first ten years of his political life Saklatvala argued for reforms in India, rather than for revolutionary change. He was always adamant that a free and socialist India was the ultimate objective, but argued that the immediate demand should be for limited reforms, obtainable within the prevailing political and social system. Even after he joined the Communist Party his practical proposals for India were couched in reasonable and non-revolutionary terms. The party advocated the abolition of colonialism, a policy of which Saklatvala wholeheartedly approved, but that did not prevent him from putting forward proposals that were less far-reaching. For example, in his advice on India to Labour MPs and the first Labour government, he made no call for Independence, but instead opted for a policy that would have left largely unaltered India's status as a dependent colony (see pp48-49).

Much of the emphasis of his anti-imperialist work was on drawing the attention of the British labour movement to the injustices of colonial rule. It was with this aim in view that Saklatvala was instrumental in establishing the Workers' Welfare League of India, in 1917. The aim of the League was to interest the British labour movement in Indian conditions of work, and to encourage the growth of trade unionism in the subcontinent. There is some disagreement as to the part that Saklatvala played in the formation of the League. Arthur Field stressed in a letter written twenty years after the event that Saklatvala was not one of the original founders of the League:

> He [Saklatvala] had a strange illusion, repeated several times publicly, that he 'founded' the Workers' Welfare League of India in 1918. He did not found it and it was founded in 1917.[38]

However, there is strong evidence that even if Saklatvala was not in attendance at the inaugural meeting of the League, he had joined within a few months of its formation. When the League declared its aims, which were published in circular later in 1917, Saklatvala was listed as the Secretary of its India Committee. The League's objectives for India were very much in accord with Saklatvala's own thinking; it is not known if the aims were written by him, but they were similar to the kinds of demands he was putting forward at the same time in the ILP.

Apart from concerning itself with workers' conditions in India, the League also wanted to ensure that there was no conflict between industrial development in the subcontinent, and the home country. The League stated in a leaflet that co-operation was necessary in order 'to prevent the industries of India being worked against the industries of this country', Saklatvala's background made him very concerned with this last issue. As an employee of the Tata Company, and one who had been previously involved in the development of India's iron and steel industry, he had first-hand knowledge of the effects of competition between British and Indian industrialists.

The League was organised in two sections, the British

and India Committees. Saklatvala was the secretary of the Indian section, and Arthur Field was the General Secretary. In these early days it was very much a body that concerned itself with gathering information about working conditions in India. It made a special appeal to trade union branches to investigate conditions in India, and to report their findings to the appropriate League Committee. In the long term the League hoped to be able to persuade the British trade union movement to send a commissioner to India, to investigate conditions of work. This did eventually happen, but it was not until November 1927 that the TUC finally sent a delegation.

Within a year of the League's formation, in 1918, the Montford Report was published, an enquiry into the government of India at all levels. The League decided to make direct representations to the various parliamentary committees examining how the report's recommendations could be implemented. Its proposals to the Joint Committee for Indian Reform were submitted by Saklatvala, and supported by Duncan Carmichael. The statement was extremely critical of the report, accusing the writers of omitting any reference to the appalling conditions of labour prevailing in India:

> The British Parliament and British public will certainly not learn from the Report that a totally inadequate rate of pensions, of from twelve to eighteen pence a week, is accorded to the widows of Indian soldiers who sacrificed their lives in France and other parts of the world. Nor will the Report enlighten them on the wages of from sixpence to twelve pence a day in factories, mines and docks, and on merchant vessels; of the long working day of twelve hours; of the absence of insurance and compensation for accidents; of the employment of child labour from the age of ten, and of women's labour, at a still worse pay. One looks in vain for some reference to the wretched conditions of housing for the workers in places unfit for human habitation, inimical to the decencies, and not conducive to the health or comfort of the occupants. Yet these conditions are more general in India than in any other country in the world, and might at least have found a reference in the Report.[39]

The League proposed a number of amendments to the

Government of India Bill; these amendments, submitted by Saklatvala on the League's behalf, showed his moderate approach to colonial matters at this time. His concern was to improve the lot of the Indian labourer within the existing social and imperial structure. The question of social change, or Indian independence, was not raised, either by Saklatvala or the League, in any of their early deliberations or proposals. Instead, they called on parliament to amend the bill so as to give Indian workers certain rights. The most important of these were the right to vote, the right to join a trade union, and an increase in wages for government employees.

Although the League's proposals were not accepted, it was the first time that a labour organisation in Britain had made a direct intervention at parliamentary level to make known its views about Indian working conditions. Much of the credit for this must be given to Saklatvala, who, as the Secretary of the India section of the League, saw the importance of attempting to influence legislation.

Saklatvala also conducted the struggle for reforms in India within the ILP. He made use of the ILP's paper, *Labour Leader*, to popularise his ideas about the need for legislation to help India's workers and peasants, writing a two-part article for the paper entitled 'British Capital and Indian Labour'. In these articles Saklatvala spelled out his ideas not only on the importance of colonialism to the labour movement, but also on the necessity for putting forward a practical programme of reforms. Although he argued the case for socialism, he once again restricted his specific demands to what was obtainable. He did not press for Indian independence, or an Indian Socialist Republic; instead, he sought to influence the readers about the justice of the claims of the Indian workers and peasants, urging support for their right to vote, the abolition of child labour, the right to join a trade union, and a minimum wage. This was almost an exact replica of the proposals that he had put forward to the Montford enquiry. He even tried to win allies amongst British and Indian employers by emphasising the benefits that would come from better treatment of workers:

I would like to point out for the benefit of my readers ...

who do not accept the whole socialist position, that it has
been proved in every part of the world, and in every
industry without exception, that bad wages and long hours
do not pay the capitalist in the long run.

At all three annual conferences of the ILP at which he was
a delegate, Saklatvala spoke on the issue of India. But he
was not only concerned with the subcontinent; he linked
the struggle in India with that of other colonies. At the
1919 annual conference he spoke in support of a
resolution which called for independence for India,
Egypt, and Ireland. In many of his speeches he argued for
both Indian and Irish freedom, seeing the two demands as
inseparable.

Ireland, especially after the signing of the Treaty in
1921, was to be an important issue in Battersea, where
there was an active Irish community. Saklatvala was only
one of two MPs to vote against partition, and he won much
support in the constituency for his consistent stand for a
free and united Ireland. He raised the question a number
of times in the House of Commons and made his position
clear when speaking in a debate on unemployment
insurance in Northern Ireland:

> The one obvious lesson for the workers of Northern
> Ireland is that they should join hands with the workers of
> Southern Ireland and live in a happy state as one whole
> united Ireland.[41]

During the troubles in Ireland after the signing of the
Irish Treaty, a number of Irish men and women living in
England were detained and deported back to Ireland. On
several occasions in Parliament Saklatvala raised the issue
of the deportees. He was applauded for his actions, and
remembered for his persistence, by Irish residents in
Battersea, even after his death. In appreciation, one of
them wrote to Beram Saklatvala, saying that Saklatvala
had taken the first step to offer help to the Irish
deportees.[42]

It was the issue of imperialism which was a major factor
in Saklatvala's break with the ILP in 1921. He had been a
consistent opponent of the war, and, like many in the

party, was outraged by the actions of the Second International in not condemning the war as imperialist and against the interests of the workers. His decision to leave the ILP and join the Communist Party was a product of his lack of faith in the ILP's capacity to fight imperialism.

Saklatvala was also disappointed in the Labour Party's approach to imperialism. On the positive side, although Saklatvala's advice was often not heeded, he did ensure that imperialism was raised as an issue in the Labour Party, both locally and nationally. He was a member of three of the Labour Party's Advisory Committees, including the Advisory Committees on International Questions, to which was submitted *The British Labour Government and India*. He was thus able to issue a number of memorandums which, even if they did not change party policy, at least brought to the attention of Labour MPs many of the problems concerning India. As the spokesperson for the All India TUC, he was able to exert an influence in the trade union movement, which in turn affected the Labour Party. His continued demand for a trade union enquiry into Indian labour conditions finally came to fruition when the TUC delegation visited India in 1927. During the period that Saklatvala was active in the Labour Party, he was one of a very small number of people who were concerned and knowledgeable about colonial affairs. Although often defeated, he made sure that the issues of imperialism, and particularly Indian social conditions, regularly appeared on Labour Party conference agendas. For his persistence he was commended by the Indian Association in Britain, who said of him:

> Saklatala's record of work on behalf of India, beginning as far back as 1912, needs no eulogy. He has done yeoman service in exposing the treacherous character of the India policy of Mr Ramsay McDonald and other Labour politicians and in bringing about the realisation among British workers of the need to be more genuine and thorough-going in their ideas of freedom for India.[43]

Even after he joined the Communist Party, he was still a consistent advocate of winning reforms in India without upsetting its political stability. His long-term objective remained a free and socialist India, but he recognised the need for a practical programme of reform. At the time of the first Labour government, he acknowledged that the government's role in relation to the administration of India would be a difficult one, and he was sympathetic to the problems that it was likely to face:

> It should not be assumed that the present Labour Government basing its moral reputation on socialist principles is not a Labour Government in its unpleasant task as an imperialist administrator.[44]

Even within these constraints, the government could still institute a number of changes. In his advice to the Labour Government embodied in *The British Labour Government and India*, he advocated a number of proposals with a dual purpose: they would help many of the poorest sections in Indian society and at the same time win these groups over to Labour's aims. He wanted to create a mass Labour Party in India, that would take the leadership of the Nationalist Movement:

> The good results of application of Labour principles would be so apparent that they will shortly value and even enhance them. Whether they do, or not, the Labour Government will bring into existence a new mass party and mass psychology in India, which will submerge the present minority expression of confused aristocratic and reactionary thought passing under the name of national rights.[45]

He proposed to the government an eleven point plan, for immediate implementation, a mixture of reform and the extension of democratic rights. The proposals showed Saklatvala's wide knowledge of India, but they also were evidence of his interest in fiscal matters. At the core of his proposed reforms were an extension of the franchise and the eradication of cheap labour, with the government taking the initiative. The government of India, he argued, as employers on a large scale, should introduce a minimum wage. They should also abolish the system of impressed labour. Saklatvala had had first-hand experience of this when prospecting for minerals for the Tata

Company at the turn of the century, and he was adamant that the system should be done away with:

> It is no use quibbling over words. A regular system exists by which Government officials simply seize persons to do work in their camps when they are on tour. The same facilities are granted freely to representatives of large firms, mostly European, to seize labour for work on exploration, prospecting etc. The practice then spreads to regular agents going out on behalf of Companies into remote districts to fetch men for industrial work by doubtful methods. The Labour Government should abolish this custom at its source, namely, the touring Government officials, and facilities of police etc granted to private firms in this respect.[46]

He favoured legislation to protect trade unions, and he wanted the instigation of a National Wages Board composed of representatives of employers and employees.

The most radical of his proposals was the demand for a Commission for Mass Education. Here Saklatvala showed his sympathy for revolutionary Russia. He proposed that a commission be established consisting solely of Indians, but assisted by two or three experienced members of working class organisations in Britain, people who were prominent in research and educational work. This commission, he argued, should travel especially in the agricultural villages of Russia and Siberia to study the method adopted there for quickly spreading mass education.

Saklatvala's proposals on India to the Labour Government were practical and comprehensive. Although not implemented, they probably marked the zenith of his influence over Labour's India Policy. Soon after they were published, in 1924, the Labour Party annual conference voted to expel the Communists, and Saklatvala was no longer considered a Labour Party spokesperson on India. But his suggestions were worth examining, because they reinforce the claim that, in spite of Saklatvala's revolutionary commitment, he was prepared to make a realistic assessment of what was possible under a Labour government. It was a great disappointment to Saklatvala that the first experience of Labour in power achieved so little as far as India was concerned. There were no political reforms, and neither was anything done in the field of labour legislation. The government's failure in this area increased Saklatvala's hostility towards the Labour Party.

At local level too Saklatvala tried to insure that his ideas were implemented, by creating links between Indian and British workers. When he was first adopted as the Labour candidate for Battersea North, in June 1921, one of his first actions as the candidate was to address a meeting at Caxton Hall, Westminster, organised for, and by, Indian residents in Britain. The meeting expressed every confidence in Saklatvala, and asked the Battersea Labour Party to meet a delegation of Indians, so that the issue of India could be raised amongst the Battersea electorate.

During the aftermath of the Bombay Cotton Strike in 1923, Saklatvala took steps to try to ensure that competition between the jute workers of Bombay and their principle British rivals in Dundee should be kept to a minimum. He travelled to Dundee to try to enlist support. He wrote to E D Morel, the Labour MP for Dundee (the same Morel who was responsible for the 'Horror on the Rhine incident'), explaining the problem:

> Once upon a time there was unity of financial and capitalist interest between Calcutta and Dundee when the development in Calcutta was on a very small scale. The Calcutta jute industry is not only growing immensely in magnitude, but is altering from its friendliness to Dundee into one of formidable hostile competition. Both groups would fight each other using their labour as the principal weapon, and as their invariable victims.[46]

Morel was highly dubious of Saklatvala's intentions, and in a letter to the Secretary of the Dundee Labour Party he dismissed his efforts as 'communist propaganda'. Without support from Morel nothing came from Saklatvala's endeavours, but it did show that he was prepared not only to talk about uniting Indian and British workers but also to take practical steps towards achieving this aim.

He took up the same theme a year later when addressing the Scottish Trade Union Congress. The Workers' Welfare League of India had won the right to represent the Indian Trade Union Congress in Britain. As the Secretary of the Indian section of the League, Saklatvala was able to speak on the Indian TUC's behalf at trade union conferences. He made particular reference to the jute industry of Bengal, and how necessary it was for the workers there and those employed in Dundee to make common cause. This was particularly important because of the Bombay Cotton Strike. Saklatvala made an urgent appeal for international solidarity:

> Unless there was a uniform standard of wages in the Jute Industries of Bengal and Dundee, the black worker terrorised in Bengal would deprive the Scottish worker and his children of the necessities of life. The position was that they had to make their Trade Union not only strong, but real. They must be unions of human beings in the trade without geographical barriers. He appealed to them to set aside all their little quibbles and arguments amongst themselves and to understand that International Trade Unionism was not the ultimate development, but the first essential.[47]

This was to be the last Trade Union Congress addressed by Saklatvala. The expulsion of the Communists from the Labour Party meant that he was no longer looked upon as a spokesperson for Indian labour. The Workers' Welfare League, which was heavily influenced by Saklatvala, continued as the Indian TUC's representative in Britain until 1927; but after this the increasing antagonism towards the Communists led to its status being revoked.

It was during his time in the Communist Party that Saklatvala did much of his work in the movement against imperialism. It was the one area too where he made a theoretical contribution and, although he was overshadowed by R Palme Dutt, Saklatvala's ideas did have an important effect on the thinking of the British Party. In the broad anti-colonial movement in which he was involved he acted in a very non-sectarian way. It was only after the Communist movement's change of strategy, in 1928, that he began to pursue the policies of the 'New Line' in the fight against colonialism. In his anti-imperialist work, unlike his approach to the Labour Party, he was not an early proponent of an independent line. He favoured the building of a broad alliance in the colonies, including members of the national bourgeoisie. He also rejected the Communist International's view that India's industrial development was being held back by British imperialism. On both counts his ideas were influential in the British Party which meant that for the first few years of the CPGB's existence its colonial strategy was a variance with that of the Communist International. In an article in *Labour Monthly* written soon after he joined the Communist Party, Saklatvala had taken to task those who viewed India solely as an agricultural backwater:

> There is a vague idea that India is an agricultural country, is industrially dormant, and is only slowly awakening to modern industrialisation. But 15% of the population of 300 millions makes up a number of 45 million people in India living by Industrial and Commercial activity.[48]

In his dialogue with Gandhi six years later, part of Saklatvala's attack concentrated on Gandhi's belief in 'Village India'. He argued that the industrialisation that was taking place was inevitable, and would be a unifying factor in the Sub-Continent:

> No man has succeeded nor shall one succeed in stopping modern industrialisation, and the economic factor is the one common factor that applies to, and that unites, men and women of various social, national, religious and communal textures.[49]

For Saklatvala, India's salvation lay through a rapid industrialisation that would be hastened by a socialist revolution. He had little time for Gandhi's adherence to the Charka (hand spinning) Movement:

> The methods adopted by other countries of organising labour and peasantry and guiding and leading the workers in factories or farms to obtain their rights have produced far more benevolent and efficient results in human life than the two annas a day Charka Movement will ever do. The Government's schemes of drainage, scientific manuring, carrying on agricultural work by machinery will add

ten times more to the economic prosperity of the peasantry
than the Charka.[50]

The CPGB, through the direct experience of leading party
members like Saklatvala, and the more theoretical
contribution of Palme Dutt, had little time for the CI's
view that imperialism held back colonial industrialisation.
When a vote was taken at the 6th Congress of the
Comintern, the British Party was in a very small minority
over this issue, but it was nevertheless prepared to stand
out for its own line against the combined weight of the
world's leading Communists, and its rejection of the CI's
view of colonial industrial development was very much
due to Saklatvala's influence on the party's colonial
strategy. His intimate political knowledge of India,
together with his personal involvement in the country's
industrial development, led him from an early date to
reject the view expounded by the Communist International. This rejection, which was also a rejection of Roy's
early thinking on the subject, came to dominate the CPGB.

During the period of the first Labour government,
Saklatvala played a major role in the campaign for the
release of the Cawnpore Prisoners. These were a group of
Indian trade unionists and communists who had been
arrested in 1924. There was a strong campaign by
Communists and other left-wingers for the release of the
prisoners. When they were brought to trial in 1925, a joint
deputation of prominent Communists and Labour
left-wingers arranged for an interview with the Parliamentary Under-Secretary of State for India. The
deputation consisted of George Lansbury and J Maxton
from the Labour Party, and Saklatvala, Willie Gallacher,
Clemens Dutt and Arthur MacManus from the Communist Party. There was further publicity about the
trial in the Labour and Communist press, with articles
appearing in *Workers Weekly*, the *Daily Herald* and *Labour
Monthly*. Saklatvala, along with Lansbury, MacManus, and
Maxton, sent a cablegram to the Provisional Governor of
India urging that the trial should be delayed until the
accused could be supplied with legal assistance. As a
consequence of the agitation, it was decided to establish a

joint Indian Defence Committee.

The protests were not successful and four of the prisoners were sentenced to four years vigorous imprisonment. M N Roy, one of the accused and India's leading communist, escaped jail because he was out of the country at the time. But although the agitation about the Cawnpore Trial was a failure, the broadly based Labour-Communist India Defence Committee was a forerunner of the much more successful League Against Imperialism, established three years later. Many of those involved in the League, including Saklatvala, Lansbury and Maxton, were also those who had worked together for the release of the Cawnpore detainees.

Throughout the period Saklatvala continued his association with the Workers' Welfare League of India. The League worked closely with the Communist Party and prominence was given to the League's activities in the party press. It was well established in the labour movement, and by 1927 had gained the affiliation of 78 trade union branches. Saklatvala remained the secretary of the League's India section, and the League continued its role of trying to influence the British labour movement about the conditions of India's workers and peasants. Before the Communist Party's change of policy in 1929, the League could draw on considerable support from the trade union movement and, until 1928, Communists and Labour left-wingers worked together in considerable harmony in the League. But because of Saklatvala's influence, and the League's open association with the Communist Party, in that year the All India Trade Union Congress, at the behest of a visiting TUC delegation, decided that the League should no longer be its mouthpiece in Britain. This role was taken over by the British TUC. This severely curtailed Saklatvala's influence amongst the more moderate trade unions; it also served to heighten his antagonism towards the trade union and labour leadership. After his ten years of endeavour in the League to focus British labour's attention on India, he had been given a slap in the face. According to the Comintern, the decision was taken because the General Council of the Trade Unions was the 'agency of imperialism'.[51] Saklatvala

did not as yet totally agree with that position, but he was
rapidly moving in that direction.

The League Against Imperialism

Despite his growing hostility towards the Labour Party
Saklatvala continued with the policy of seeking Labour-
Communist unity on colonial issues. One of his most
important achievements in this sphere came on the eve of
the CPGB's turn toward the 'New Line'. While he was
touring India, the League Against Imperialism was
established in Brussels, in February 1927. It was a
worldwide organisation uniting the national liberation
movements of the colonial and semi-colonial countries
with the progressive forces in the imperialist countries,
and was an extremely representative body.

The British delegation to the founding congress
consisted of a number of Labour left-wingers and
Communists, including George Lansbury, Ellen Wilkin-
son, John Beckett, Fenner Brockway, John Stokes and
Harry Pollitt. Although Saklatvala could not be present,
his reputation meant that he was elected to the League's
International Executive Committee, in December 1927.
From then on he played an active part in the work of the
League, both as a member of the International Executive,
and within the British Section.

The formation of the League's British Section took
place at a meeting in the House of Commons in April
1927. The initiative was largely the work of Communists
and Labour Party members, particularly Labour MPs.
Fenner Brockway was elected Chairman, and Reginald
Bridgeman Provisional Secretary. The motion to establish
the British Section was proposed at the meeting by George
Lansbury, and seconded by Harry Pollitt; the first
provisional committee comprised Communist Party members and Labour Party members in almost equal numbers.

At the British section's first conference, in July 1928,
Saklatvala claimed credit for an earlier attempt to create a
League Against Imperialism; his efforts, had come to
nothing because of the Labour Party's unwillingness to act.
He told the delegates that he had made such an attempt at

the end of 1926:

> Mr Saklatvala said that at the end of 1926 he tried to secure the interest of a small selected group of the Party, Mr Lansbury, Mr Thurtle, and Miss Wilkinson. While they professed agreement with the principles of the league they seemed to suspect that the movement originated from Moscow and was supported by Russian gold. A meeting was arranged and at this meeting Mr Thurtle asked a great number of prepared questions on these points. Inquiries were afterwards made on the Continent and at a later meeting the Labour Party members who attended it 'quarrelled like children and went away'.[52]

The League was again to be accused of being a Communist front, this time by the Socialist International. The provisional committee took the accusations seriously and ordered an enquiry. Fenner Brockway, at a League meeting in the House of Commons, in July 1927, gave a report of their findings:

> Two points have been generally raised in connection with the League which it was best to face at the outset. The first was that the League was Communist inspired and financed. The Provisional Committee have made careful enquiries into this charge and considered that it had been disproved. Of the Executive Committee of the League, only two were members of the Communist Party, and as far as finance was concerned, the Brussels Congress had cost £1,780, sterling, and of that sum to the best of knowledge the only contribution from any organisation with Communist associations was the sum of £30, sterling from the Workers International Relief. The work of the League since the Brussels Congress has been financed from loans and sources unconnected with the Communist Party.[53]

The Secretariat of the Socialist International continued to maintain that the League was Communist inspired, and because of this they were opposed to Brockway's Chairmanship of the provisional committee of the British Section. Brockway argued that even if it were true that the League had been initiated by Communists, its work was so important that it would be foolish for the Labour Party to stand aside because of that. The meeting supported

Brockway and agreed the provisional committee's findings without dissent. There were a fair number of Labour MPs present, and only a few Communists. Saklatvala was not at the meeting; he had just undergone a throat operation, and was busy preparing for the Parsee initiation service for his children, which was to take place the next day. However, by the time the first conference took place, both Lansbury and Brockway had resigned from their positions in the League, because of pressure from the Labour Party and the Socialist International. Maxton resisted these pressures and took over Lansbury's post as International Chairperson in November 1927.

In one of its first attempts to build unity between workers in Britain and the empire, the League organised a series of public meetings in 1928, in protest against the Simon Commission of Enquiry into the Government of India. The enquiry, which included two Labour Members, Attlee and Hartshorn, was condemned by the Indian National Congress, who organised a boycott and a series of demonstrations. The League held a public meeting in Clement Attlee's Limehouse constituency and a resolution was passed calling on Attlee to resign from the Commission. Saklatvala and Maxton spoke at the meeting, and so too did representatives from the Indian National Congress.

International sectarianism

Although by 1928 Saklatvala still supported joint Labour-Communist cooperation in the League, he did not conceal his hostility towards the Labour Party. Although he shared a platform with Maxton, and welcomed his contribution to the League, at the same time he denounced the ILP of which Maxton was a leading member, and made veiled attacks on Maxton's integrity. In an article for the *Anti-Imperialist Review*, which was the journal of the League's International Secretariat, Saklatvala stated:

Shall we forget that both those worthies (Attlee and Hartshorn) are, and are permitted to continue to be, members of the British Independent Labour Party, that

Party that, with characteristic political perfidiousness, desires India to believe it to be an organisation opposed to the Simon Commission and to imperialism.[54]

In an obvious reference to Maxton, he went on:

Several active members of the British Independent Labour Party are assiduous in acting as decoy birds, misleading Indian politicians into the belief that there is still hope in this section of the British Labour Party, and that they respect India's self determination, when one hundred and twelve of their own members are really and truly responsible for the most treacherous anti-Indian decisions of the Labour Party in Parliament.[55]

Even by the beginning of 1929, after the CPGB had adopted its 'New Line' strategy, the League still retained some semblance of Labour-Communist unity. A mixed group of Labour and Communist Party members were chosen to attend a League Conference in Cologne; the group consisted of Saklatvala, Maxton, Reginald Bridgeman, the Labour candidate for Uxbridge, Alex Gossip, the Furniture Workers' leader, and A J Cook, the Miners' leader. They were detained at Ostend, on route to the conference, and it was apparent from newspaper reports that, as far as the authorities were concerned, all involved in the League were viewed with equal suspicion.[56] Saklatvala, Maxton and Bridgeman were apprehended by Belgian officials, allegedly because their papers were not in order. Evidently, the Belgian Minister of Justice thought that Bridgeman and Maxton, as well as Saklatvala were Communist MPs. Cook and Gossip were not detained, but they stayed with their colleagues, protesting against their treatment. They were later released, but there was no apology and no adequate explanation given for their detention.

The British Section of the League became an early victim of the 'New Line'. Maxton, who was one of the League's inspirers, and had done so much on its behalf, was forced out of the position of chairperson in September 1929. Allegedly this was because he had not carried out 'a rigorous enough attack on the ILP's pro-imperialist policy'. At a League Executive Committee meeting in Berlin, in May 1930, the British Party representatives, Saklatvala and Robin Page Arnot, reported on his explusion. They claimed that while Maxton 'had no hesitation in using anti-imperialist language internationally, he was lending support to the imperialist policy of the Labour Party by his policy and tactics in Britain'[57]. This action of the Communists, with Saklatvala very much to the fore, led two other League stalwarts, A J Cook and Mardy Jones MP, to resign in protest.

Although the League's International Executive supported Maxton's expulsion, it sent a letter to the British Section arguing that the League should remain a broad organisation. The letter from the EC, which Saklatvala supported, is an indication of the contradictions that there were in his thinking at this time. Like Communists generally he wanted joint activity around specific issues, but only on his own terms. In his view all broad organisations should accept Communist leadership and Communist policy.

Nowhere was this contradiction more apparent than in the London Branch of the Indian National Congress. Until Saklatvala's rejection of the policy of a broad colonial alliance there had been general agreement on the tactics to be employed. But now that he had rejected such a strategy, and was in outright opposition to Gandhi, increasing tensions developed within the branch. Saklatvala had been active in the London organisation for some years and in 1929 he had been elected as the London Branch's delegate to the Indian National Congress. (He was unable to attend, having been refused a visa by the Labour Government.) But in an article for the *Daily Worker* in 1931, Saklatvala gave vent to the hostility felt by the Communists for their former Congress allies. The branch was organising a conference, and Saklatvala made his feelings clear about the event:

The reactionary Congress leaders and the crowd of London Indian sycophants who were too ready to attend Royal Garden Parties, feasts in honour of State Secretaries, and ex-viceroys, and all imperial functions, have all become united with Gandhi, and are staging a Political Conference in London. We trust the British Workers will not be misled by this pretence.[58]

He attacked all those in the Indian National Congress who were not members of the Communist Party:

> Last year under independent control, the London Political Conference had passed out and out anti-imperialist resolutions. This year it will not only be presided over but influenced and wrangled by Gandhi's right-hand coadjutant, Vithalvahi Patel, the ex-speaker of the Indian Assembly. He will be assisted in all the arts of forcing upon the audience a sham programme by Mr Bhavan Lotwalla, the pseudo socialist of Bombay and Mr Deep Narian Singh of Behar, a rich landlord, who in private conversation pretends to be a Communist and in public remains an ardent supporter of Gandhism. There will also be a display of Left Wing Socialism from some young Indians who profess to love Communism but hate or fear to join the Communist Party. They are like the false prophets of Russia, Ireland and Egypt, who made the people believe that out of the Dumas, Dail Eireanns, Constituent Assemblies and other Parliamentary whatnots, will evolve and emerge a workers and peasants republic, without any proletarian revolution and without any mass action against their own nationalist capitalist bloodsuckers.[59]

Saklatvala informed *Daily Worker* readers of a resolution he intended to move at the conference. This resolution was yet another indication of the extreme sectarianism of the Communist Party during this period. It stated:

> In the opinion of this conference the genuine political, economic and social emancipation for the masses of India, and India's liberation from the British yoke, lies only in the formation of a Soviet system after the Russian fashion and that such a measure can be obtained only through the organisation of the workers and peasants of India along Communist lines and principles.[60]

When the conference met, the Communist supporters were in a minority, Saklatvala's resolution was defeated, and one supporting Gandhi passed by almost two to one. What happened next was described in the *Daily Worker*:

Then followed two resolutions, one demanding the release of the Meerut Prisoners, the Garhwali riflemen, and all political prisoners, and the other demanding withdrawal of Indian Troops from Burma, and cessation of the war in Afridas. It was at this point that uproar took place and Patel tried to close the proceedings. After stormy scenes the reception committee resumed the conference under the chairmanship of Comrade Saklatvala. 23 delegates stayed behind and decided to establish an anti-imperialist organisation embracing Indians in Britain.[61]

The conference was the culmination of the Communists' two year struggle to win control of the branch. It was, however, something of a phyrric victory, for the branch was disaffiliated by the Indian National Congress in August 1931. In response to this, the Communists were involved in the establishment of a short-lived new organisation, the Independence of India League. This new body had similar aims to the Indian National Congress, but once again Saklatvala and the CPGB were keen that it should pursue their New Line strategy. Saklatvala, who had been elected to the provisional committee whose job it was to draw up the constitution was reported as saying that 'He was against any half-way house attitude – Indian Merchants and Stockbrokers would never carry through a revolution against the British in India. Only the toiling masses with the proletariat in the van would make a clean sweep'.[62]

In spite of his move to sectarianism after 1928, Saklatvala made a great contribution to the movement for colonial freedom. Throughout his political life, and in the three political parties to which he at one time belonged, he set himself the aim of bringing to the attention of the British labour movement the plight of India's workers and peasants. For Saklatvala, the interests of British and Indian workers were inextricably linked. He was forever attempting to forge unity between both labour movements. His activities, over almost two decades in the Workers' Welfare League of India, are an excellent example of the attempts to build such a united front. While for Saklatvala the struggle against imperialism was important in its own right, it was always a fight that had to be conducted on two fronts. He was always at pains to explain how the battle against colonialism must be linked to the fight for socialism. He believed that once capitalism was overthrown and socialism established, empires would disappear and India would win its freedom. It was this perspective that guided his contribution to the fight against colonialism, during his years of active political involvement in the British labour movement, and led to both the achievements and problems of his anti-imperialist activity.

Notes

[1] E D Morel, *The Horror on the Rhine*, UDC August 1920.

[2] *Ibid.*

[3] *Labour Leader*, 24 February 1921.

[4] *Ibid.*

[5] *The Communist*, 8 April 1922.

[6] *Ibid.*

[7] *Ibid.*

[8] Report of the 1919 Annual Conference of the ILP, p76.

[9] Report of the Twentieth Annual Conference of the Labour Party, June 1920, p156.

[10] *Daily Telegraph*, 18 October 1924.

[11] *Daily Herald*, 3 December 1923.

[12] *Ibid.*

[13] *South Western Star*, 16 April 1926.

[14] S Saklatvala, *The British Labour Government and India*, TUC and Labour Party Joint International Department, Advisory Committee on International Questions, Paper No 9.

[15] Report of the Seventh National Congress Communist Party of Great Britain, May 1925, CPGB 1925, pp196-197.

[16] Saklatvala's Message to the First Indian Communist Conference, 1925, contained in *Documents of the History of the Communist Party of India*, Vol 2, 1923-25, Communist Party of India, 1974.

[17] *Ibid.*

[18] M N Roy, *Memoirs*, Bombay 1964, p379.

[19] Report of Revolutionary Organisations in the U.K. Report No 268, August 21st, 1924. Contained in Ramsay MacDonald's Private Papers.

[20] National Archives of India F103/IV J&P(s) 7847, 17 May 1923, contained in Sir Cecil Kaye, *Communism in India, op cit,*, pp233-34.

[21] *Ibid*, Deposit 64, p48.

[22] *Ibid*, pp233-234.

[23] *Ibid.*

[24] *Communist Papers: Documents selected from those obtained on the arrest of the Communist leaders on the 14th and 21st October 1925*, HMSO 1925.

[25] Signed letter dated 25 September 1925, from the International Peasant Council (Krestintern) to A MacManus, regarding a section formed in Moscow for work among Hindu Peasants, contained in Communist Papers, *op cit*.

[26] Signed Report by R W Robson on a Colonial Conference held in Amsterdam, July 11th-12th, 1925. Contained in Communist Papers *op cit*.

[27] *Ibid*.

[28] *Bombay Chronicle*, 16 January 1927.

[29] *Amrila Bazar Patrika*, 19 February 1927.

[30] *Bombay Chronicle*, 15 January 1927.

[31] *Documents of the History of the Communist Party of India, Vol 2, op cit.*

[32] *Is India Different? Correspondence on the Indian Labour Movement and Modern Conditions*, S Saklatvala and M K Gandhi, CPGB December 1927.

[33] *Ibid*.

[34] *Ibid*.

[35] *The Communist*, 28 March 1928.

[36] Mary McCarthy, *Generation in Revolt*, Heinemann 1953, p106.

[37] *Sunday Worker*, 6 November 1927.

[38] Letter from Arthur Field to Beram Saklatvala, dated 13 February 1937.

[39] 'The Empire Labour', statement submitted to the Joint Committee on Indian Reforms by the Workers Welfare League of India, 25 January, 1919.

[40] 'For British Trade Unionist and British Indian Labour', *Labour Leader*, 4 July and 9 October 1919. Later reproduced as a pamphlet.

[41] *Hansard*, Vol 192-135, 22 February 1926.

[42] Letter from Delia MacDermott to Beram Saklatvala, 20 February 1937.

[43] *Workers Weekly*, 26 March 1926.

[44] S Saklatvala, *The British Labour Government and India*, TUC and Labour Party Joint International Department, Advisory Committee on International Questions, Paper No 9.

[45] *Ibid*.

[46] Letter from S Saklatvala to E D Morel, 24 January 1923. Contained in Morel's papers at London School of Economics.

[47] *Annual Report of Scottish Trades Union Congress*, April 1924.

[48] *Labour Monthly*, November 1921.

[49] *Is India Different?, op cit.*

[50] *Ibid*.

[51] *Report of the Sixth World Congress of the Communist International*, CPGB 1928, p943.

[52] *South Western Star*, 13 July 1928.

[53] Report of the National Conference of the League Against Imperialism and for National Independence (British Section) held in February 1931.

[54] *Anti-Imperialist Review*, Vol 1 July 1928.

[55] *Ibid*.

[56] *Daily Chronicle*, 16 January 1929.

[57] Report of the National Conference of League Against Imperialism, February 1931.

[58] *Daily Worker*, 26 June 1931.
[59] *Ibid.*
[60] *Ibid.*
[61] *Daily Worker*, 29 June 1931.
[62] *Daily Worker*, 28 January 1932.

Chapter Eight

The New Line Years

During the last six and a half years of Saklatvala's life, from his election defeat in 1929 to his death in January 1936, there was no let up in his political activity. Although he was no longer an MP, and was therefore less in the public eye, his commitment to the cause of socialism was as great as ever. Freed from the responsibilities of parliament and his Battersea constituency, Saklatvala spent his last years campaigning and speaking for the Communist Party throughout the length and breadth of Britain. He was involved in every by-election which the Communist Party contested, and was himself a parliamentary candidate on two occasions. He also challenged unsuccessfully for a seat on the London County Council, and the St Pancras Borough Council. Even after he suffered a heart attack, while visiting the USSR in 1934, he still continued to play a full part in Communist Party activity. He died on 16 January 1936, from a second heart attack, but he was still addressing meetings a fortnight before his death.

This last period of Saklatvala's life is of particular interest from the standpoint of the politics of the Communist Party at this time. 1928 saw the party's total acceptance of the 'New Line' and all that that entailed, but in 1935 this policy was rejected and renewed overtures to the Labour Party were made. Throughout these years Saklatvala was a faithful exponent of the party line. He was a fervent supporter of the 'Class Against Class' strategy, which he expounded with particular vigour during two election campaigns; and he also pursued the new line strategy with enthusiasm in his dealings with nationalist groups abroad. However, when the CPGB, towards the end of Saklatvala's life, revised its strategy and abandoned the 'New Line', he seemed to have accepted the about-turn without reservation. One of his last political acts was during the 1935 general election campaign, when he sent a letter to the *South Western Star* urging his supporters in Battersea to vote Labour, and offering his services to the Labour candidate.

The demise of the 'New Line', was the result both of a series of directives from the Communist International to all its member parties, and of the experiences of British Communists themselves in combatting fascism. After Hitler came to power in Germany in February 1933, the Executive Committee of the Communist International immediately issued instructions to all the Communist Parties of the world to work for an anti-fascist united front with their own Social Democrats. Previously social democrats had been castigated as 'social fascists', and commitment to democracy considered bourgeois. However the experience of fascism convinced the communist movement that democracy was an important issue, and that it was necessary for all democratic forces to work together for the overthrow of fascist regimes. Had this recognition occurred earlier it would have greatly assisted the democratic cause.

In Britain, Oswald Mosley and his British Union of Fascists were mounting a challenge to the organisations of the labour movement. The Communists began to look around for allies, and were prepared to unite with others on the left in the face of this new danger. As well as the problem of Mosley and his blackshirts, after 1932 the National Government became increasingly right-wing. The Communists were pushed into a position where they needed to build alliances. The 'class against class' policy did not change overnight; it was more a gradual process, but from 1933 onwards the signs were there that the strategy would ultimately be abandoned.

After his defeat at the May 1929 general election, Saklatvala was involved in many campaigns. One of these was the campaign to launch the *Daily Worker*. The Communist International had criticised the CPGB for not campaigning enough to establish a Communist daily paper. Internally too, party members were sceptical of the leadership's apparent reluctance to act. Saklatvala was one of those who saw the importance of a communist press. In an article in the CP's weekly paper, *Workers Life*, entitled 'Make Everyone Buy It', he said:

> Where would the Capitalist Movement have been without a Capitalist Press – now come up you lads and lasses, work for your solution. To work for it have first a good fighting press of your own, there is your 'Workers Life'. Buy it and then see that everyone buys it and then ask for a daily copy.[1]

This was almost two years before the *Daily Worker* began publication. He returned to the theme eighteen months later, when speaking at a Minority Movement conference. It is reported that he told the delegates that he had decided to cease buying the *Daily Herald* and would instead buy six copies of *Workers Life* to distribute to sympathisers, and he called upon all the other delegates to do the same.[2]

The *Daily Worker* followed four months later, in January 1930. It was an important part of the 'New Line' strategy: if the Communist Party was to replace the Labour Party as the leadership of the working class, it was imperative that the party have its own daily paper to act as an organiser and disseminate the party line in the day to day struggles of the workers. Most important of all, it would act as a recruiting agent for the party. The steady growth of the Communist Party throughout the 'New Line' period was partly due to the increasing circulation of the *Daily Worker*. If the 'paper' was to survive, the first six months were crucial. Saklatvala, because of his period as an MP, was one of the best known British Communists, and he made a commitment to help in the sales drive. Shortly after the paper started publication it carried a photograph of Saklatvala under the heading 'Book Sak for Campaign'.[3] In the accompanying article he urged support for the paper and offered his services as a speaker in the drive for increased sales, and for the next three months he toured the country on behalf of the Communist Party, in an effort to popularise the new Communist daily.

His workload was remarkable: during late February and early March he spoke at meetings in Coventry, Birmingham, Edinburgh, Fife, and Aberdeen; he then returned to London for two weeks to campaign in his own constituency, before leaving again. During late March, April and May, he spoke at meetings in support of the *Daily Worker* in the following towns and cities; 26 March Wigan, 30 March Derby, 2 April Croydon, 5 April Nottingham, 25-29 April West Wales, 17-21 May Liverpool, 24-25 May Thanet.[4]

The Shettleston By-election

Saklatvala's nationwide tour on behalf of the *Daily Worker* came to an end on 25 May. Two days later the paper announced in its front page editorial that Saklatvala had been chosen to contest the forthcoming Shettleston (Glasgow) by-election. This must have come as something of a shock to Saklatvala's supporters in Battersea. There had been a rumour some time before the 1929 general election that he would give up his old constituency and contest St Pancras instead.[5] To refute these allegations Saklatvala had declared, 'nothing shall entice me away or buy me away from Battersea'.[6] After referring in a disparaging way to Ramsay McDonald's relinquishment of his Aberavon constituency in order to contest Seaham, Saklatvala went on:

> I don't run away from you because of circumstances and conditions through which my chances are getting spoiled. There are constituencies in which I am just as well known as in Battersea. My loyalty is this, whether my position is easy or difficult, here is my place and here I am going to stay.[7]

But by 1930 times had changed – the Communist Party was keen to challenge the Labour Party at every opportunity, and if that meant taking Saklatvala away from Battersea, then it would have to be done.

The decision to fight Shettleston was first mentioned by the *Daily Worker* on 17 May 1930. The sitting MP, John Wheatley, an ILP left-winger, had died, and the paper, in

a typical onslaught on the Labour Party, outlined the
reasons why the by-election should be contested:

> A great strike of wool workers is in full swing against the
> wage cutting and rationalising Labour Government and
> Labour Party in alliance with the employers.
>   The Labour Government is striving to crush the Indian
> revolution by bloody military repression; 31 leaders of the
> workers and peasants of India are still in the dock after 13
> months. The record of the Labour Government stinks in
> the nostrils of every class conscious worker.[8]

The *Daily Worker* also argued that Shettleston should be
considered a priority because it was 'the home of the Lefts
of the Labour Party and the ILP. In no constituency is it
more urgent that a revolutionary fighter be brought
forward to raise the banner of the class war and colonial
independence'.[9] The paper went on. 'Here will be focused
the fight for the release of the Meerut Prisoners, the fight
for working class solidarity with the Indian revolution, for
full support to the woollen strike, for socialism against
capitalism'.[10] From this description of the ideal Communist candidate Saklatvala was an obvious choice; and ten
days later an editorial announced 'Sak for Shettleston',
and he was confirmed as the Communist Party's nominee.

The Shettleston by-election gives a good insight into the
Communist Party's pursuit of the 'New Line' in the
electoral field. As the *Daily Worker* had already made clear,
one of the reasons for fighting the by-election was that
Glasgow was a stronghold of the Labour left. In order to
win the undisputed leadership of the labour movement
the Communist Party had to not only replace the Labour
Party, but also defeat Labour's left wing. The Communists'
attack, in contrast to previous years, was not simply
confined to the Labour Party's right wing; left-wingers too
were criticised. The entire Labour Party was seen as
another capitalist party. In fact they argued that the
Labour lefts were even more dangerous than the right,
because they nurtured illusions in the working class about
the possibility of achieving socialism through the Labour
Party. This approach can be seen in the *Daily Worker* on the

day of Wheatley's death. Under the headline, 'A Sham
Left Dies', the article concluded:

> The passing of Wheatley will not be regretted by the
> revolutionary workers. It serves to remind us of the
> pressing necessity of a relentless struggle against those Left
> leaders who are the most dangerous enemies of the
> working class.[11]

When the announcement of Saklatvala's candidature was
made, an optimistic *Daily Worker* editoral claimed that the
basic issue raised by Saklatvala was the fight for the
overthrown of the Labour government and the advance
towards a revolutionary workers' government.[12] How this
was to be achieved by a party with less than three thousand
members the paper did not say, but this unrealistic
assessment of events epitomised the whole election
campaign. The *Daily Worker* carried stories about
Shettleston on its front page almost every day. In one
edition, just before the election, the paper declared:

> A motley crew is supporting McGovern during the last few
> days, including Cabinet Minister Lansbury, and Under
> Secretary Johnstone, in addition to the Clydeside Gang.
> This is causing many workers to appreciate for the first
> time the treacherous role of the Leftists. The Labour Party,
> which expected a walkover, is now panic-stricken in the
> face of almost certain defeat.[13]

Inside the paper another story about Shettleston stated
emphatically, 'thousands of workers in Shettleston, and
especially the women, will vote for Saklatvala'.[14]

John McGovern, the Labour candidate, was an ILP
left-winger, and as such came in for a number of scathing
attacks by the Communists. He was also denounced as a
'sham left', as well as being 'another capitalist nominee'.
The Labour government was described by Saklatvala on at
least one occasion as fascist: in an appeal to *Daily Worker*
readers in the constituency, he wrote, ...'The fight at
Shettleston is not only a Shettleston fight. It is a workers'
fight for all Britain and for oppressed India against the
fascist Labour Government'.[15] By the time his election

address was issued, three days later, he had toned down his attack. The Labour Government was no longer fascist, but it was still capitalist: his appeal to the electors concluded with the warning that 'any vote now for Labour or so-called "left wingers" is support for the MacDonald/Thomas policy of capitalisation and workers ruin'. His entire election address did not mention one local issue; it was simply a straightforward attack on the Labour Party, urging the electors to follow Communist leadership. It consistently referred to Labour's betrayals, and the need to establish the Communist Party as the party of the working class.

The Communist Party, through the pages of the *Daily Worker*, continued with the assertion of impending triumph right up until election day. The paper claimed that the Communists were winning many recruits during the campaign, and that Shettleston workers were turning towards Saklatvala. It is true that public meetings seem to have been well attended and it was evident that Saklatvala was still a popular orator. Two days before the election the paper reported that a meeting in a school had overflowed into the playground, with an audience of at least 1000 attending the overflow meeting. In addition the paper reported that four other well attended meetings provided 'dress rehearsals for tonight's 20 meetings'.[16] However these meetings did not represent mass support; the result when it came was something of a blow. McGovern had won, although with a greatly reduced majority, and Saklatvala, with less than 1,500 votes was bottom of the poll, behind even the Scottish Nationalist. McGovern received 10,699 votes; Templeton, the Conservative received 10,303; McNicol, for the Scottish National Party, received 2,572; and, bringing up the rear, Saklatvala polled 1,459.

Despite the smallness of their vote, the communists still adhered to the correctness of their new strategy. In their objective of replacing the Labour Party as the workers' choice, they had not been successful, but they were pleased that Labour's vote had declined. The day after the election the *Daily Worker* cheered Labour's narrow majority, claiming that the result showed the growing disillusionment of the workers with the Labour Government. Saklatvala elaborated the party's position in an article assessing the campaign:

> The most significant thing is the drop of nearly 9,000 in
> the Labour vote. Thousands are fed up and disgusted with
> the Labour Government and see through the 'left wing'
> sham. The Labour Government is losing support, yet we
> are not getting these masses behind us in sufficient
> numbers.[17]

Saklatvala called for 'intense activity' by the Communist
Party in those constituencies that were dominated by the
Labour left. Disappointed though he was at the result, it
did not diminish his belief in electoral intervention as an
important part of the Communists' 'New Line' strategy.

The Shettleston by-election also revealed the Communist Party's inconsistency in conducting the electoral fight.
Saklatvala, despite his previous protestations of loyalty to
Battersea, allowed himself to be put forward as a
candidate in a constituency nearly five hundred miles
from where he lived. He had no knowledge of the area,
and was not involved in the local labour movement. This
must have caused some resentment amongst potential
communist voters, that they should be treated as voting
fodder. Neither can it have helped to increase his
following in Battersea.

Back to Battersea

In spite of this cavalier approach to his old constituency,
the area was still considered by the Communist Party to be
a priority. When the elections for the London County
Council took place in March 1931, Saklatvala and Ellen
Usher, a local party member, were selected as the
Communist candidates for the two Battersea North seats.
The selection process for the Communist candidates was
almost an exact replica of the tactics employed at the 1929
election, to try to secure broad support for 'Workers
candidates'. There is no evidence however that in
Battersea this support was anything other than the local
Communist Party branch. The party organised a Workers'
Electoral Conference in the borough, and the delegates
were asked to endorse Saklatvala and Ellen Usher as the

candidates. There were no other nominees, and the
conference was little more than a rubber stamp for the
candidates already selected by the Communist Party.
There was regular canvassing, a number of poster
parades, and an eve of poll rally in the Nine Elms Baths,
but the enthusiasm that marked Saklatvala's earlier
campaigns was lacking. Even the *Daily Worker* had to admit
that on one 'mass canvass' only four comrades turned out.
It is clear, from the daily appeals for support that
appeared in the paper, that Saklatvala's active supporters
in the constituency had declined. In the end the Municipal
Reform candidates won both seats, with the candidates
receiving 4,781, and 4,647 votes respectively. The Labour
candidates were narrowly defeated, receiving 4,107 and
3,969. This was a smaller margin that Saklatvala's own vote
of 728. Mrs Usher received 535 votes.

The Communists were now totally isolated in the local
labour movement. What support they had had amongst
Labour Party members had diminished with the onset of
the 'New Line'. Even so, the following that they could
muster was enough to ensure that Battersea North
returned two Municipal Reformers to the London County
Council. Saklatvala's seven hundred votes effectively
denied to the Labour Party this traditional Labour seat.
The Communists, in splitting the anti-Tory vote, had
certainly not endeared themselves to Labour activists in
Battersea.

Even after this setback the Communist Party still
persisted with the view that Battersea was a winnable seat,
in spite of the fact that the local Communist Party branch
was small, and the factors that had led to Saklatvala
winning the constituency were no longer present. Under
the heading 'Battersea Is Not Pulling Its Weight', the *Daily
Worker* carried the following report:

> Strong criticism can be levelled at the Battersea Local.
> Here, in a constituency where the Communist Candidate
> received the votes of 6,000 workers in the General
> Election, there is obviously no drive for the paper. Poster
> displays are conspicuous by their absence. Only a fraction
> of the quantity we can expect to sell in this district are being
> distributed. Many newsagents confessed amazement at the

passivity of the daily campaign in Battersea. This passivity
is also expressed in the fact that the Battersea Local, which
had developed mass influence among the workers in South
West London, has contributed no more than £7.11s.2d. for
the Daily Fund.[18]

Two days later the Battersea branch replied to the
criticisms:

> We welcome the criticisms of the Battersea Branch in
> Wednesday's issue of the Daily Worker and resolve to
> remedy the situation as far as lies in our power at the
> earliest possible moment. We wish however, to draw your
> attention to the following points; The number of active
> comrades in the Battersea Local does not exceed 9, several
> of whom live in Balham which is a 3d train ride from
> Battersea. ...The myth that Battersea is 'Red Battersea', or
> that 6000 votes for Saklatvala is any criteria by which to
> judge the work of the local, should be ended once and for
> all.[19]

Nevertheless when a general election was announced in
October 1931, Saklatvala was again a candidate for
Battersea North. The election had been precipitated by
the decision of MacDonald and a number of other Labour
leaders to form a National Government. The Communist
Party put forward 26 candidates, and where there was no
communist standing, as at the 1929 general election,
communist supporters were asked to abstain from voting.

Saklatvala's campaign in Battersea, unlike previous
occasions, was a fairly low key affair, with none of the big
meetings and enthusiasm that marked his earlier contests.
By now the disaffiliated Battersea Trades Council and
Labour Party had ceased to exist, and there was no
Battersea Workers' Electoral Committee to help campaign
for Saklatvala's return. There was no pretence that
Saklatvala's candidature was backed by any organisation
other than the Communist Party. There were still a few
Labour councillors who supported him, and one of these,
C Powell, chaired his adopted meeting in the lower town
hall. Powell made it clear that he was there in a personal
capacity, however, and soon after the election he lost his
council seat when he stood as an independent.

The *Daily Worker* reported Saklatvala's adoption meeting, as it did most of the other Communist candidates, as a 'Workers' Conference'. The Communist Party strategy was to try and obtain as much support as possible for revolutionary candidates from amongst the labour movement. This was only possible in two cases, Reginald Bridgeman in Uxbridge, and John Strachey in Aston. In these instances the candidates won support for their nomination from others in the local labour movement, and not just the Communists, neither of them were Communist Party members and they went forward as 'Workers' Candidates'. In every other contest the Communist candidate received very little backing outside the party organisation.

Even before his adoption meeting Saklatvala was gaining publicity for himself by intervening at a Battersea Labour Party event. A report in the *Daily Worker* of what happened showed the animosity that now existed between the Communists and others in the Battersea labour movement:

> When the Labour Party, at its mass meeting in the Battersea Town Hall last night, refused to permit an amendment to be moved to their resolution, the workers refused to permit the meeting to continue. Two MPs, W S Sanders and W Bennett were shouted down, the workers booing and shouting. In preference to permitting the workers to voice their opinion through an amendment the Labour Party closed the meeting and extinguished the lights. But the meeting was carried on in darkness with Saklatvala as speaker.[20]

There was no such unruly behaviour at the Communists' one big election meeting in the Borough; Harry Pollitt spoke at the Town Hall along with Saklatvala, and according to the *Daily Worker* seventeen hundred came to hear the two Communist leaders speak. There seems to have been a shortage of helpers however; almost every day in the *Daily Worker* an advert appeared asking for volunteers to assist with the campaign. The adverts implied that Saklatvala had a good chance of success:

Workers in the daytime are urgently needed. All comrades
in the locality should volunteer, as with a big drive North
Battersea can be won back for communism.[21]

Saklatvala's election address, as usual, did not concern
itself with any local issues. In line with Communist Party
strategy much of it was devoted to an attack on the
Labour Party and the previous Labour government.
There was however one new addition, and that was the
need to establish Workers' and Soldiers' Councils. This
was the first time in any of his election material that such a
demand had been made.

> At this stage we are coming out to you once again as the
> Communist Party to organise our fight on a class basis, with
> a united front to lead the masses to mass action inside and
> outside Parliament. We have no schemes of assisting
> Bankers, helping profiteers, and asking the starving
> families to make sacrifices. Our scheme is to demand that
> the wages of Soldiers, Sailors, Postmen, Policemen,
> Teachers, Clerks, or Industrial Workers shall not be
> decreased by a single penny. ...Workers of Battersea, our
> demands cannot naturally begin and end with the ballot
> box. They must be continued and pushed forward by mass
> demonstrations and mass action, by united Councils of
> Workers, Soldiers and Sailors.

The address, like that of all the other Communist
candidates, was uncompromising in its condemnation of
the Labour Party, and particularly the Labour
government:

> The workers must not forget the rotten policy of the last
> Labour Government for two and a half years. Every
> member of Parliament supports the Government of the
> Capitalists. To vote for the Labour candidates means a vote
> for a vicious capitalist offensive ... The advice given to the
> workers by the leaders of the Labour Party and trade
> unions, not to fight, is actually support of the fight of the
> capitalists against the workers.

For Saklatvala only the Communist Party could resist the
attacks by the employers. He told the electors of North
Battersea:

> All workers who want to fight against the policy of the
> capitalist ... will give their votes to the candidates of the
> Communist Party. Every vote for the candidates of the
> Communist Party is a demonstration of readiness to fight
> against the capitalist offensive – a fight which can be
> carried on uncompromisingly only by the Communist
> Party.

When the results were declared, Saklatvala's vote declined
still further to 9 per cent of the poll and he lost his deposit.
The seat was won by Marsden, the Conservative candidate
with 18,688 votes; Sanders, for Labour, received 11,985,
while Saklatvala received 3,021.

The areas where the Communists did best in this
election were the mining constituencies of Scotland and
Wales. In West Fife, Gallacher received 22 per cent of the
vote, and in Rhondda East, Arthur Horner gained over
ten thousand votes. In future it was in these areas, where
there was a tradition of class struggle, that the
Communists were to pin their electoral hopes. Constituencies like Battersea, products of a bygone era of
Labour-Communist unity, were to be steadily jettisoned.

At this election the National Government was returned
with a massive majority, and the number of Labour MPs
was reduced to 52. In spite of this decisive setback for the
labour movement, the Communists welcomed the result,
interpreting it as yet another blow to the Labour Party.

1931 was the last time that Saklatvala contested
Battersea as a parliamentary candidate. He was to have
stood at the 1935 general election but at the last moment
the Communist Party decided to withdraw most of its
candidates. He was a candidate in Battersea for the
London County Council Elections in 1934, but apart from
that he paid little attention to the area. Instead he
concentrated his efforts on a number of nationwide
speaking tours and propaganda drives. Now that it was
recognised that the factors that had made Battersea a
potential area for party growth were no longer present,
Saklatvala was free to put his oratorical skills to use in
other directions. From November 1931 until his death, he
was involved in every parliamentary by-election where the
Communists had a candidate.

The party propagandist

Immediately after the 1931 election contest in Battersea Saklatvala was off addressing meetings in other parts of the country. At a meeting in Nottingham he spoke to an audience of over 700, and 74 applied to join the Communist Party. A month later he was up in Scotland to speak at a meeting in Alexandria in the Vale of Leven, a Communist stronghold. There were nearly 1,000 present at the meeting and 200 applied to join the Party. During 1932 there was hardly a part of the country that was not visited by Saklatvala speaking on behalf of the Communist Party. His workload was tremendous, and was reminiscent of his campaigning tours on behalf of the Independent Labour Party over a decade before. Now that he was freed from his parliamentary responsibilities and his commitment to the constituency, he reverted to his real love – oratory and public propaganda.

At the beginning of 1932, he left for Lancashire, with another veteran Communist campaigner, Tom Mann. From there he went on to Scotland. A notice in the *Daily Worker* for just one day's itinerary shows his exhaustive workload.

Irvine	– 12:15 P.M.
Kilwinning –	2:00 P.M.
Daruel	– 7:00 P.M.
Kilmarnock –	8:00 P.M.[22]

The Scottish tour was something of a triumph, and the *Daily Worker* reported in a headline on its front page, 'Scotland's 765 New Communists – Saklatvala's Successful Campaign'.[22] The paper went on to record that nine meetings in Scotland addressed by Saklatvala brought in 765 new members, 420 of these being obtained in the City Hall, Glasgow, where 2,600 'workers packed every inch of space'.[24]

From Scotland he went directly to Ireland, where he helped James Larkin Junior in his unsuccessful campaign to win a seat in the Irish Dail. He was only there for a few days before being sent to Sheffield to address a series of meetings on the 'World Crisis', and over the next few

months he made speaking tours, to Cumberland and
Doncaster.

While concentrating his efforts during this period on
recruitment, Saklatvala did not neglect his work in the
anti-imperialist movement. He took part in two well
conducted campaigns, the fight to free the Scottsborough
Boys, and the struggle for the release of the Meerut
Prisoners. Saklatvala was extremely active in the Meerut
campaign, as could be expected; but he also played a major
part in the agitation around the Scottsborough Boys, and
during this campaign it became apparent that he was
regarded by the Communist Party as their public relations
man in developing international solidarity. The Scottsborough Boys were a group of black youths from the
American South, who were accused of raping two white
prostitutes while on a train in Georgia. Mrs Wright, a
mother of one of the boys, at the invitation of
International Labour Defence, an organisation in which
Communists were very active, undertook a speaking tour
of Europe. At first she was denied a visa to visit Britain,
but after pressure it was granted and she addressed a
number of meetings. On her arrival at Waterloo Station
she was met by Saklatvala and Bob Lovell. There were a
large number of supporters present and Saklatvala read
out a resolution welcoming Mrs Wright, and calling for the
immediate release of the boys. She stayed in Britain for
almost two weeks, and at her first meeting, in Holborn,
Saklatvala was one of the main speakers. He was also
present at Liverpool Street Station when she left for
Sweden. There were over a thousand supporters at the
station, and Saklatvala gave the farewell speech. As so
often happened he took the opportunity to emphasise the
unity of the world's workers, when he stated that 'The
British workers have shown by their reception to Mrs
Wright that they have broken down the barriers dividing
them from the Negro races'.[25]

The Meerut prisoners were a group of Indian trade
unionists and Communists, including two British Communist Party members. Saklatvala had been involved in the
campaign for their release since they were first arrested
in 1929. The trial, which had taken nearly two years

to complete, was by the end of 1932 drawing to a close, and British communists were keen to mobilise as much support as possible for the prisoners' release. Saklatvala played a major part in this campaign. The League Against Imperialism organised a big public rally at the Memorial Hall in Farringdon Street, London, at which Saklatvala and Harry Pollitt were the main speakers. Over 500 people attended the meeting. The following month, the Communist party organised a major meeting in Sheffield. Jim Larkin Junior came over from Dublin and spoke about the situation in Ireland, while the other main speaker, Saklatvala, drew attention to the Meerut Prisoners.

When the sentences on the prisoners were announced they drew wide indignation from the labour movement. They ranged from three years vigorous imprisonment to transportation for life. Phil Spratt was to be transported for seven years and Ben Bradley for ten. The *Daily Worker*, which had given much space to the Meerut campaign, carried a major article by Saklatvala. He was scathing of the trial:

> By savage and appalling sentences, after a monstrous trial, the British Raj in India has proclaimed to her 350 million conquered slaves that henceforth the study of the mighty triumph of Communism in the U.S.S.R., which in seven brief years has put to shame the inhuman results produced by one hundred and fifty years of British Rule in India, will be visited upon the heads of Communists in India with a revengeful ruthlessness.[26]

Saklatvala's own union, the National Union of Clerks, protested against the sentences and organised a public protest meeting in Kingsway Hall, London, addressed by Saklatvala and the General Secretary of the Union H M Elvin.

Throughout 1933, British Communists kept up their campaign on behalf of their Indian comrades. Saklatvala addressed meetings in support of the Meerut Prisoners in Glasgow, Stepney Shoreditch and Hammersmith. The worldwide campaign achieved some success when at the end of 1933 some of the prisoners were released and others had their sentences reduced. Ben Bradley was one of those freed, and it was Saklatvala, who, at Victoria Station, welcomed him back home on behalf of the Communist Party.

Saklatvala was still the secretary of the Indian section of the Workers' Welfare League of India, and continued to speak at meetings on the League's behalf. He also remained active in the League Against Imperialism, which continued to function despite some internal dissension after the Communists' change of line. He constantly sought to raise the issue of India and Indian independence in all the campaigns in which he was involved. At the height of the Communist Party's agitation for the release of Ernst Thaelman, the German Communist leader imprisoned after Hitler came to power, Saklatvala urged the party not to forget the plight of Indian prisoners who had been jailed by the British. In a letter to the *Daily Worker* he wrote:

> Are not the British friends who are making such noble efforts for giving publicity to the oppressive and unjust imprisonment of Comrade Thaelman aware that at this moment the British Viceroy of India is holding in prison in Bengal, and other parts of India, nearly 100 persons who have not been tried, and are even not intended to be tried, and held in prison for a few months to a few years?[27]

Thaelman's arrest was part of the development's of fascism in Germany; and this development had signalled the Communists Party's move away from the 'New Line'. An early example of this change of strategy was an incident that occurred in Battersea. Saklatvala, who had previously been very vocal in his condemnation of the local labour movement, now made a complete turnabout. He was incensed when an Anti-Nazi meeting was organised in the borough in July 1933, to which the Communists were not invited. He wrote a strongly worded letter to the organisers of the meeting accusing them of using Hitlerite tactics:

> If some of you in Battersea are ready to condemn part of Hitlerism do you support the remainder of the acts of brutality of the same Hitler against the working class and

the Communists in particular? If not, why is your protest
not broad enough to cover Hitler's inhuman action against
all his victims?

In your organising of the present meeting you further
betray strong partiality for Hitlerism in this later respect.
You have carefully selected men and women of all parties,
MPs and ex-MPs, and yet with all Hitler's characteristics
you too have unjustly excluded Communists who have
similar rights to attend and address meetings such as yours
in Battersea.

Our Jewish comrades, who also form a large section of
the working class, and who have contributed their due
share in the building up of Communism in the world, can
receive very little real help and moral support from half
Hitlerites.

I therefore beg you to announce to your meeting – if
such little acts of justice are possible to be done by your
colleagues – my most emphatic protest against the obvious
exclusion of Communists from this meeting in Battersea.

I trust even an eleventh hour attempt will be made to rid
yourself of the spirit of persecution common to Hitler and
your committee, and you will invite Communist Party
speakers.[28]

Saklatvala's appeal had an effect, and when the meeting
took place he was included amongst the speakers. The
meeting, organised by the newly formed Relief Committee
for the Victims of German Fascism, was one of the first of
many broad-based Anti-Nazi protest meetings. In the new
situation, Communists welcomed such initiatives and
increasingly began to adopt a strategy of uniting with
anyone who was opposed to fascism. Saklatvala was one of
the first to highlight the dangers in Nazi Germany
through the Workers' International Relief Organisation.
He signed an appeal issued by the WIR in March 1933,
just after Hitler came to power. The appeal was headed,
'Help Workers and Jews under Fascist Terror'.

Although the Communists had begun a reappraisal of
their 'Class Against Class' strategy, they did not
immediately drop their hostility towards the Labour Party.
In March 1933 they decided to contest the by-election in
Rhondda East, a Labour stronghold. Saklatvala was sent to
Wales to work in the constituency on virtually a full-time

basis. It was an ideal constituency for the Communist Party
to contest, a mining area incorporating the notoriously
militant pit village of Maerdy. And in Arthur Horner they
had an ideal candidate – he was a long standing party
member with a good record of activity in the South Wales
Miners Federation. The Communist Party held a large
number of meetings in the constituency, and at one of
these, Saklatvala made it clear that the Communists'
attitude toward the Labour Party, and particularly the
Labour government, remained substantially unchanged:

> Saklatvala at Porth held a crowded audience until a late
> hour with an exposure of the Labour Government's record
> of robbery of the workers in order to pay the War Lords
> and Law Lords. Murmurs of indignation arose from the
> audience as Saklatvala piled up the facts regarding the
> Labour Government's colossal expenditure on the
> slaughter of colonial peoples who revolted against
> oppression – it found millions for this and for preparation
> for future war while it was unable to meet the demands of
> the unemployed for decent maintainance.[29]

The result when it was announced was impressive. Horner
received 11,228 votes, while the successful Labour
candidate received 14,127. It was an extremely good result
for the Communist Party and it helped to reinforce the
view that in some areas it was possible for the Communists
to supersede the Labour Party as the party of the working
class.

Six months later the Communists decided to contest
another by-election, this time at Clay Cross in Derbyshire.
Once again Saklatvala was sent to the constituency to help
in the campaign. Clay Cross, like Rhondda, was a strong
Labour area, and in spite of their appeal for unity, the
Communists still hoped to build an independent electoral
base there.

It was ironic that during the campaign the Labour
left-winger who responded to the Communists' call for a
united front was none other than John McGovern, the MP
for Shettleston who had been so roundly condemned by
Saklatvala only two years before. McGovern was a member
of the ILP and his intervention came about as a direct

result of the Communist Party's softening attitude towards the Labour Party and the ILP. The ILP had made the most positive response to the Communists' appeal for unity when they had approached the Labour Party and TUC for joint action against fascism. The approach had been rejected by both those organisations, but had been sympathetically received by the ILP. Negotiations then took place between the two parties about the necessity of organising joint action, with one result being that McGovern made a public declaration of support for Pollitt, the Communist candidate at Clay Cross. The *Daily Worker* gave a good deal of publicity to McGovern's plea to the Clay Cross electors to vote Communist, and McGovern spoke on Pollitt's behalf at a number of meetings, writing a letter to the *Daily Worker* calling on Labour supporters in the constituency to vote for Pollitt rather than Henderson, the Labour candidate.

In his work in the constituency, Saklatvala devoted much of his attention to the anti-imperialist struggle. As usual he was addressing a large number of meetings and at these he constantly referred to the need for solidarity between British and Indian workers. From reports in the *Daily Worker* Saklatvala had lost none of his old magnetism:

> In another village Saklatvala is speaking. How the workers listened to Sak as he so graphically describes the conditions of our comrades in India. His telling exposure of the results of generations of imperialism, his descriptions of the magnificent way the Indian workers fight literally on their stomachs against their exploiters make a tremendous impression, and as he winds up he shows the special tasks we have in Britain to build up the bonds of British and Indian workers solidarity, so that by mutual help and assistance we can defeat our common enemies.[30]

The Communists' more friendly appraisal of left unity did not prevent Saklatvala from informing the electors that only the Communists, and the Communist candidate, had a solution to their problems:

> Only Pollitt fights for the unity of British and colonial workers, both in the daily struggle of today and for the mutual exchange of their common resources after the

workers' revolution, when the period of socialist construction is entered upon.[31]

Clay Cross was not a constituency where the Communists had been involved in campaigning over a period of time, and neither was Pollitt a local labour movement figure. The election result showed that these factors were the important ones for communists when it came to winning votes. Pollitt received 3,404 votes compared with Henderson's 21,931. This result was disappointing, comparing very unfavourably with Rhondda.

Although Communist policy was beginning to change, it still continued with its attacks on the Labour Party, and persevered in its efforts to build an electoral base at Labour's expense. In January 1934 in the London County Council elections, Communist candidates contested in eight Boroughs. One of these was Battersea North, where Saklatvala was the candidate, along with William Johnson, the organiser of the Battersea Trades and Labour Council's Unemployed Association. Even, after an absence from the borough of over two years, Saklatvala could still attract a large crowd. At a public rally in the town hall, the *Daily Worker* claimed that over 1,200 people came to hear Saklatvala speak. The paper also reported an organised attempt by local fascists to disrupt the rally.

Saklatvala and Johnson paid particular attention to housing in the borough and the Communist Party in other parts of London also made housing an important issue. Previously Communist election material, particularly during the height of the Class Against Class period, had confined itself to making general statements about the need for the revolutionary overthrow of capitalism; now there was a much more realistic approach, calling for reduction in council rents, slum clearance, and a programme of building houses, schools and hospitals. Another positive aspect of the campaign in Battersea was that the Communists attacked the Municipal Reformers for their decision to reduce the rates. This was a new development: since the start of the 'New Line' the Communists had spent most of their time denouncing the Labour Party, rather than the Tories.

The result was disappointing. Saklatvala obtained 577 votes, and his election partner Bill Johnson 526. The Labour candidates each received more than 8,000 votes, while the Municipal Reformers polled around 4,500. Although Saklatvala could get large attendances at meetings, and had represented the constituency in parliament for a number of years, he now fared no better than Communist candidates in other constituencies. Because of this poor result, the Communist Party began to reassess its endeavours in the borough. After the LCC election, Battersea was no longer considered a prime election target. At the borough council elections seven months later, in November 1934, the Communist Party did not stand any candidates in Battersea. Instead, Saklatvala contested a seat for the St Pancras borough council. He was not elected. The most significant feature of the elections however was that the Communist Party, for the first time in five years, pledged grudging support to the Labour Party. The Communists were contesting 60 seats in London, but agreement had been reached with the ILP to support each other's candidates. Where there was no Communist or ILP candidate standing the voters were told to vote for Labour candidates who pledged themselves to build up the united front of struggle. The New Line had been effectively broken. Although the Communists were not yet prepared to give unequivocal support to Labour candidates, their recognition of differences within the Labour Party was itself a turn away from the old strategy.

In the 1935 general election, *Daily Worker* readers were informed that Saklatvala was not to contest Battersea; a report appeared in the paper, that in both North and South Battersea the Communist Party's offer of individual help had been cordially accepted.[31] This was in line with the party's policy for a united front against the Tories. Some of Saklatvala's old supporters, unaware of the Communist Party's change of line, were confused about why Saklatvala was no longer a candidate. In order to explain the position he wrote a letter to the *South Western Star*. Like the Communist Party, he now accepted the need for a rapprochement with Labour, and for the return of a

Labour Government. He told the electors of his old constituency:

> I have been honoured or doubted by some of my friends in
> North Battersea with enquiries as to why I have not
> appeared on the scene in my former constituency in this
> General Election ... I entirely agree with the policy of my
> Communist Party that the gravity and the peculiarity of the
> situation makes it clear that during this election I can
> render that service essentially by standing off and,
> paradoxical as it may appear, I am as much in the service of
> working class Battersea by not asking from the electors for
> a quota of Labour votes. It is no fear of defeat or loss of
> prestige that keeps me back. If the local Labour Party
> arrangements make it possible, I would readily give my
> active participation in the election in the Borough by
> speaking and working for the Labour Candidates.[32]

At this election, apart from the contests in Rhondda East
and West Fife, the Communists called on their supporters
to unreservedly vote Labour. The conditions that gave rise
to the 'New Line' had, in the opinion of the CPGB,
unquestionably altered. Because of the continuous
provocation from the British Union of Fascists, and their
view that the National Government might resort to
Fascism, British Communists, learning from the experiences of Germany, sought unity at any price.

During 1934 Saklatvala made an extensive tour of the
USSR, as part of a workers' delegation which left Britain in
April 1934 and returned in August. He did not spend a
great deal of time with his fellow tourists; instead, he went
off to visit the Soviet Far Eastern Republics, to see how
they compared with India. He sent a report to the *Daily
Worker* on his way home:

> I have finished a long and most interesting tour on the
> spot. I have learned things of which I could never have got
> a real grasp by 'collecting' information at home. New
> Russia is a wonderful place, but new Soviet Asia even more
> so. One can never fully realise the tremendous extent of
> human development made possible by the revolution ...
> No worker who sees for himself can leave anything but a
> friend of the Soviet Union, and one who is anxious to
> spread the truth among his mates.[33]

Confirmation of this admiration for the USSR was given by P Chaterjee of the Indian National Congress. On Saklatvala's death, Chaterjee wrote an obituary for the *Daily Worker*, reporting a letter written to him by Saklatvala: 'I have visited all the middle regions of the USSR and it is here among the Asian races that one discovers the mighty efforts of Communism for human liberation'.[34]

During the trip to the Soviet Union Saklatvala suffered a heart attack. However, on his return he continued to speak at a large number of meetings. The Communist Party organised a series of public events that were devoted to the achievements of the Soviet Far East. Saklatvala spoke on such topics as 'The Achievements of Jews in the USSR', 'Democracy in Asia', and 'Minorities in the USSR'. His list of speaking engagements was as great as ever, in spite of his heart attack. On his return, according to one of his children, he had aged considerably. However, he could still find the energy to address a mass meeting in Manchester Free Trade Hall, at which four thousand people turned up to hear him, together with Pollitt and Maxton – it was a joint ILP/CP event, and was the biggest public meeting in the city for ten years.

The last years

Throughout the last years of his life Saklatvala's commitment to the Communist Party was as great as ever. Despite the obvious debilitating effect of a heart attack, he continued to address meetings on every conceivable subject. Just taking those events that were advertised in the *Daily Worker*, during 1935, he spoke at 19 public rallies and meetings; he also made a speaking tour of West Fife, and engaged in substantial work on behalf of Gallacher and Pollitt at the general election. After the election he spoke at the victory rally at Shoreditch Town Hall, which celebrated Pollitt's 13,655 votes at Rhondda East, and Gallacher's election in West Fife. This was just two months before his death. His last recorded meeting was at Ashton-Under-Lyme, on 5 January 1936. He suffered a second heart attack, and died at home on 16 January 1936.

I emphasise this record of activity during his last few years because it has been suggested that towards the end of his life Saklatvala had differences with the Communist Party, and may even have renounced his membership. Rumours of Saklatvala's differences with the Communist Party were referred to by Fenner Brockway in *Inside the Left*.[35] Malcom Muggeridge also mentions them in *Chronicles of a Wasted Time*; and Saklatvala's late son Beram maintained that during the last years there were differences, and that Saklatvala came back from the USSR with a number of reservations. These claims cannot be substantiated by an examination of Saklatvala's work record. His commitment to the Communist Party, if meetings and public statements are anything to go by, remained as great as ever. It is possible that the alleged differences had their origin in a short article in the *Empire News* in April 1931, which claimed that Saklatvala was disillusioned with the CPGB. An article in the *Daily Worker* reported Saklatvala's response:

> A fortnight ago a Sunday newspaper called the 'Empire News' published a paragraph in which Comrade Saklatvala was represented as having told a 'friend' (who needless to say remained anonymous) that 'the Communists of Great Britain as a whole had too little vigour and energy to arrive anywhere'.
>
> Comrade Saklatvala sent a letter to the 'Empire News' in which he said, 'I wish to state emphatically that I have made no such remark openly or in confidence to any person, for the simple reason that my conviction is exactly opposite of your statement. I am myself an active member of the CPGB, not for any personal gain, but for the opportunities it affords for working for the emancipation of the working class, and while I appreciate the very difficult task that lies before the British Party, I am also aware with what unceasing vigour, energy, perseverance and industry my comrades, the British Communists, have been carrying on their task for the last ten years.
>
> During the last three or four months I have heard such comments made to me by critics of the Party or of the Communist Movement in general, and I have explained to more than half a dozen friends, even recently, how they

fail to appreciate the true worth and the arduous work of the CPGB.'

Comrade Saklatvala asked that this letter should be published, but he has so far received only the information that it is 'receiving attention'.[36]

If there were disagreements they certainly didn't show themselves on the event of Saklatvala's death. Two days after he died the *Daily Worker* carried a full page of tribute by Harry Pollitt, an article entitled, 'He Will Live Again in the Work to Come'. There were also two columns headed 'British Labour Mourns Saklatvala', which were devoted to tributes from all sections of the labour movement. It is unlikely that the Communist Party would have given such publicity to Saklatvala's achievements if there had been a serious rupture between him and the party.

The funeral ceremony, which took place at Golders Green Crematorium, brought together representatives of the many strands of Saklatvala's extraordinary career. Harry Pollitt, the General Secretary of the Communist Party in a moving portrayal of his life said of him:

> Sak was a comrade who could have chosen the easy path to great riches, to a political career and to a high place in society, but who consciously chose the path of anti-imperialist struggle and revolutionary Communism.[37]

Condolences were received from Ben Tillett, George Lansbury, and Clement Attlee, all leading figures in the Labour Party. George Elvin, the General Secretary of the National Union of Clerks, Saklatvala's old union, paid tribute to his work. Both Georgi Dimintrov, on behalf of the Communist International, and Ivan Maisky, the Soviet Ambassador in Britain, sent their regards. Pundit Nehru, of the Indian National Congress, who Saklatvala had denounced during the early part of the 1930s, also mourned his passing. Messages of sympathy were received from all those sections of the labour and anti-imperialist movement with which he had been involved.[38]

The other side to Saklatvala was also revealed at his death. After the highly political funeral march and the speeches at the Crematorium had died away, his ashes

were taken to Brockwood in Surrey, where they were
interred, according to Parsee rites, at the Parsee burial
ground within Brockwood Cemetery, where other
members of the Saklatvala family were buried as well as
the Tatas, who were close relations. At this strictly Parsee
ceremony, something of Saklatvala's socialist conviction
managed to break through in the simplicity of the event:

> The coffin, covered with a purple pall on which lay the red
> flag, was placed on a metal platform in front of which
> stood two Parsee ministers, M H Vjifdar and M J Dastoor,
> wearing white suits of homespun cloth with round white
> caps on their heads.
>   Close to the edge of the platform was a large silver cup in
> which a fire of sandalwood chips burned and was fed by
> the ministers. Incense and spices were added from time to
> time. The service, in the sacred language of the Parsee's,
> was intoned by the ministers.[39]

For twenty years Saklatvala had been virtually a full time
revolutionary. From 1916 until his death, he had given his
every waking moment to the cause of socialism and
national liberation. His life had split neatly into two, half
spent in India, and half in Britain. Yet there was a direct
relationship between these experiences. He had been able
to bring to the British labour movement an understanding
of developments taking place in India; and the cause of
India's national liberation was enhanced by Saklatvala's
efforts in Britain. His dual commitment to socialism and
colonial freedom was the product of a life lived on two
continents; it was also the result of a conviction that these
two objectives were inseparable. Saklatvala's endorsement
and support at three general elections by the labour
movement in Battersea was precisely because he combined
these twin strands of revolutionary socialism and
anti-imperialism. He had achieved notoriety as an MP,
partly because he was an Indian, but partly because he was
the Communist Party's first long serving representative in
the House of Commons. However, his years in Parliament
were only part of his overall political contribution. His
activity spanned an important period of labour movement

history, and his political legacy should now finally receive the recognition it deserves.

Notes

1 *Workers Life*, 9 March 1928.
2 *Workers Life*, 30 August 1929.
3 *Daily Worker*, 18 Feb 1930.
4 See *Daily Worker*, March-May 1930.
5 *South Western Star*, 14 Dec 1928.
6 *South Western Star*, 16 Nov 1928.
7 *Ibid*.
8 *Daily Worker*, 17 May 1930.
9 *Ibid*.
10 *Ibid*.
11 *Daily Worker*, 14 May 1930.
12 *Daily Worker*, 27 May 1930.
13 *Daily Worker*, 25 June 1930.
14 *Ibid*.
15 *Daily Worker*, 20 June 1930.
16 *Daily Worker*, 26 June 1930.
17 *Daily Worker*, 1 July 1930.
18 *Daily Worker*, 22 January 1930.
19 *Daily Worker*, 24 January 1930.
20 *Daily Worker*, 6 October 1931.
21 *Daily Worker*, 19 October 1931.
22 *Daily Worker*, 30 January 1932.
23 *Daily Worker*, 4 February 1932.
24 *Ibid*.
25 *Daily Worker*, 9 July 1932.
26 *Daily Worker*, 18 January 1933.
27 *Daily Worker*, 27 August 1935.
28 *Daily Worker*, 7 June 1933.
29 *Daily Worker*, 28 March 1933.
30 *Daily Worker*, 14 August 1933.
31 *Daily Worker*, 21 October 1935.
32 *South Western Star*, 1 November 1935.
33 *Daily Worker*, 20 July 1934.
34 *Daily Worker*, 22 January 1936.
35 Fenner Brockway, *Inside the Left*, Allen and Unwin 1942, p139.
36 *Daily Worker*, 9 May 1931.
37 *Daily Worker*, 22 January 1936.
38 *Ibid*.
39 *South Western Star*, 24 January 1936.

Appendix

The New Line and CPGB Policy

Saklatvala's active political life spanned the years from 1917-1936. This was an eventful period in socialist history beginning with the Russian revolution and the formation of the Communist International. The Communist Party of Great Britain was formed in 1920 and Saklatvala joined the new party a year later. His political involvement therefore coincided with the formative years of British Communism. During this time, the British Party underwent two major policy revisions. From its formation until 1928, it advocated affiliation to the Labour Party, and a united front between Communists and Labour Party members. After 1928 began the 'Class Against Class' or 'New Line' period, of hostility to social democracy and all members of the non-communist left. This period came to an end in 1935, less than a year before Saklatvala's death.

Saklatvala's contribution and involvement in these policy reviews enables a number of lessons to be learned. It casts doubt upon the conventional myth of the period by communist and non-communist historians alike, that the strategy of the CPGB was determined almost solely by the whims of the Communist International. The British Party was an independent body, and developed its strategy according to its own situation rather than to any external directives. In its differences with the comintern on the strategy for fighting against imperialism, it remained defiant of the Communist International until its overwhelming defeat at the hands of the Sixth Congress in 1928.

Saklatvala's activities during the latter part of the period also bring into question the popular view of this period. This time is generally regarded as a particularly barren one for British Communists, with a loss of membership and a tailing off of militancy. If Saklatvala's activities are anything to go by, and there is no reason to believe that he was unusual as a Communist militant, the 'New Line' period, was, in fact, a fruitful one for British Communists. It was a time of increased membership, and lively CPGB initiated campaigns. Saklatvala's activities reflected the party's new sense of purpose at this time, with its aim to establish itself, against all others, as the independent leadership of the working class.

The 'New Line' policy, of which Saklatvala was an early advocate, has received a good deal of attention from marxist and non-marxist historians. The general consensus has been that the strategy was imposed on a reluctant British Party by the Communist International. Walter Kendall, in *The Revolutionary Movement in Britain*, has argued that the party's very formation would not have been possible unless it had been nurtured and financed by the Communist International. He claims:

> If the Communist International had not been backed by all the resources of a great national state, if there had been no couriers, no instructors, no false time-scale for the fusion, no travel to Congresses in Moscow and above all no subsidies on a large scale, it is impossible to believe that a Communist Party of any importance could have been created. The CPGB thus became a stranger in its own country, an artificial creation which owed its existence, its form and its character, to the CI which had given it birth and had provided the sustenance which alone made its continued existence possible.[1]

That the British Party was dominated by the Communist International, has also been the line of approach by Communist historian Noreen Branson. Referring to the New Line period, Branson claims that the new approach 'did not emanate from within the British party but from the Communist International'.[2] Other writers have argued that the CPGB was not simply subservient to the

Communist International, but, through that organisation to Moscow as well. Brian Pearce, in his *Early History of the Communist Party of Great Britian*, claims:

> It is plain that the Soviet Bureaucracy contrived to secure the connivance of the CPGB officials in transforming what in 1922-1924 had been a party full of promise of becoming the Marxist Leadership of the British Workers into a servile instrument of their will that they were henceforth able to use as they fancied, ruining it in the process as a Communist Party in the true original sense.[3]

A similar argument is pursued by Henry Pelling: 'With the British party reduced to an almost slavish submission to Moscow, the control of the Comintern over its policies could assume a quasi-military character.'[4] Macfarlane, in his comprehensive study of the period, *The British Communist Party*, states that the main thrust for the change in CPGB policy came not from within the party itself but from the Communist International. Referring to the discussion around the 'New Line' he writes: 'How did it come about that the critics triumphed over the party leadership in 1929? Clearly the main reason was the introduction of the Comintern's 'New Line' policy'.[5]

The theme running throughout the work of all the writers of the period is that the strategy of the CPGB was determined more by external factors than by internal ones. Saklatvala's party involvement indicates that the CPGB, although a disciplined section of the Communist International, changed its policy not simply because of directives from that body, but because of changes that were taking place within the British labour movement. There were two factors involved in the CPGB's changing assessment of the situation between 1920 and 1935. One was undoubtedly the worldwide strategy of the Communist International, but the other, equally important, was the party's own appraisal of the objective situation in Britain. Saklatvala's activities help illustrate the importance of this second factor.

That this was the determining factor was alluded to at the time by the British Party itself, who went to some lengths to refute those who alleged that the 'New Line' was imposed on British Communists, in contradiction to the internal political situation. The preface to *Communist Policy in Britain* (1928), which was a party statement on the 'New Line' stated:

> This report explodes all the fairy tales and the mischievous assertions of the enemies of the working class that the British Resolution of the Comintern Plenum, as well as all the resolutions of the staff of the World Revolution are 'Orders from Moscow', forced on the sections of the Comintern in the various countries. This report shows clearly in what manner and by what means the Plenum came to the conclusion that it was necessary to change the tactics of the British Communist Party in conformity with the changes that were taking place in the correlation of class forces in Great Britain, as well as in the relations with the British Working Class. This report will show to all unprejudiced readers that, in fulfillment of its function of general staff of the forces of world revolution, the Plenum of the Comintern discussed very carefully not only the general lines of the development of class forces, but also all concrete problems brought to the fore by the interest of the British proletariat at the given stage in the development of its struggle.[6]

The statement showed quite clearly that even after the Communist International's intervention, it was Britain's changing situation that was responsible for the change of line.

The 'New Line' strategy was to replace the Labour Party as the party of the working class. In the communists' view, the Labour Party had become another capitalist party, and because of its working class support, was even more dangerous than the Tories. Labour left-wingers, because they harboured illusions amongst the working class of pushing the Labour Party in a left direction, were the worst offenders of all. In a situation of capitalist crisis the ruling class relied on the Labour Party to offset revolution and keep the working class in its place – hence the Communists' 'New Line' slogan 'Social Democrat equals Social Fascist'.

This policy was first adopted at the party's Tenth Congress in January, 1929. But for almost a year before this decision discussion about a change of strategy had been taking place with the Executive Committee of the

Communist International. All historians who have studied the CPGB during this period agree that there was no interference by the CI until after the party's ninth congress, which took place in October 1927. It was only after that congress took place, they argue, that outside intervention forced the party to change its line. Noreen Branson writes:

> The first intimation that the Executive Committee of the Communist International wanted a different political line was contained in a telegram to the British Party which was sent off before the party's 9th congress but did not arrive until it was over ... the congress was no sooner over than the telegram arrived followed by a letter from Bukharin, President of the Comintern, which made clear that the attitude of the parties to their respective social democratic parties was to be reconsidered.[7]

Saklatvala's political development shows that there was already, before 1927 discontent within the British Party over its attitude towards the Labour Party. Saklatvala, a Communist activist, an MP, and a member of the Party's Executive Committee, was not unusual in his resentment of a too soft approach towards the Labour Party. By the time of the ninth congress many of the 'New Line' ideas put forward by Saklatvala in his letter to the EC of 1925 had been incorporated into party strategy. The ninth congress accepted the view that, for the first time since 1922, the Communist Party should stand candidates against Labour. It was a view with which Saklatvala was in total accord. At the first EC meeting of 1928, Saklatvala urged the standing of fifty party candidates at the next general election. He also argued that the CP should contest a large number of municipal seats at borough council elections. None of these actions would help the CPGB in its fight for affiliation. Some time before the Communist International's intervention Saklatvala had expressed the idea that the Labour Party was no longer a workers' party. In 1925 he had claimed:

> We should adopt the attitude that the Labour Party has now deserted its original function and turned itself into a Liberal Reformist Group like the Irish Nationalist Party,

and that the real political crusade for Socialism has been abandoned by the Labour Party. Therefore the Communist Party must now set itself up as the only avowed anti-Capitalist party.[8]

By 1927 the CPGB had adopted the same approach, and the party's ninth congress resolution proclaimed:

> The growing middle class and bureaucratic control of the Labour Party which is directed towards making the Labour Movement safe for capitalism must be energetically combatted. This corruption of the Labour Movement has been especially evident in the Parliamentary Labour Party and in its support given to the Baldwin Government in all its anti-working class activities.[9]

Saklatvala's close connection with the first Labour Government had only served to strengthen his anti-Labour views. The Communist Party also, by 1926, had grave doubts about the possibilities presented by Labour in power. After the general strike it dropped its pre-strike demand for the return of a Labour government. At the ninth congress the party no longer gave blanket support for a Labour election victory. Instead, it claimed a Labour government could only have any chance of success after there had been a change in the Labour Party leadership:

> A strong and powerful Labour Government can only be realised when the Labour Party and the T.U.C. fight in a united manner for the immediate demands and necessities of the working class. This involves a complete change in the present leadership and the replacement of these liberal leaders by honest working class fighters prepared to utilise the whole resources of the movement to defend the workers from the attacks of the capitalists. Only in this way can the spirit and energy by developed that will ensure the return of a Labour Government basing its whole strength upon the organised power of the working class.[10]

The most significant feature of the ninth congress was the recognition that the Communists' expulsion from the Labour Party was likely to be a feature of political life, at least for the foreseeable future. Up till 1927 the

Communists had confidently expected that their read-
mission to the Labour Party was just a matter of time.
They did not believe that the resolution to expel them,
passed at the 1924 and 1925 Labour conferences, would
ever be properly implemented. *Workers Weekly* in 1925 had
confidently proclaimed that 'the Conference decision is
not being carried out because it can't be carried out. That's
the plain truth of the matter'.[11] Johnny Campbell, one of
the party's leaders, told the party's seventh congress in
June 1925:

> This latter resolution has in very few cases been put into
> operation. The Labour Party Executive were justified in
> believing when this resolution was passed that it was quite a
> simple matter to expel the communists. They soon
> discovered however, that it was not merely a matter of
> turning out the communists, but also of dealing with
> hundreds of left wing workers in the localities. As a
> consequence of the fact that the workers in their localities
> work with the communists and appreciate our will to fight
> capitalism, the resolution is never likely to be put into
> operation.[12]

By 1927 the communists' appraisal of the situation had
changed. The Left Wing Movement, initiated by
Communists and Labour left wingers to fight against the
expulsions, had been unsuccessful. After 1926, the whole
issue of Communists in the Labour Party was no longer
even included on the agenda at Labour Party conferences.
It was not until 1936 that Communist Party affiliation was
again discussed at a Labour Party conference. The
Communists, at their ninth congress, recognised that their
exclusion from the Labour Party was now nearing
inevitability. They admitted for the first time that the
threat of disaffiliation was forcing many Labour Parties to
operate the ban on Communists. The delegates were told:

> Generally speaking local Labour Parties have applied the
> Liverpool decision, 24 Labour Parties and Labour Party
> sections have been disaffiliated for refusing to do so, or on
> other pretexts, although a few relatively important Labour
> Parties have not yet applied the decision and have so far
> managed to avoid disaffiliation.[13]

This recognition that, for the time being anyway, they could no longer operate within the Labour Party, led the Communists to fundamentally revise their strategy.

There was discontent with the old line of tailing along behind the Labour Party, and by 1927 many Communists wanted a more independent role for their own party. The strategy first advocated by Saklatvala in 1925 was now much more acceptable. During the intervening two years the Communists had suffered a whole string of defeats in their overtures towards the Labour Party. Saklatvala had been particularly affected by the turn of events. The Battersea Labour Party and Trades Council had been disaffiliated. An official Labour candidate had been selected to stand against him in the constituency at the next election. His views on India had been rejected by the Labour leadership. His application to be considered as a part of the Labour Parliamentary Group had been turned down. From prison he had witnessed the betrayal of the general strike by the leadership of the labour movement. These negative experiences of Labour, and Labour in power, were to a lesser extent shared by many other Communists. It is worth remembering that as late as 1927, two years after they had been officially expelled, almost one in five of Communist Party members were still active Labour Party members. It was estimated that of the party's 7,377 members at the time of the ninth congress (October 1927) no fewer than 1,455 were active in their local Labour Parties, and 252 were delegates to local Labour Parties and Trades Councils.[14] Like Saklatvala, over the past two years they had seen their endeavours come to nothing, as the effects of disaffiliation and expulsion began to take effect.

Saklatvala realised after the 1925 Labour Party conference that a change of policy towards the Labour Party was necessary. He was now convinced that the Communists' claim for recognition by the larger organisation had suffered a major reversal. Without any prodding from the Communist International, the ideas he expressed, both as a grass roots activist and as an EC member, began to gain ground. By 1927 it was recognised by the party generally that a change had taken place in the

Labour Party. In a letter to the membership, written before any formal discussion with the ECCI, the Executive Committee pointed out the changes that had taken place during the past few years:

> The new situation manifested in 1927 has been that the masses, raised to a higher peak of class struggle by the experience of the first Labour Government, Red Friday and the General Strike, have learned by that experience. The betrayal of May 1926 and onwards has not left them helpless before reaction.[15]

The events of 1927 had proved, the EC argued, that opportunities were there for the Communists to defeat the reformist leadership of the Labour movement:

> Whenever the party influence was brought to bear in an organised fashion for a direct appeal to the masses, the response was immediate and, particularly as the year went on, more and more successful, in spite of the reformists' bitterest opposition – the success of the party in rallying and concentrating the leftward trend of the masses had been dependent above all on the vigour, determination and wholeheartedness with which the party banner had been unfurled and an uncompromising fight against the capitalist reformists conducted on political lines.[16]

The party's aim must be, said the EC, to become the undisputed leaders of the working class:

> Our aim must be to help the workers to break loose completely from the spiritual yoke of reformism, to realise finally that the Communist Party is their only leader and to transform their partial success of 1927 into a definite counter-offensive against capitalism in the shortest possible time.[17]

It was not until their tenth congress, in January 1929, that the Communists finally accepted the complete reversal of strategy known as the 'New Line'. And there was a further congress at the end of that year, when many of the old leadership were replaced, because they were not sufficiently enthusiastic for the new policy.

The adoption of the 'New Line' was not an instantaneous process. It was a product of the crisis in communist strategy brought about by their continuous rejection by the Labour Party. There was intervention by the Communist International to get the CPGB to adopt a harder line towards the Labour Party, but that was only half the story. As Saklatvala's political involvement shows, there was already grassroots support for a change of line. It also proves that many of the ideas of the 'New Line' were not so new. They had been expressed by Saklatvala at a much earlier date. He realised in 1925 that a change of strategy was necessary. Yet it was not until three years later that the policies he advocated finally became incorporated into CPGB strategy.

The aim of the 'New Line' policy was for the CPGB to replace the Labour Party as the party of the working class. If this was to be achieved, one important area where the Communists must make gains was in the electoral arena. Saklatvala's efforts in this field have already been chronicled. At the General Election of 1931, the Communist Party put forward 26 candidates, and where there was no Communist standing, as at the 1929 election, Communist supporters were asked to abstain from voting. With a membership of just over 3,000 it would need a considerable effort to mount anything like an effective campaign, and this showed the importance the Communists attributed to their electoral fortunes. They did much better at this election than two years before: they increased their overall vote by almost 50 per cent. The 26 Communist candidates received 74,826 votes, compared with 50,632 votes for 25 candidates in 1929. The areas where the Communists made the most headway were the mining constituencies in Scotland and Wales. In West Fife, Willie Gallacher received 22 per cent of the vote, and in Rhondda East, Arthur Horner gained over 10,000 votes. The Communist vote in those two constituencies was a serious challenge to the Labour candidate. It was in the Rhondda in the 1945 General Election that the Communists, although unsuccessful, received one of their highest ever votes, and in West Fife, in 1935, Gallagher won the seat and held it for the next fifteen years. Much of the credit for these later, although limited, successes, must be attributed to the 'New Line' strategy, and the need to build the Communist vote. One other important virtue of the Communists' wider participation in elections was that it contributed to an increase in party membership. The *Daily Worker* reported that during the 1931 general election campaign 2,000 new recruits had been made for the party. This, when compared with an overall membership figure of just 3,054 in June 1931, was no mean achievement.

When Saklatvala contested Shettleston, in June 1930, although his vote was less than 1,500 the resulting campaign attracted people into the party. In an interview for the *Daily Worker*, he emphasised the importance of such contests for party recruitment,

> We have won 1,460 sincere supporters and created a communist local of 37 members and a group of the Young Communist League. Our task is clear, with these new members we must work amongst our 1,460 voters, and with their assistance win over the thousands who have turned away from the Labour Party.[18]

Saklatvala had been a consistent advocate of more Communist electoral contests. His advice to the Executive Committee in 1928, to increase the number of parliamentary and municipal candidates, was followed up a year later, during the 1929 general election campaign, with a further plea. He optimistically told a public meeting in Battersea, that the Communists could push Labour into second place.[19] His advice was not heeded, but the notion that the Communist needed to build their electoral support was an intrinsic part of the 'New Line'.

A major criticism of the 'New Line' by contemporary analysts has been that the Communists suffered a loss of membership during the period. As we have seen, Saklatvala's recruitment drives were very succcessful, and his public rallies well attended, and they resulted in a rush of recruits. It could be argued that he was the exception rather than the rule, and that the Communist Party during this time did find recruitment difficult. A look at the membership figures for the period from 1929, when the strategy was first adopted, to its demise in 1935, reveals that there was a substantial growth in party membership at this time. One of the reasons for the adoption of the 'Class Against Class' policy had been the Party's falling membership, which since the end of the general strike had slumped quite dramatically. This point was made clear in the party statement on the 'New Line', 'Communist Policy in Britain'.[20] During the 'New Line' period this decline was halted, and the Communist Party's membership showed a respectable increase.

The reasons for the growth of the Communist Party during the early 1930s are many. There was a disillusionment amongst active Labour supporters because of the defection of MacDonald, Snowden, and Thomas, and this was not helped by the reactionary policies being pursued, with their support, by the new National Government. It seemed to many on the left that what the Communists had been saying about the Labour Party, and the nature of its leadership, was true. Unemployment was also a factor in the party's growth. It had increased by 50 per cent in just over a year, and in January 1932 stood at 2,995,000 – 22 per cent of the workforce – the highest figure reached in the pre-war years. Another factor in the party's growth was a new sense of purpose in the Communist Party itself. The 'New Line', despite its sectarianism, did give the Communists a certain direction. From the party's formation until 1929, the Communists had no clear role. Were they to be a ginger group within the Labour Party, as their affiliation strategy implied? Or were they to be an independent party in their own right? Between 1920 and 1929 this was never really decided. After the adoption of the 'Class Against Class' policy, the Communist Party had a definite aim: it was to replace the Labour Party as the party of the working class. With this clear and simple objective, the drive for membership took on a new meaning, and a new importance.

During 1931 and 1932, at the height of the 'New Line', the Communist Party showed that it was capable of organising major public events at which thousands of recruits were made. There was an interest in Communist Party policies and this was reflected in the large turnout at public meetings organised by the party. Between June and

December 1931, the *Daily Worker* reported that 5,000 new recruits had been made for the Communist Party.[21] Saklatvala played an important part in this recruitment drive. His commitment and level of activity during this period are phenomenal, and he was a good example of the dedication shown to the party by full time party activists at the time. The attendances he achieved at meetings, and the number of recruits made by just this one propagandist, were a reflection of the renewed vigour with which the Communist Party was now conducting its campaigns.

These Communist Party recruitment campaigns were partly in response to Pollitt's exhortation to the party membership to redouble their efforts to gain recruits. At the end of January 1932, he had said in the *Daily Worker* that 3,000 new members and a doubling of the paper's sales were not good enough in view of the capitalist offensive.[22] During 1932, Communist Party membership continued to rise, to reach a peak of 9,000.[23] The pages of the *Daily Worker* were full of reports of packed public meetings. One new convert wrote to the paper informing the readership how he had been recruited: 'I am one of Preston's 97 new recruits to the Communist Party enrolled last Tuesday week when Comrade Saklatvala addressed a mass meeting here.'[24]

There seems little evidence to support the claim that during this period the Communist Party was either moribund or in decline. It remained a small party with very little influence outside the organised labour movement, but that had always been the case since its formation. The adoption of the 'New Line', in terms of membership, did not lead to a decline. On the contrary, the party's membership began a steady upturn and its recruitment capability, as evidenced by reports in its daily paper, was large. In the early days of the new policy, party membership stood at 2,555 but by the time of the thirteenth congress, in February 1935, which effectively brought to an end the 'Class against Class' years, party membership had increased to 7,700. In the space of five years the CPGB had trebled in size. During the early 1930s a wider audience was prepared to give the party a hearing, and an increasing number were prepared to join.

However, there was a problem in retaining these enthusiastic recruits. An exasperated Idris Cox, in charge of membership, reported to the party's Executive Committee, in July 1932:

> There is no doubt that a big proportion of the new members have left the party since January of this year. The present total membership of the party is roughly at the same level as November of last year.[25]

Saklatvala's activity during this period cannot be seen in isolation from the upsurge in party militancy generally. The Communists' attacks on the Labour Party, far from being an obstruction, actually aided them in winning recruits. When, a few months after Saklatvala's death, the Communists applied for Labour Party affiliation, their application received a more favourable response than before. After six years of unmitigated onslaught on the Labour Party, during which it had been accused of 'propping up capitalism' and of being an agent of fascism, the Communists could still gain wide appeal for their attempts at affiliation. The *Daily Worker* reported that over one thousand labour and trade union organisations supported this application.[26] When it was discussed at the 1936 Annual Labour Party Conference, the motion for affiliation was rejected by 1,728,000 votes to 593,000.[27] Although this was a substantial vote against, it compared favourably with the results achieved during the early 1920s. Previously the highest vote in favour of Communist Party affiliation had been at the 1923 conference, when a similar motion was rejected by 2,880,000 to 366,000 votes. The 'softly softly' approach towards the Labour Party which had been practised until 1928, paid less dividends than the policy advocated in later years. Saklatvala's appeals for unity at the 1922 and 1924 Labour Party conferences fell on deaf ears; in retrospect he, and the Communist Party, might have received a better response had their attacks on the Labour Party and its leadership been more forthright. The Communists had, by 1935 made substantial progress towards Labour Party affiliation. Clearly, external factors had played a part, and the rise of fascism had affected the thinking of large sections of the labour movement. Many Labour Party members and others on the left also saw the necessity of a united front. Nevertheless, the 'New Line' had struck a chord amongst some sections of the organised working class: the Communists' continuous attacks on the Labour Party had won them some sympathy, particularly after the debacle of the 1929-31 Labour Government. Despite all their sectarianism, the Communists came out of the 'New Line' period closer to achieving Labour Party affiliation than at any time during the 1920s. If this was a measure of their success, then it compared very favourably with their less sectarian phase.

Notes

[1] Walter Kendall, *The Revolutionary Movement in Britain*, Weidenfeld and Nicholson 1969, p297.
[2] Noreen Branson, *History of the Communist Party of Great Britain, 1927-41, op cit*, p17.
[3] Brian Pearce, *Early History of the Communist Party of Great Britain*, Socialist Labour League 1966, p61.
[4] Henry Pelling, *The British Communist Party: An Historical Profile*, Adam and Charles Black 1958, p54.
[5] L J Macfarlane, *The British Communist Party: Its Origins and Development until 1929*, McGibbon and Kee 1966, p24.
[6] *Communist Policy in Great Britain: The Report of the British Commission of the Ninth Plenum of the Comintern*, CPGB 1928, p7.
[7] Noreen Branson, *History of the Communist Party of Great Britain,1927-41, op.cit*. p18.
[8] Letter from S Saklatvala to the Polit Bureau of the CPGB, dated 7 October 1925. Contained in *Communist Papers. Documents selected from those obtained on the arrest of the Communist Leaders on the 14th and 21st October, 1925*, HMSO 1926.
[9] *Report of the Ninth Congress of the Communist Party of Great Britain*, October 1927, CPGB, 1927, p96.
[10] *Ibid*, p .
[11] *Workers Weekly*, 6 February 1925.
[12] *Report of the Seventh National Congress, Communist Party of Great Britain.* 1925, CPGB 1925, p26.
[13] *Report of the Ninth Congress of the CPGB, op.cit*, p17.
[14] *Between the Fifth and the Sixth World Congress: Report of the Executive Committee of the Communist International*, 1928, p127.
[15] Letter from Executive Committee CPGB to all Party members, contained in *Workers Life*, 27 January 1928.
[16] *Ibid*.

[17] *Ibid.*
[18] *Daily Worker*, 1 July 1930.
[19] *South Western Star*, 1 March 1929.
[20] *Communist Policy in Britain, op.cit*, p161.
[21] *Daily Worker*, 1 January 1932.
[22] *Daily Worker*, 20 January 1932.
[22] *Communist Review*, August 1932.
[24] *Daily Worker*, 30 June 1932.
[25] *Communist Review*, August 1932.
[26] *Daily Worker*, 8 August 1936.
[27] *Report of the Thirty Sixth Annual Conference of the Labour Party*, October 1936, p211.

Index